# QUEEN MOTHER

# QUEEN MOTHER

An Alternative Portrait
of Her Life and Times

Penelope Mortimer

ANDRE DEUTSCH

This revised edition first published as
*Queen Mother An Alternative Portrait of
her Life and Times* in 1995 by
André Deutsch Limited
106 Great Russell Street
London WC1B 3LJ

This book first published as
*Queen Elizabeth The Queen Mother* © 1986

ISBN 0 233 98972 2

CIP data available for this title
from the British Library

Printed by WSOY, Finland

For my grandchildren

'It has been my experience that the pleased incredulity with which the public reacts to the elementary demonstrations on the part of Royalty that they are, after all, like other people is matched by the public's firm refusal to treat them as such.'

HRH the Duke of Windsor, *A King's Story*


'Nor do I apologise for my analyses of the Royal Family's circumstances and actions; we have no access to its members as real persons, and can only speculate. We can only chip away at the myths that encrust them, and look very carefully at the roles we force them to play. It is only hagiography that kills its subjects stone dead.'

Adam Mars-Jones, *Lantern Lectures*

# Contents

# Author's Note

When I set out to revise my 1986 biography of the Queen Mother I thought it would be a relatively simple matter of putting right the odd typographical error and bringing the book up-to-date to cover the last decade of the Queen Mother's life.

In fact as I began to check the old book I realised that I wanted to change far more than I thought. Perhaps authors should not re-read their old books since clearly it can be dangerous. In effect the desire to make modest changes turned into an uncontrollable urge to rewrite virtually the whole book. Thus any old reader returning to the work will find little to recognise and new readers should start here.

# PART ONE
## LADY ELIZABETH BOWES-LYON

# Chapter One

The cool showery weather at the beginning of August 1900 came as a relief after July's heatwave, particularly to women like Cecilia, Lady Glamis, waiting for the birth of her ninth child in her parents' Grosvenor Gardens apartment. The last few weeks had brought a raffish, Mediterranean look to London. Horses had taken to sun-bonnets; servants were humanely provided with straw hats, Homburg-shaped for butlers, boaters for footmen. The Great Canadian Water Shoot at the Earls Court Woman's Exhibition was besieged by young people whose delighted screams through the splash and spray drowned the brave noise of the Swedish Hussar Ladies Band and The Maine Ladies Naval Orchestra. At the Royal Aquarium, 'London's largest, coolest Palace of Amusements', ladies fully dressed in stockings and elaborate bathing costumes swam slowly round and round, their heads held high. Grass was as scorched as the South African veldt and at Church Parade in Hyde Park there were plenty of alpaca jackets, some slightly immodest gowns and a noticeable lack of gloves. Even the old Queen, who normally moved from place to place like clockwork, was rumoured to be feeling 'quite languid' at Osborne, and planning to go to Balmoral early if the intense heat persisted.

The weather, always a newsworthy subject, had temporarily taken over the headlines, competing with casualty lists from Frederickstad and the Chinese crisis and passionate arguments in Parliament concerning a statue of Oliver Cromwell. As the weather broke, there was a succession of notable deaths and disasters – first HRH Prince Alfred, Duke of Edinburgh and Duke of Saxe-Coburg-Gotha passed on from natural causes at Rosenau, then King Humbert of Italy was assassinated, followed four days later by an assassination attempt on the Shah of Persia. The *New York Herald* asserted that within the past few months twenty-seven anarchists had left

America with the avowed purpose of laying low every crowned head in Europe.

It was once more a wet, windy, unreliable world. Cricket was interrupted by rain. Horses plodded bare-headed through the familiar drizzle. The Water Shoot lost customers to the Gravity Railway and Mlle Marguerite's Performing Lions. Madame Tussaud's produced Lifelike and Realistic Portrait Models of the late Duke of Saxe-Coburg and the late King Humbert of Italy to show the crowds on Bank Holiday Monday, 6 August, by which time Lady Glamis's daughter was two days old.

Exactly where in London the future Queen Elizabeth the Queen Mother was born is the subject of speculation. There is a theory that the event took place in an ambulance. The first petrol-powered buses were not in operation until that year and those, for some odd reason, were in Norfolk, so it is reasonable to assume that ambulances were still horse-drawn and none too easy to summon in an emergency. However, it is recorded that when Mrs Miller Mundy caught her foot in some matting at Earls Court and 'one of her knee-caps broke right across, giving forth a loud report like that of a gun', causing her excruciating pain, an ambulance was summoned, so it was obviously possible. Cabs were hailed by one's butler blowing a whistle – a single blast for a taxi, two for a hansom, three for a four-wheeler – and perhaps the same method applied. If that is what happened and it arrived in time, did it clop calmly on through the traffic while Lady Glamis was delivered of her daughter or did it pull up in Hyde Park? What was its intended destination anyway? The official answer from Clarence House is that they have no idea.[1]

Wherever the whereabouts of his wife and youngest daughter, Lord Glamis was in Scotland by 23 August, making nine runs out of his side's total of 303 for 9 declared in the Glamis v. Strathmore cricket match.[2] There he resolutely stayed until the third week in September. When he finally returned to the family home, St Paul's Walden Bury near Hitchin, the six-week-old Elizabeth was neither christened nor registered, non-existent in the eyes of God and man. Lord Glamis was immediately sent off to the Registrar's Office at Hitchin where he paid a fine of 7/6d for failing to report the birth on time. It was then, upset, perhaps, by the drain on his pocket and distraught by the fuss, that he stated the child had been born at St Paul's Walden Bury. Unless he was not at all certain himself, it must have seemed the easiest way out. Under the Forgery Act of 1861 the Queen Mother's father could have been sentenced to penal servitude for life, but since nobody questioned the matter for the next eighty years he got off, in this world at least, scot-free.

Next came the christening, performed by the Reverend Tristram Valentine, the incumbent of St Paul's Walden Bury, after matins on Sunday, 23 September. As the godparents forgot to sign the register all of them, except Lord Glamis' spinster sister Maud from the Cotswolds and Lady Glamis' second cousin Mrs Arthur James, have been forgotten. Venetia James and Cecilia shared the same great-grandfather, William, 3rd Duke of Portland, perhaps the only Prime Minister never to have made a speech in Parliament. Very much part of the *haute-monde*, which the Glamises and Bowes-Lyons were not, and a close friend of the Prince of Wales' future companion, Alice Keppel, Venetia also received her share of Royal attention until she made the mistake of concealing herself in a giant Easter egg and popping out with a whoop and a curtsy as the Prince and Princess of Wales were passing by. Edward was furious, Alexandra not amused.[3]

Venetia would become notoriously mean and severe in her later years, but in September 1900, as far as renouncing the vain pomp and glory of the world was concerned, she seems an improbable choice for a godmother, wafting into the village church with her leghorn, her veils, her boa and her eighteen-inch waist, looking down her pretty little nose at the gawky Bowes-Lyon boys in their tweed knickerbockers and thoroughly upsetting the Reverend Valentine with her dimpled smile and flashing ankles. There were one or two tense moments. Rev Valentine misheard, or misunderstood, the infant's name – Elizabeth Angela Marguerite – and had to scratch it out and replace it on the baptismal certificate; then he omitted to state that the father was a Lord, and had to squeeze that in later.

Queen Victoria died at Osborne on 22 January 1901. The former Prince of Wales, now King Edward VII, travelled from his mother's deathbed to London on 25 January for his Accession Council and made history by rejecting the prepared speech and improvising his own. As nobody took down what he said Lord Rosebery had to reconstruct it from memory for the records. That same day King Edward was proclaimed from St James's Palace with ritual that had not been used for over seventy-two years:

> Whereas it has pleased Almighty God to call to His Mercy Our Late Sovereign Lady Queen Victoria, of Blessed and Glorious Memory, by whose Decease the Imperial Crown of the United Kingdom of

Great Britain and Ireland is solely and rightfully come to the High and Mighty Prince Albert Edward: We, therefore, the Lords Spiritual and Temporal of this Realm, being here assisted with these of Her late Majesty's Privy Council, with Numbers of other Principal Gentlemen of Quality, with the Lord Mayor, Aldermen, and Citizens of London, do now hereby, with one Voice and Consent of Tongue and Heart, publish and proclaim, That the High and Mighty Prince Albert Edward, is now, by the Death of our late Sovereign of Happy Memory, become our only lawful and rightful Liege Lord Edward the Seventh, by the Grace of God, King of the United Kingdom of Great Britain and Ireland, Defender of the Faith, Emperor of India: To whom we do acknowledge all Faith and constant Obedience, with all hearty and humble Affection; beseeching God, by whom Kings and Queens do reign, to bless the Royal Prince Edward the Seventh, with long and happy Years to reign over Us. God save the King!

Crowds roared, trumpets sounded, the band played the National Anthem, a salute of guns boomed out from Hyde Park and the Tower. This event, unnoticed by the five-month-old baby at St Paul's Walden Bury, would play a significant part in her future.

By the time Elizabeth was fourteen months old her mother was pregnant again. David Bowes-Lyon was born on 2 May 1902, four weeks before the end of the Boer War and eight weeks before the scheduled date for King Edward's Coronation. Unfortunately the King succumbed to acute appendicitis and the ceremony was postponed at the last minute, causing great inconvenience to foreign potentates and an unseemly riot in Hemel Hempstead, where the rustics felt cheated of a free dinner. It was appropriate to the dawn of a new era that the Coronation, which finally took place on 9 August, was celebrated with more jubilation by the troops just returned from South Africa than by the Almanac de Gotha. Edward, the sunny King, rose benevolently over the first decade of the twentieth century and settled in to what seemed to many people an eternal noon of peace and prosperity.

Of course there were skirmishes abroad and anarchists under the bed, deplorable goings-on in Russia and some very nasty murders. French aviators dropped out of the sky like flies. Undomesticated members of the working class were troublesome and a few hysterical women, amusingly dubbed 'fooligans', didn't seem to realise where their buttered bread came from. These, however, were little more than the midges and mosquitoes of a summer day. Real people, proper people, the sort of people one knows, never saw the dark or felt the cold. A million lights came on at dusk, and those who were not actually basking in the Royal Presence – the gentry, the respectable, affluent middle classes, domestic servants of superior rank and all good children – retired into their various fortresses, cosy and warm as Leonard Woolf's 'nursery with its great fire, when the curtains were pulled and the gas lit and Nurse settled down to her reading, and occasionally far off could be heard the clop-clop of a horse in hansom-cab or four-wheeler . . .'4 The sense of safety, of being protected from all outside worlds, may have been in direct proportion to the sense of peril, but few people said so.

In February 1904 the old Earl of Strathmore died and Elizabeth's father succeeded to the title, becoming the 14th Earl of Strathmore and Kinghorne, Viscount Lyon and Baron Glamis, Tannadyce, Sidlaw and Strathdichtie, Baron Bowes, of Streatlam Castle, County Durham, and Lunedale, County York. As a result of his considerable inheritance, Lord Strathmore rented a splendid Adam mansion in St James's Square. Elizabeth and David were the first of the family to grow up with a sense of wealth and privilege – a London home 'for the season', St Paul's Walden Bury and the vast folly of Glamis for the rest of the year. Elizabeth acquired a French governess, Mlle Lang, and attended Madame d'Egville's dancing class in Knightsbridge. She was small for her age, inclined to puppy-fat, with long dark hair tied back with a satin bow and an expression, in front of the camera at any rate, of mischief alternating with wistful charm. She was an excellent dancer, one-two-three-hopping through the polka, twirling to the waltz – if it had been allowed, she could have performed a vigorous can-can.

London was an endless party for these little Honourables: soldiers wore scarlet when they came calling on housemaids; uniforms of every kind, from postmen to Field Marshals, were gilded and braided and bobbled; Peter Yapp's in Sloane Street sold sailor hats for children with HMS VICTORY emblazoned on the ribbon, surmounted by a gold star. If you were extremely grand, like the Buccleuchs of Montagu House or their neighbours, the Fitzwilliams, your prams were decorated with the family crest and painted in the family colours, and on special occasions you rode out with Mama and Papa in one of the family coaches: 'The harness was shining silver, and there were a wigged coachman and footman in front and two postillions behind all in livery, with red breeches and white stockings.'5 Everything was remarkable to a child with a firm grip on her governess' hand and muffins at home for tea: knife-grinders, crossing-sweepers, buskers, cripples, chimney sweeps, beggars, urchins, the whole colourful pageant of the un-washed poor; brass bands and barrel organs and parades. Perhaps, if you're very good, Mama might take you for a birthday treat to the Coliseum.

Whenever it was that Elizabeth saw her first music-hall, something about Vesta Tilley and Marie Lloyd and Gertie Millar struck a rousing chord in the little girl's fantasies – their clothes, their command of the stage, their glamour and rollicking good humour behind the footlights. Actresses, thanks to their Sovereign, had become socially acceptable; Seymour Hicks was inundated with replies when he rashly offered jobs to the twelve prettiest society girls to send him their photographs and débutantes were rushing to the stage, happy to find the theatre almost indistinguishable from their daily lives. Had she been a few years older Elizabeth could easily have become another Zena Dare.

As it was, she used her talents effectively enough. Lord David Cecil remembered being introduced to her at a children's party at Lansdowne House:

> I turned and looked and was aware of a small, charming, rosy face around which twined and strayed rings and tendrils of silken hair, and a pair of dewy grey eyes. Her flower-like mouth parted in a grave, enchanting smile, and between the pearly teeth flowed out tones of drowsy melting sweetness that seemed to caress the words they uttered. From that moment my small damp hand clutched at hers and I never left her side . . . Forgotten were all the pretenders to my heart. Here was the true heroine. She had come. I had seen and she had conquered. . . I remember her playing in the Park, racing beside her yellow-haired brother, her hair flying in the wind, her cheeks bright with the exercise, her clear infectious laugh ringing out; or sitting demurely at the tea-table; or best of all, at a fancy-dress party dressed as a Vandyck child, with high square bodice and stiff satin skirts surrounded by a bevy of adorers. . .[6]

Remembered rapture so affected Lord David's prose style that it is hard to believe the child was normal. If in all this excitement she occasionally wet her knickers, sulked, howled, refused to eat her bread-and-butter pudding, her contemporaries discreetly forgot it. Photographs of these angels should by rights have the sunny sanctity of a Margaret Tarrant print. Perhaps it's the primitive lighting, but some of them give a shadowy impression of Henry James' Miles and Flora – solemn faces, a hint of innocence about to be corrupted or already, perhaps, doomed; good as gold and sly as little foxes.

Of all the Strathmore homes, St Paul's Walden Bury was best

suited to an Edwardian childhood – shabby, comfortable, taking its ageing beauty for granted. Lady Strathmore engaged a new nursery maid, Clara Knight, when David was born. The seventeen-year-old farmer's daughter from Hertfordshire would spend the rest of her life caring for Strathmore children and grandchildren and must have had an incalculable effect on Elizabeth and David. Both would write nostalgically about 'THE WOOD', 'THE HARNESS ROOM' and 'THE FLEA HOUSE' which

> could only be reached by a very rotten ladder, the rungs of which would certainly have broken if an adult had attempted the ascent. Consequently our nurse was unable to come up and retrieve us . . . In it we kept a regular store of forbidden delicacies, acquired by devious devices. This store consisted of apples, oranges, sugar, sweets, slabs of chocolate Meunier, matches and packets of Woodbines. Many other things there were besides, and to this blissful retreat we used . . . to have recourse whenever it seemed an agreeable plan to escape our morning lessons.[7]

Less agreeable, but perhaps more dramatic, were the secret hideouts and ghostly companions at Glamis. Once they were installed in this remote fortress Lady Strathmore would set about cheering the place up, a dispiriting task what with the gloom and the bloodstains on the floor. Sir Henry Channon remembered 'the whole castle heavy with atmosphere, sinister, lugubrious';[8] Lord Gorrell, by temperament more inclined to look on the bright side, insisted that 'it was all so friendly and so kind, days of such wholehearted and delightful youth under the gracious guidance of Lady Strathmore . . . the old castle re-echoed with fun and laughter.'[9] All the boys except Patrick, now Lord Glamis and a captain in the Scots Guards, would be back from Eton and Oxford for the summer. The Strathmore sons 'were wild',[10] and the eldest daughters, Mary and Rose, often flounced off to their bedrooms, only to appear again all smiles as carriage-loads of visitors streamed through the lofty front door. Meanwhile, escaping from Clara and Mlle Lang, the two youngest children raced and toddled through spook-laden passages, past sealed up doors behind which might be the Monster, mumbling and dribbling, or the Room of Skulls, in which a number of Ogilvys had been immured until, after eating the flesh off their own arms, they died of starvation and crumbled into a heap of bones.

'Was there a secret at Bly,' Henry James' heroine in *The Turn of the Screw* wondered anxiously, 'a mystery of Udolpho or an insane,

9

unmentionable relative kept in unsuspected confinement?' There certainly was at Glamis. Thomas Lyon-Bowes, Lord Glamis, and his wife Charlotte produced their first son and heir on 28 September 1822, or so the reference books – including Burke's Peerage – said. But was he their first? Debrett thought otherwise and slipped in a son who was born, and reputedly died, on 18 October 1821. Luckier for him, and for all the succeeding Earls, if he had. The child was shaped like an egg, covered in hair, with spindly little arms and legs – according to the superstitions of the time, a monster. Unfortunately, hoping for a swift release and not wanting their little maverick to be eternally damned, the parents had the child baptised. He thrived, growing hairier and more egg-like every day. Now they had given him an immortal soul they couldn't just smother him or dump him in the river. What to do? The vast, largely uninhabited castle of Glamis provided the answer.

In 1684 the first Earl of Strathmore, a man with a passion for hiding, had built a secret room 'within the charter house', about ten feet wide by fifteen feet long. The story is that this dank and gloomy cell became the rightful Lord Strathmore's home for a hundred and fifty years. Only the current Earl, his eldest son, the family lawyer and the agent of the estate knew of his existence or where he was kept. In Elizabeth's grandfather's time a tactless workman told the Clerk of the Works that he had found a door opening onto a long passage and didn't like the look of it; before he knew what was happening he was pensioned off and dispatched to Australia. Rose Granville, Elizabeth's elder sister, said in her old age, 'We were never allowed to talk about it . . . Our parents forbade us ever to discuss the matter or ask any questions about it. My father and grandfather absolutely refused to discuss it.'[11]

Whatever fun and games were indulged in by the women and younger boys of the family, the Earls themselves were a melancholy lot. Each of them, on their succession, was taken by the lawyer and the agent through the secret door and down the long corridor to be introduced to the indestructible freak, its hair now grizzled, its antique rags smelling to high heaven. According to various records, they never smiled again. Augustus Hare, writing of his visit in 1877, recounts that the Bishop of Brechin was so upset by Lord Strathmore's gloom that he offered his services as an ecclesiastic to try and dispel it. Lord Strathmore thanked him kindly, but said 'that in his most unfortunate position, no one could ever help him.' 'Silent and moody, with an anxious, scared look on his face,'[12] Elizabeth's grandfather must have made his brother's monstrous presence felt throughout the castle, even though his lips were sealed. It was said that Elizabeth's father was so alarmed by this that he himself 'absolutely refused to be enlightened' when the time came. Whatever the truth of the matter, the idea of this unhappy, geriatric monster lurking in their home must have affected the Strathmores profoundly. Perhaps, in his way, he was their most influential ancestor.

No wonder the children whispered, darting quick looks over their shoulders in case they were being overheard: the place was packed with secrets and stories about secrets. Linen women and kitchen maids loved to tell the tale about a guest who, strolling on the lawn after dinner one night, saw a girl at one of the upstairs windows gripping the bars and looking white-faced out into the darkness. As he watched, she disappeared. At one minute before midnight there was a piercing scream, then silence. A few moments later the door of one of the towers opened and a hideous old hag 'with a fiendish face' staggered out with a sack on her back. At the sight of the guest she lolloped across the lawn and into the woods, her black cloak billowing, the sack bumping as she ran. Years later the guest came across 'the girl at the Glamis window' in a convent in Italy. Her hands had been cut off and her tongue cut out as a punishment for disclosing family secrets.

*Struwelpeter* was nothing to the dreadful warnings of the Strathmore ghosts. Elizabeth was told that if she dared look out of the night-nursery window late at night she would see the tongueless woman running across the park, pointing in agony to her bleeding mouth. The moral was clear: never admit to knowing secrets; never tell them.

Elizabeth had already given an impeccable performance as brides-maid at brother Patrick's wedding in the Guards' Chapel and would be much in demand now that the rest of the elder siblings had reached marriageable age. She had also met the Prince of Wales' children, David, Bertie, Georgie and Mary, at Lady Leicester's, making Royal history by palming off her cherries on the speechless Bertie's plate. In September 1908, since Mlle Lang was taking an extended holiday, Elizabeth and David, dressed in identical tussore smocks, were sent to Constance Goff's kindergarten in Marylebone High Street – a curious choice for a girl of eight, but perhaps the pair refused to be parted. It soon became clear that the curriculum did not cover instruction in the accomplishments proper to her station. By the following Easter Mlle Lang had been recalled, piano lessons begun at the Matilde Verne school in the Cromwell Road and visits planned to Lady Strathmore's mother, who lived near Florence with her unmarried daughter Violet, and an admirable person to introduce a girl to the more difficult aspects of Florentine art.

This suited Elizabeth very well. She was alone with David again, Clara in charge of their comforts, Mlle Lang fruitlessly imploring them from the bottom of the Flea House ladder. Christmas at St Paul's Walden Bury, off to St James's Square for pantomimes and parties, starring in Madame Verne's children's concert, being lifted 'on and off the piano stool oftener than was necessary' by Madame Verne's sister, 'just because she was so nice to take hold of.'[13] Not that she was allowed to overlook the fact that she was unusually fortunate – Lady Strathmore was a devout Christian and it was as necessary to support suitable charities as it was to be seen in the right place at the right time wearing the right clothes. Elizabeth, a tender-hearted child, would have been upset by the death from starvation of three-year-old Charles Leaning from Hoxton, if she had known about it. Mr Leaning, a scaffolder, had been out of work for nine weeks. His wife earned five shillings a week making boxes; their rent was four shillings. The Leanings and their five children lived – or not – on the remainder. When the boy died his mother was at the police court being fined for not sending one of his brothers to school; since she was unable to pay the fine, Mr Leaning was sent to prison.[14] This happened at strawberry-time, a month before Elizabeth's ninth birthday, and was the sort of thing they prayed about most fervently, along with requests for the King's continued health and their own safety from damnation. 'The rich man in his castle/The poor man at his gate/God made them high or lowly/And ordered their estate/*All things bright and beautiful. . .*'

Back to Glamis again for the summer. Going to bed at Glamis might be perilous, but the ghosts, unlike those of Bly, considerately absented themselves during daylight hours. The children played cricket, rode their ponies, went on picnics, learned the mazurka and the minuet from old Mr Neal, who tucked his violin under a long white beard. They visited neighbours and entertained guests: 'The Countess sat down at the piano,' their local minister recalled, 'and played a few bars of a quaint old minuet. Suddenly, as if by a magician's touch, two little figures seemed to rise from the floor and dance, with admirable precision and grace . . . These little children were the Hon. David Lyon and Lady Elizabeth Lyon, the youngest son and daughter of the house. The former had donned part of the dress of the family jester and the latter had assumed the robe and cap of a little girl of the period of James I.' After half an hour ('brief but supreme,' to the minister, at least), 'the music stopped and the little dancers, making a low bow and curtsey, clapped their hands with delight . . . Choruses of praise were heard on every side, and Lady Elizabeth, on being asked . . . the name of the character she had adopted, said with great *empressement*, "I call myself the Princess Elizabeth." '[15] The nine-year-old child had already set her sights higher than the Coliseum.

# Chapter Two

At the end of April 1910 King Edward caught a cold. King Edward was ill, dying, with his wife and Alice Keppel at his bedside. On 6 May King Edward was dead. Mourning was back after only nine years, though this time it took some bizarre forms. Alice Keppel threaded black ribbon through her daughter's underwear;[1] a desolate hostess tied a large black crepe bow round a tree the King had planted in her garden five years before; a grocer in Jermyn Street filled his window with black Bradenham hams.[2] At nine o'clock on the morning of 9 May King George V's accession was proclaimed from St James's Palace:

> Whereas it has pleased Almighty God to call to His Mercy our late Sovereign Lord King Edward the Seventh, of Blessed and Glorious Memory . . . We, therefore, the Lords Spiritual and Temporal of this Realm . . . with Numbers of other Principal Gentlemen of Quality . . . do now hereby, with one Voice and Consent of Tongue and Heart, publish and proclaim That the High and Mighty Prince George Frederick Ernest Albert is now, by the Death of our late Sovereign of Happy Memory, become our only lawful rightful Liege Lord George the Fifth . . . God Save the King!

Crowds roared, trumpets sounded, the band played the National Anthem, a salute of guns boomed out from Hyde Park and the Tower and the King's eldest sons, David and Bertie, watched from the garden wall of Marlborough House.

For the beginning of a new era it was more like a damp Sunday afternoon than a promising dawn. Lovely ladies, gay blades, gamblers and wealthy pimps leapt with extraordinary alacrity into the shadows, leaving their places in the sun to the landed gentry, sporting peers, decorous dowagers and the clergy. God, a fitful element during King Edward's reign, rejoined the monarchy in the social firmament. Respectable domesticity became the order of the day, the nights were long and peaceful. The widowed Queen, wandering disconsolately about Sandringham House wearing black and silver and a silver widow's cap could not reconcile herself to it. Georgie was not born to be King.* Mary was a nice enough girl, but a poor relation after all. Encouraged by her sister Dagmar, Dowager Empress of All the Russias, Alexandra made clear that she still considered herself to be First Lady in the land. To add to their recognisable image, King George V and Queen Mary had a mother-in-law problem.

Their Coronation took place a year later, on 22 June 22 1911. Among the acts of God around at that time were killer earthquakes in Turkestan, volcanic eruptions in Italy, Alaska and the Philippines, a Finnish village carried bodily out to sea, a 54 miles-per-hour gale and 1.1 inch of rainfall in fifteen minutes on a July day in London. The King's sister Louise and her husband were shipwrecked off the coast of Morocco, a Commander F G Brine washed overboard and drowned. The French Premier was shot by a madman, the Russian Premier assassinated by an anarchist, the Persian Minister of Finance was assassinated. Republics were proclaimed in Portugal and China, Italy declared war on Turkey, there was civil war in Mexico. Riots broke out for one reason or another in Bombay, Hankau, Liverpool, Rome, Tunis, Cardiff, Hull, Brazil, Dundee, Lisbon, Llanelly and Tredegar. In Britain there were strikes of shipbuilders, seamen, dock labourers, railway workers, car-men, transport workers, postal employees, carters, taxi drivers and schoolboys.

It was a busy year for royalty. Britain had the Festival of Empire, the Coronation Exhibition, the Pageant of Empire, the Pageant of London and the Coronation. Prince Edward received the Order of the Garter and was invested as Prince of Wales at Caernarvon, miserably dressed in white satin breeches and a mantle and surcoat of purple velvet edged with ermine. ('Your friends will understand that as a Prince you are obliged to do certain things that may seem a little silly,' his mother said).[3] The new King and Queen invited 100,000 children to tea at the Crystal Palace, which would later be sold to Lord Plymouth for £210,000. Then there was the Durbar at Delhi, Emperor George and Empress Mary sitting on 'a lofty white many-tiered pedestal . . . on two golden thrones under a twenty-foot purple and gold canopy supported by twelve slender bronze columns

* King Edward VII's eldest son, Albert Victor, Duke of Clarence and Avondale, died in 1892 at the age of twenty-eight. He was engaged to Mary of Teck who, eighteen months later, married his only brother, George.

and surmounted by a dazzling golden dome', and the Emperor's eagle
eye noted that the Gaekwar of Baroda did not observe correct court
etiquette when making his homage. King Vajiravudjh was crowned
King of Siam in Bangkok. Unfortunately there was distinct coolness
between King Alfonso of Spain and his aunt, the Infanta Eulalia,
owing to the publication of her autobiography.

Balloons were clearly out-dated – the remains of the 'Hilderbrandt',
containing the bodies of two aeronauts, were found petrified under
the ice in a Pomeranian lake. Among the relatively few aviators
surviving the last decade M Pierre Prier made history by flying
from London to Paris without stopping. A young French airman
committed suicide after shooting the secretary of Hendon aerodrome;
this tragedy appeared to have no connection with the inauguration
of the first aerial mail between Hendon and Windsor. The Congress
of International Law confirmed the right to use aerial warcraft in
war and its blessing resulted in a very entertaining demonstration
of military aerobatics. Down to earth, the Reverend Swann and Mr
E Manning rowed across the Channel within days of each other and
Mr T W Burgess swam it. The *Lusitania* completed the round trip to
New York and back in just over twelve days and the first unsinkable
liner, the *Titanic*, was launched from a British shipyard. Suffragettes
kept up their clamour and Members of Parliament voted to give
themselves a salary for the first time. Winston Churchill became
First Lord of the Admiralty; Dr Sun Yat Sen became President of
China and abolished the pigtail. Prince Albert, aged fifteen, shot his
first woodcock, his first partridge and his first grouse.

Shortly after they had watched the Coronation procession, Elizabeth and David were taken by their spinster Aunt Violet to stay
with their maternal grandmother, Mrs Scott, at the Villa Caponi
near Florence. Mrs Scott was very High Church and went in for
incense and red damask wallcoverings in her private chapel. She
was also Ottoline Morrell's aunt and used to have her to tea with
little Bertie Russell at her house on Ham Common, which reeked
of tiger lilies.[4] Aunt Violet duly conducted the children round the
Trecento frescos, the tombs of the Medicis, the Pitti Palace and the
Boboli Gardens.

Soon after their return to Glamis Elizabeth's 24-year-old brother
Alec died from an unspecified illness. Almost a year later David
was sent off to prep school in Broadstairs, a bracing seaside resort
mainly populated by small boys worrying their way to Eton, knees
chapped by the east wind and the necessity of constant prayer. The

establishment chosen by Lord Strathmore was probably St Peter's Court, already graced by the presence of the young Princes Henry and George. Elizabeth had been living with her parents' mourning all year; her desolation was now extreme. 'David went to school for the first time on Friday,' she wrote to a friend, 'I miss him horribly.'[5] Smeared letters were sent off to Broadstairs by every post; she lost weight, looked peaky; her twelve-year-old heart was breaking. Lady Strathmore, unused to this sort of thing from her youngest daughter, realised something must be done.

Patrick, the eldest Strathmore son, was nearly thirty, Jock and Fergus already in the army, Michael up at Magdalen, Mary married to the 16th Baron Elphinstone. Twenty-three-year-old Rose was still at home, but she was a beauty and much occupied. If Elizabeth had been a boy she would have been preparing for Eton. The Buccleuchs of Montagu House were considering sending their daughters Alice and Sybil to boarding school – not to Heathfield, which would be proper, but to some insignificant institution in Malvern.[6] Lady Strathmore could not contemplate such a step. She finally and reluctantly decided on the Misses Birtwhistles' academy in Sloane Street as a passable, if temporary, distraction.

Although Elizabeth won a literature prize during her eight months' schooling in Sloane Street her greater achievements were entertaining distinguished old gentlemen like Lord Rosebery and Lord Curzon when they visited 20 St James's Square. She had already learned the knack of appearing to listen with sympathetic interest to crashing bores. 'The most astonishing child for knowing the right thing to say,' a friend wrote to Cynthia Asquith. 'Had she been consciously rehearsing for her future she could hardly have practised her manners more assiduously.'[7] School took up too much time. A temporary German governess was engaged to get them through the Easter holidays; Elizabeth persuaded her to stay, and Fraulein Kathie Kuebler took over her instruction in everything from piano to modern science.[8]

This was to be the extent of Elizabeth's education. Owing to Fraulein Kuebler's unhappy nationality the whole of it, modern science and all, was packed into less than eighteen months.

# Chapter Three

'Never have the prospects for world peace been so bright. Never has the sky been more perfectly blue,' David Lloyd George, Chancellor of the Exchequer, declared on 1 January 1914. Such statements are always ominous. In fact, the war had been going on for some time. In the autumn of 1912 Serbia, Greece, Montenegro and Bulgaria had declared it on Turkey, who was already fighting it against the Italians in Tripoli. Turkey, making a hasty peace, hurried home to declare it on Serbia and Bulgaria. Tsar Nicholas, one of King George's many cousins, took sides by sending a message of congratulation to King Peter on the successes of the Serbian army. Sir Edward Grey, the British Foreign Minister, said the Powers could scarcely intervene unless requested by both parties, though since there were half a dozen parties involved this seems unreasonable. Nevertheless British battleships and destroyers were ordered to Turkish waters, just in case.

There were abortive Peace Conferences in St James's Palace; the war survived them. Members of the imperial family kept in constant touch. George and Nicholas attended the wedding of their cousin Kaiser Wilhelm's daughter in Berlin, where George suspected that 'William's ear was glued to the keyhole' every time he and Nicholas tried to have a private chat.[1] There were diplomatic notes and ultimatums and blockades and when the Turkish business seemed to be settled the war went on between the Balkan countries themselves. It was unstoppable and sooner or later – or so it seemed to a few realists, if not to Lloyd George – Germany and Austro-Hungary would have to go to the defence of Turkey while Russia and her allies defended the Slav states.

By Christmas 1913 everyone was out to get everyone else. Six months later Gustav Princip and his friend Cabrinovic, Bosnian Serb students who believed a bullet in an Archduke was worth 10,000

18

casualties in war, were equipped with hand grenades and revolvers by the Serbian army and smuggled across the Drina. Two days later they shot the Archduke Franz Ferdinand, heir to the throne of Austria, and his wife at Sarajevo.

Kaiser Wilhelm, racing at the Kiel Yachting Week, was deeply upset and went home to Berlin, but otherwise nothing much happened. After writing 'Terrible shock for the dear old Emperor' in his diary, King George took Bertie to review the fleet at Spithead.[2] M Poincaré, the French President, was enjoying a series of brilliant State parties and preparing to visit St Petersburg. The Tsar was concerned with his son's illness, his wife pestering him to call in some crazy monk from the steppes. Glamis was getting ready for the Season, twenty-eight guest rooms to be polished as well as a dozen rooms for the ladies' maids in the service wing; the French chef was planning his menus, an army of local women scrubbing the bloodstains. Three-and-a-half weeks of peace and quiet; then on 23 July Austro-Hungary sent an ultimatum to Serbia charging her with tolerating terrorist propaganda against the Empire and accusing Serbian officers of planning the Sarajevo murders. The Emperor demanded that an inquiry, partially staffed by Austro–Hungarian officials, should be instituted forthwith. The time limit was forty-eight hours.

Serbia was reasonable but stubborn, and offered to submit her case to the Hague Tribunal. On 26 July King George cancelled his visit to Goodwood. On 28 July Franz Joseph declared war on Peter of Serbia. On 1 August Kaiser Wilhelm declared war on Tsar Nicholas. On 3 August he declared it on M Poincaré and marched into Belgium. On 4 August it was Elizabeth's fourteenth birthday. The family took her to the Coliseum to see Charles Hawtrey and Fedorovna, and the King wrote in his diary, 'I held a Council at 10.45 to declare war with Germany, it is a terrible catastrophe but it is not our fault . . . the cheering was terrific.'[3]

There was no conscription, as in Germany and France, but any decent young man knew where his duty lay and those who weren't so sure were soon shamed into it. The Bowes-Lyon boys and their contemporaries had no shadow of doubt. The three eldest sped back to their regiment; Michael abandoned Magdalen for the Royal Scots. David was only twelve (he was never to be a fighting man anyway), and at Eton, where the Sixth Form soon dwindled to a few sickly intellectuals. The Glamis neighbours – Dalhousies,Southesks, Butes,

Monymusks, Douglases and Stuarts – became sonless almost overnight.

They did, however, gain a great many daughters-in-law. There was a lemming-like stampede to the altar. Fergus and Jock Bowes-Lyon were married within a fortnight of each other, one in Sussex and one (to a girl who sacrificed the name of Hepburn-Stuart-Forbes-Trefusis) in Scotland. The clergy had never had it so good, turning out prospective widows every half an hour. The smaller jewellers ran out of wedding rings, confetti was at a premium; no time for the niceties, just a brief collision to ensure an heir, then back to the barracks and to Mother.

Elizabeth told Cynthia Asquith what she remembered of those suddenly purposeful days, 'the bustle of hurried visits to the chemists for outfits of every sort of medicine, and to the gunsmiths to buy all the things that people thought they wanted for a war, and found they didn't,'[4] – a bizarre image of queues outside John Bell and Croydon, ladies staggering home with armfuls of rifles and ammunition. A week later, properly equipped, she and her mother set off for Glamis, leaving Rose to train as a nurse.

Glamis was used as a hospital and Elizabeth spent the next four years encouraging wounded officers. Relinquishing all hopes in the field of modern science, Fraulein Kuebler had returned to Germany. She would have been pleased to know that her pupil passed the 'Oxford local' examination – the ancestor and rough equivalent of the O-level and GCSE – but perhaps she was never told. The athletic Miss Boynard took over in the following spring. They played a great deal of tennis.

In the 1960s a neighbour of the Strathmores, James Gray Stuart, third son of the 17th Earl of Moray, wrote an imaginative autobiography. As far as World War I is concerned it seems safe to assume that his descriptions were largely accurate. 'I duly joined my battalion of the Royal Scots at Weymouth on 15 September,' he wrote, 'and was happy to find a number of good friends from both Scotland and Eton among my comrades. . .' They were toughened up on the parade ground for four months, route-marching round Portland Bill to harden their feet. 'It was a sketchy sort of training, but it was all we got and all there was time for.'[5] By the New Year of 1915 the Royal Scots were at the front line in Belgium. At Glamis, as in every other home in the kingdom, the main interest was in letters from overseas.

Those from the Bowes-Lyon sons and young Stuart must be

packed away in some attic or vault, but it isn't difficult, from other records, to see what they were like. Billy, the second son of the Duke of Buccleuch, wrote to his sister Alice that summer:

> Dear Alice,
>     You might let my father know that several articles arrived safely, viz 1 Fowl in tin; 2 tins of sardines; 3 tins of herrings; 1 tin of rolled ox tongue; many tins of cream, cocoa etc. also such items as Dubbin.
>     We live entirely on the tinned stuff from England as the only meat out here is pork and the ration beef is not very tempting.
>     The asparagus is very good: but the best of all was the fowl in a tin.
>     What I particularly want is a tinned ham, or a big corned beef to have as a midday meal, and some *salad oil* or *mayonnaise sauce* would be very useful.
>     Cakes are also very useful. In fact send the same as now only more.
>     We have had a quiet time in the trenches with only a few casualties. I am only about 12–16 miles from Walter but cannot arrange to see him.
>     Love from Billy.[6]

The Strathmores would have read *The Morning Post* and the discreet Scottish papers, so may at first have taken such letters at face value. The masses, who relied on news from Bert and Alf and the *Daily Express*, knew both more and less of the real truth:

> As they pressed forward to the attack they were suddenly swept by a diabolical fire from two machine-guns posted at either end of the German trench . . . In this zone no man could live. But . . . [they] . . . were men of grit. They did not stop. They got as far as the wire. They hacked at it, tore at it with their hands until they were raw and bleeding and their uniforms rent to tatters. From their starting point right up to the wire they left a deep lane of their dead and dying 120 yards long, a sight so poignant that men, coming suddenly on that bloody trail, broke down and wept at the sheer pity, the undying glory of it.

Jingoism, well-bred insouciance, stupidity, courage, suffering, genocide – better to stay with Lady Elizabeth among her wounded Tommies. There are many heartwarming descriptions of her life at this time – the sing-songs and whist, the way she wrote letters for them and bought their 'baccy' at the village shop and asked them in 'that sweet quiet voice', 'How is your shoulder?', 'Do you sleep well?', 'Does it pain you?', 'Why are you not smoking your pipe?', 'Have you no tobacco?', 'You must tell me if you haven't and I'll get some for you' – a veritable phrasebook of the language of womanly concern. With a score of lonely men to adore her and no competition, she would have been the envy of any teenaged girl. One day she dressed twelve-year-old David in a skirt, veils, furs and a becoming hat, and took him round the ward, introducing him as her cousin. He played his part with natural talent and the patients much enjoyed the masquerade.

In September 1915 Fergus came home on leave to see his two-month-old daughter for the first time. Three days after his return to France he was killed at the disastrously mismanaged Battle of Loos. The Rev J Stirton's sermon at the parish church of Glamis the following Sunday was taken from John 14: 'I will not leave you comfortless; I will come to you. Yet a little while and the world seeth me no more; but ye see me; because I live, ye shall live also.' On 8 October the *Forfar Review and Advertiser* published a long poem by a pseudonymous 'Walter C. Howdon':

O brother mine, O comrade dead,
O sunny-hearted son,
What wreath shall crown your comely head
When valour claims her own?
Brother o' mine, twas ever yours
To win the favoured goal; You had the courage that endures,
The great all-conquering soul.

Twas yours to join the great crusade,
Twas mine to creep along;
And while you flashed a radiant blade
I spun an empty song.
Twas yours to take the high lone road
As mine to take the low,
And the proud charger you bestrode
Went where the God-led go.

O brother mine, O comrade dead,
O loyal-hearted son,
What wreath more meet for your dear head
Than the proud love you've won?
And for your requiem ours to sing
And that triumphantly – For you, O Death, where is thy sting?
Grave, where thy victory?

Lady Strathmore, unconvinced, sensibly collapsed, leaving the running of the hospital and household to her daughter Rose, now a qualified nursing sister, and the industrious Elizabeth. It was fairly strenuous, 'knitting, knitting, knitting . . . crumpling up tissue paper until it was so soft that it no longer crackled, to put in the lining of sleeping bags. . .'[7] Every morning, wearing little lace caps, Lady Strathmore and her youngest daughter prayed together in their private chapel. Elizabeth put her hair up and cut herself a wispy little fringe to complement the dewy, flirty eyes; if she was anything like a normal adolescent the effect would, she hoped, make up for the fact that her legs were too short and plump. In fact, if photographs are anything to go by – and in those days they all had a strange, probably deceptive magic – Lady Elizabeth Bowes-Lyon was a tease, and very fetching in what looked like outfits from the local rummage sale: an Orphan Annie whose Daddy was worth well over £100,000 a year.

Fund-raising for the Red Cross, running the local Girl Guide company, strawberries and cream at Eton, champagne and white chiffon for sister Rose's wedding at St James's Piccadilly (Elizabeth and David gave the bride four silver toast racks, Venetia James parted with a Venetian mirror that had probably seen better days, Lady Sackville made do with a stamp-damper); Michael reported killed and three months later found to be a prisoner – general rejoicing. It had at last been officially recognised that this was no gentleman's war. Heroes must be conscripted, even butlers and footmen and chauffeurs, unless they were mentally or physically deficient. The plight of the average Lady was piteous, 'There are only two housemaids,' Cynthia Asquith complained, 'so we can only have breakfast and tea in.'[8]

The situation abroad was pretty grim too. The Battle of the Somme was an experience Captain James Stuart and thousands of others would never forget. At some places the Allies advanced seven miles; in others, not an inch. For these seven miles the British lost 420,000 young men and the French more than 200,000; German losses were given as 450,000, but the equation was still rocky.[9] America had joined in after nearly three years of shilly-shallying, but on the other hand Russia had more or less retired in order to have a revolution. The terribly unfair thing, to a young girl just entering the marriage market, was that casualties were about three times heavier among junior officers than among common soldiers. The prospects, as Elizabeth approached her eighteenth birthday, seemed bleak.

It all ended in November 1918 exactly as it had begun, with cheering crowds and brass bands and balcony appearances and lumps in the throat. Perhaps the demonstrations were a little less sunny. 'Omnibuses were seized, and people in strange garments caroused on the open upper deck. A bonfire heaped against the plinth of Nelson's column in Trafalgar Square has left its mark to this day. Total strangers copulated in doorways and on pavements.

The celebrations ran on with increasing wildness for three days, when the police finally intervened and restored order.'[10] It is improbable that Elizabeth and her friends witnessed these Rabelaisian scenes. There would be Victory balls and dances to look forward to, even if it wasn't easy to dance with a man with only three limbs, and she was determined to make the most of it. 'Elizabeth Lyon is out now, and Cecilia has had a dance for her,' wrote Lady Buxton to a friend, adding with a sigh, 'How many hearts Elizabeth will break.'[11]

# Chapter Four

Albert Frederick Arthur George, the second son of George Duke of York and Princess Mary of Teck, was born on 14 December 1895 at York Cottage, Sandringham. The only error his father made was not to time things better. It was the thirty-fourth anniversary of the death of the Prince Consort and the seventeenth anniversary of the death of Princess Alice, a day dedicated to mourning at Windsor. George waited anxiously for a reprimand, but although 'Gan-gan' Victoria let it be known that she was 'rather distressed that this happy event should have taken place on a darkly sad anniversary'[1] she bravely looked on the bright side and gave the infant a bust of his sanctified great-grandfather as a christening present. The ceremony went off without a hitch, apart from one-year-old Prince Edward bursting into howls of jealousy or boredom or prescient grief and having to be removed to the vestry.

Some extraordinary combination of Teck and Wettin mixed with a brew of Saxe-Coburg-Gothas and Wurttemburgs and Schleswig-Holstein-Sonderburg-Glucksburgs had produced the exquisite changeling Edward, known as David. Born a year later, his brother Albert, known as Bertie, was to become a knock-kneed, stammering second-best with a chronic digestive complaint and an uncontrollable temper. As a baby, he was stuck up on top of a pillar by Cosmo Gordon Lang, who sourly remarked that the child 'was evidently not accustomed to such robust amusement.'[2] Shortly after this terrifying experience his position in the family was made even more awkward by the birth of a much-longed-for girl, Mary. The wretched Bertie seemed doomed to a lifetime of vertigo in high places and mediocrity everywhere else.

These children seldom saw their parents. On Bertie's fifth birthday he received a letter from his father: 'Now that you are five years old, I hope you will always try & be obedient & do at once what you are told, as you will find it will come much easier to you the sooner you begin. I always tried to do this when I was your age & found it made me much happier.'[3] If Bertie could read by then he probably thought this a normal birthday greeting. It's all there was, anyway, unless he was lucky enough to be staying with his grandparents at Marlborough House or Sandringham or Balmoral. There the indulgence and affection and fun were more than the repressed little boy could cope with; he became unruly, intoxicated by kisses and kind words, impossible to manage. The visits were curtailed. The two elder boys were turned over to an ex-footman called Frederick Finch. 'It was Finch who attended to their clothes and saw that they themselves were personally clean. It was Finch who heard their prayers morning and evening, and who tucked them up in bed, and it was Finch also who, when occasion demanded, administered condign chastisement upon their small persons.'[4] Luckily they were both devoted to him. The 'handsome, stalwart, muscular' Finch was the nearest thing to a natural parent they had ever known.

Even Finch, however, favoured the charismatic David and would later become his valet (concocting the 'pitiless remedy' for his young master's first hangover[5]), and then his butler. Very few people preferred Bertie. Among them, curiously enough, was Grandpa Edward, who wrote him countless encouraging notes beginning 'My dearest little Bertie'.[6] Lady Airlie, Princess Mary's lady-in-waiting, also favoured the unappealing little boy:

> He made his first shy overture to me at Easter 1902 . . . when he presented me with an Easter card. It was his own work, and very well done for a child of six – a design of spring flowers and chicks, evidently cut out from a magazine, coloured in crayons, and pasted on cardboard. He was so anxious for me to receive it in time for Easter that he decided to deliver it in person. He waylaid me one morning when I came out of his mother's boudoir, but at the last moment his courage failed him, and thrusting the card into my hand without a word he darted away . . . When I succeeded later in gaining his confidence he talked to me quite normally, without stammering, and then I found that far from being backward he was an intelligent child, with more force of character than anyone suspected in those days.'[7]

Mabell Airlie, a great friend of Elizabeth's mother, was thirty-six at the time, a year older than Princess Mary and a far more accessible character. It would be nice to think that little Bertie found refuge in her company.

But unlikely. He did not often brave his mother's boudoir and

had just come under the rule of his first tutor, Mr Hansell, a conscientious and high-minded person who would have disapproved of
the six-year-old Prince dallying around ladies. With the best will in
the world Mr Hansell set about teaching the left-handed child that
left-handedness was a mortal sin and showing his grieved disapproval
when the stammer became worse. 'The work in simple division sums
is most disheartening,' Mr Hansell reported, after he had been doing
his best for a year. 'I really thought we had mastered division by 3
but division by 2 seems to be quite beyond [Prince Albert] now.'
Six months later, 'I am very sorry to say that Prince Albert has
caused two painful scenes in his bedroom this week. On the second
occasion I understand that he narrowly escaped giving his brother
a very severe kick, it being absolutely unprovoked & Finch being
engaged in helping Prince Edward at the time.'[8] Bertie was caught in
a vicious circle. The more he laboured to use his right hand and save
his soul, the more inarticulate and stupid he became; the more stupid
and inarticulate he became the more his father upbraided him and his
brothers and sister mocked; the more inferior and ridiculous he felt
the more obstreperous he was, raging and weeping at the slightest
set-back or shouting and crashing about with manic exuberance,
demonstrating something that his locked tongue couldn't say.

And yet, as Mabell Airlie discovered, the left-handed child who
was trying to get out had a very modest, sensible attitude to life.
Bertie's knees were the next target. (David had excellent knees.) Sir
Francis Laking, Bt, GCVO, KCB, MD, devised a system of splints
into which the child was strapped for certain periods during the day
and, for a time, all night. 'This is an experiment,' Bertie wrote to his
mother who, as usual, was not at home. 'I am sitting in an armchair
with my legs in the new splints . . . I have got an invalid table, which
is splendid for reading but rather awkward for writing at present. I
expect I shall get used to it.'[9]

His knees, in fact, improved. Nothing else did. He continued to
let Mr Hansell down and to burst into furious tears when presented
with a simple equation. 'You must really give up losing your temper
when you make a mistake in a sum,' wrote his father with a sort of
bewildered concern. 'We all make mistakes sometimes, remember now
you are nearly 12 years old & ought no longer to behave like a little
child of 6.'[10] Somehow, this final admonishment worked. It seems
incredible, but Bertie passed his Osborne examinations and entered
the Royal Naval College in January 1909. It was the first time he
had lived among other boys, let alone slept with them. David was

already in his last term and the rigid etiquette of the school forbade him to be seen in the company of a new boy, even that of his own brother;[11] Bertie's stammer grew even worse, he was terrified, clumsy and dreadfully homesick. After six months he caught whooping cough.

This would not seem such a remarkable event in the life of a normal fourteen-year-old. Bertie, however, after his whoops had been attended by the assistant medical officer of the college, a Surgeon-Lieutenant Louis Greig, was considered to need a long convalescence. For over three months the boy lived entirely on his own – apart from Finch to see to his socks and a Mr Watt to keep up the relentless tutoring – on an estate ten miles from Balmoral.[12]* What puzzled them was that he showed no signs of loneliness or boredom. A few Scottish miles to the south the Bowes-Lyons were racketing around the countryside and Elizabeth doing her royal impersonation. A few miles north, east and west children were working on trawlers and being taken to America on sailing ships and putting in a ten-hour day in the shipyards and even going to school. All Bertie wanted, then as later, was to be left in peace to shoot and fish and be cock of his own walk across the heather. Under these conditions his stammer became little more than a hesitation, the tension slackened; he was even happy.

His grandfather died the following year. There was now the added strain of being the King's son; Bertie's place in his class at Osborne plummetted from bad to worse. 'My dear boy, this will not do,' wrote his father desperately, 'if you go on like this you will be bottom of your Term . . . It will be a great bore, but if I find that you have not worked well at the end of this term, I shall have to get a master for you to work with all the holidays & you will have no fun at all. Now remember, everything rests with you, & you are quite intelligent & can do very well if you like. . .'[12] In vain. Bertie's final position in the term was sixty-eighth out of sixty-eight.

How he got into Dartmouth on these results is a mystery. His first term was interrupted by measles, which necessitated another long convalescence at the Headlands Hotel, Newquay, under the supervision of Mr Hansell; his second by his father's Coronation. At the end of that term Bertie was placed sixty-seventh out of sixty-eight: an improvement. Two years later, out of grim determination, perhaps, rather than aptitude, he passed out of Dartmouth in sixty-first place out of only sixty-seven examinees, with a reference that stated he

---

*Prince John, Bertie's retarded and epileptic youngest brother, was isolated in a remote house on the Sandringham estate for the greater part of his short life.

was 'quite unspoiled and a nice, honest, clean-minded and excellent mannered boy.'[13] It was more than he had dared to hope for.

Bertie was now seventeen, an age at which, had he been a girl, he would have been beginning a strict training for marriage. The thought must have shuddered across his mind occasionally. Apart from his own inclinations, whatever they were, he was a Royal stallion and would have to be put out to stud sooner or later. It is hard to imagine what his sexual education could have been – probably a dutiful warning from Mr Hansell about the dangers of masturbation and homosexuality, vaguely mixed up with the Virgin birth, the habits of bees and the necessity of taking cold baths in emergencies. Even David at this time was diffident and socially immature but his looks were so startling and in such contradiction to his exalted position as Prince of Wales that women were already staring and sighing and longing to touch the fragile manikin. Bertie was handsome enough but unlike the precocious Lord David Cecil, he was terrified of girls, particularly those surrounded by bevies of adorers. At the various balls which were given for the naval cadets when they were in Quebec nothing would induce him to dance; he dug himself into a corner and stayed there.

The Navy was the last career Bertie would have chosen for himself. Apart from being paralysed with shyness in every port, he suffered dreadfully from seasickness and disliked sailing. However, it did get him away from home and there was a lot to broaden the mind and loosen the joints. Something must have happened, because by 24 November 1913 he was writing in his diary that he had danced nearly every dance at Lord Kitchener's ball in Alexandria and didn't get to bed until 3am.[14] He was also coming into contact with the common people, an experience most necessary to Royal training: 'Last night I went to a ball given by the Municipality, which was a very funny affair,' he wrote to his mother from Toulon. 'There were 6,000 guests, and it was in a theatre. There was no room to dance and you could not move at all. All the guests were ordinary people in the town and most of them got drunk at supper. I went away very early.'[15]

The young midshipman was not particularly concerned when the Archduke was shot at Sarajevo. His relatives were constantly being assassinated and although it was deplorable – 'What a good thing it was he was killed by the crowd,' he had written to his father after the lynching of 'one of these beastly anarchists' who had tried to kill the King of Italy[16] – it was not actually a case for mourning, as with poor Uncle Willy of Greece, who had been shot that spring while out for his morning stroll in Salonika. Fifty girls from Roedean visited Bertie's ship one afternoon and they had a tea-dance.[17] A month later Bertie recorded in his diary, 'I got up at 11.45 and kept middle watch until 4.00. War was declared between us and Germany at 2am. I turned in again at 4.00 till 7.15 . . . Papa sent a most interesting telegram to the fleet. I put it down in words.'[18]

Apart from whooping cough, measles and seasickness Bertie's health seems to have been better during his first years in the Navy than it was when he was small, but three weeks after the declaration of war he was attacked by violent pains in the stomach and had great difficulty breathing. The *Rohilla* was recalled from active service in the North Sea to take him to Aberdeen, where he was operated on for appendicitis. When he was due to rejoin his ship after three months' convalescence, the pain recurred. With everyone else occupied, he hung about, trailing from Sandringham to Buckingham Palace and back again, miserably depressed and no use to anybody. They gave him a job in the Admiralty, but it was only a sinecure and he had nothing to do. David had already succeeded in getting himself sent overseas and was dashing about boosting morale and being consulted by French generals. 'What does it matter if I'm killed?' he had demanded of Kitchener. 'I have four brothers.'*[19] Bertie's morale was lower than it had ever been.

At last he was allowed to return to sea, though forbidden to play football or hockey or to do any gymnastic exercises. Three months later the pain came back. He was transferred to a hospital ship for observation and the doctors sadly concluded that Prince Albert was unfit for active service. Such a humiliating and indeed unthinkable idea had never occurred to King George. He was horrified. 'The idea of the Prince's not being allowed to proceed into action with his ship would prey on his mind and undo all the good effects of his treatment,' Lord Stamfordham wrote to His Majesty's passionate dictation. 'Therefore HM cannot agree to Dr Sutton's suggestion . . . the King would prefer to run the risk of Prince Albert's health suffering than that he should endure the bitter and lasting disappointment of not being in his ship in the battle line.'[20]

In spite of what amounted to an order, Bertie was unable to get better. His complaint had been diagnosed as a weakening of the muscular wall of the stomach and a consequent catarrhal condition;

*His fourth brother, the sickly Prince John, was ten years old at the time.

the treatment was a quiet life, careful dieting, and an enema every night,[21] all of which would have been hard to provide in the middle of a naval battle. He was transferred to yet another hospital ship and inevitably finished up on the Balmoral estate in the care of the perennial Mr Hansell and a naval doctor. He did not return to sea until the following May, by which time almost half the war was over.

However, Bertie was to have one moment of glory. At 2pm. on Wednesday 31 May 1916 he was in the sick-bay of the *Collingwood* 'in a state of acute depression'[22] when he heard shouts of 'Action!' and 'Full speed ahead!' Bertie leapt out of his hammock and scrambled to his turret, where he stayed until 9pm and the Battle of Jutland was over. 'When I was on top of the turret,' he wrote to David, 'I never felt any fear of shells or anything else. It seems curious but all sense of danger and everything else goes except the one longing to deal death in every possible way to the enemy.'[23]

'In a single summer afternoon,' states Prince Albert's official biographer, 'he had passed into the full dignity of manhood.' Whatever that means, Bertie was certainly tremendously excited by the experience. 'In a war on such a scale as this,' he told David with the wisdom of a veteran, 'of course we must have casualties and lose ships & men, but there is no need for everyone at home to bemoan their loss when they are proud to die for their country. They don't know what war is, several generations have come and gone since the last great battles.'[24]

Prince Albert was among those officers commended for their services by Admiral Sir John Jellicoe in his dispatch; his health improved quite dramatically. 'Though his food that evening and night was of an unusual description,' Captain Ley wrote to King George, 'I am glad to tell your Majesty that he has been quite well since and *looks* quite well again!'[25]

Three months later Bertie was back at Windsor suffering from a duodenal ulcer. The doctors, as usual, prescribed a prolonged period of rest. He rested until the following May, his only excitements being a trip in a submarine on the Solent and receiving the Order of the Garter from his father. ('I cannot thank you enough for having made me a Knight of the Garter. I feel very proud to have it, and will always try to live up to it,' Bertie wrote. 'I am glad you say you will try & live up to the Garter,' the King replied.) Back to sea for another three months, then back to Windsor for more rest and quiet. Even Bertie began to see the endlessly repetitive pattern. Surgeon-Lieutenant Louis Greig from Osborne had turned up again and in spite of the fact that he was now second surgeon on the battleship *Malaya* strings were pulled to send him home with Bertie. Perhaps it was he who sensibly persuaded the Prince to give up the Navy. In any case, with considerable courage Bertie wrote to his father that he felt that he was not fit for service at sea. During four years of what he considered to be his country's heroic struggle he had managed to stay afloat for twenty-two months.

The operation performed at the end of November 1917, though two years overdue, appeared to be successful. At the beginning of 1918 Bertie and Dr Greig ('He is a perfect topper') were moved to the Royal Naval Air Service, pending its amalgamation with the RAF. A fortnight before the Armistice they were posted to General Trenchard's staff at the Headquarters of the RAF at Autigny. Bertie was in France at last, albeit nowhere near the front line. In what sounds like a desperate effort to assert himself again, he immediately started pontificating. 'General Trenchard won't allow anybody to talk about peace here,' he informed his father only a few days before the final shot was fired. 'I have never seen a man more engrossed in his command . . . He fairly keeps everybody up to their work.'[26] Unfortunately there was very little work left. Bertie and Greig found themselves staying peacefully and comfortably at the British Embassy in Paris, waiting to be told what to do.

They were sent to Brussels and when King George visited France he took both the sons on a tour of the battlefields, war cemeteries and devastated villages. It was decided that Bertie should remain there for a while, in case the relatives of those who had been proud to die for their country should start asking awkward questions. 'Bertie can be of far more use in this way than sitting in England where he has spent most of the war, not that this was his fault!' David scribbled to his mother. 'But by remaining with the armies till peace is signed he will entirely erase any of the unfair questions some nasty people asked last year as to what he was doing, you will remember.'[27] Queen Mary did remember. She was trying to come to terms with the death of 'poor darling little Johnnie' and to convince herself of what she told other people: 'For him it is a great release. I cannot say how grateful we feel to God for having taken him in such a peaceful way; he just slept quietly into his heavenly home, no pain, no struggle, just peace for the poor little troubled spirit.' Her three eldest sons were little comfort. David should stay at home instead of planning to 'rush about' the world; it would only make it harder for him to settle down when the time came. Harry seemed steady enough, but she had to confess she found him extremely dull. Bertie's health was a constant worry.

by now Bertie's constant companion and mentor, found his rôle as Royal Nanny exhausting and time-consuming, whatever affection and loyalty he felt towards his difficult charge. His greatest ambition was to 'put steel into' Prince Albert,[3] but he needed assistance. Major Stuart's *savoir-faire*, together with his splendid war record, were just what was needed. Greig made tactful enquiries about his plans for the future.

Stuart went home to Edinburgh to read law, play golf and lead the life of an eligible young bachelor in Scottish society. Elizabeth, 'a noticeable débutante' said Lord David Cecil with remarkable restraint, who dressed 'picturesquely, unfashionably'[4] (she was given to wearing sunbonnets and homespun skirts), was also doing the seasonal rounds. At Ascot she gave her little wave to Princess Mary in the Royal Box, quickly assessing her 'sweet frock of filmy georgette, with touches of the pale blue that is so becoming to our blue-eyed Princess' and the 'large hat of white crinoline straw with one large pink rose reposing on the brim.'[5] She was having a wonderful time, all the men at her feet,[6] twinkling and *chassé*-ing in all the most exclusive ballrooms on both sides of the border.

Dancing was no longer a formal pastime; it had become a way of life, and Elizabeth was very good at it. You could dance through lunch, through tea, through dinner, and on until breakfast. You could dance in clubs and pubs and restaurants, on roof tops and river boats and trains. It was a kind of energetic, extended foreplay, all the healthy exercise of sex with none of its unpleasantness. The music was brazenly innocent, 'heavily punctuated, relentless rhythm, with drums, rattles, bells, whistles, hooters and twanging banjoes,'[7] but nevertheless self-styled moralists thundered outrage at the 'Twinkle' and the 'Missouri Walk', the 'Elfreda', the 'Jog Trot' and the 'Shimmy'. Anything could be done with the tango, and often was, but the Blues, with its disturbing, wailing melodies and the tribal dances of the Bright Young Things, Charleston and Black Bottom, were still to come.

Prince Albert was a nifty dancer, almost as agile on the ballroom floor as the tennis court. Since so few facts are known about Elizabeth's success at this time in breaking hearts, some romantically-minded biographers have assumed, or hoped, that they came to know each other while they were both on the trot in 1919 and early 1920. Some say she popped into the Palace from time to time to dance to Mary's gramophone, but it is most unlikely that King George would have agreed to such frivolity. Bertie was a Squadron Leader in the

RAF and a token undergraduate at Trinity, Cambridge, during that winter. With his elder brother out of the country for four months in 1919 and seven months in 1920, he was also called upon to do a number of royal chores. While it could not be said that these employed him for 247 days a year, eight hours a day, give or take the odd Bank Holiday, he was reasonably busy. Elizabeth was delightfully occupied with a dozen flirtations, more and less serious. While they must have seen each other occasionally – an awkward acknowledgment from Bertie, a cool flutter of eyelashes from Elizabeth – they had little in common. She was certainly less aware of Bertie than she was of the Prince of Wales, whose name was on every girl's lips and in every mother's dreams. He was seen everywhere with Mrs Freda Dudley Ward, but it was well known that she was *persona non grata* with the King and Queen and such a liaison couldn't possibly last. What *was* it about Freda that attracted him? None of them could understand it. That the very qualities which made Elizabeth 'irresistible to men'[8] were those that made her so resistible to the Prince of Wales may have rankled a little, even then.

She was small, wistful, yielding, an instinctive mistress of the arts and crafts that please, 'mildly flirtatious in a very proper romantic old-fashioned Valentine sort of way. . . She makes every man feel chivalrous and gallant towards her.'[9] She was – the highest accolade at that time – dainty.* Her contemporaries might crop their hair, drink Sidecars, smoke De Reszke cigarettes and fling their silk-stockinged legs about, but all they got for it was a slap on the back and the endearment 'good sport', 'ripper', even 'good chap'. Elizabeth, though she would have been shocked at the familiarity, was pattable, a pet, a positive darling. The young men in her circle, back from the stench and squalor of the trenches, wanted nothing better. 'I was madly in love with her. Everything at Glamis was beautiful, perfect. Being there was like living in a Van Dyke picture . . . I fell *madly* in love. They all did.'[10]

The author of this statement remains incognito, as does the suitor who serenaded her by cracking his hunting whip under her window half the night. 'What a happy group we were,' 'Chips' Channon sighed

---

*OD: choice morsel. *The Lady*, in a single issue during 1919, lists Dainty dance frocks at Peter Robinsons, Dainty tea frocks at Debenham and Freebody's, Dainty dishes, recipes for, Dainty sewing for odd moments, Dainty trifles for Odds & Ends, Dainty voile frocks for warmer days, Dainty wear for Nursery Folk, Dainties for Invalids, Dainty lingerie, the Daintie Hair Net and the Daintiness of Aertex Cellular Clothing.

twenty years later. 'Paul. . . Gage and me, the Queen, others. . .'[11] There are many dots and gaps in these records, and a great deal of editing. The young men crowded round her in the photographs are now dead, and their grandchildren would be unable to recognise their kilted or tweeded figures, moustached, jaunty, wrinkling their eyes against the sun. We can, however, identify James Stuart. Like his ancestor, the bonny Earl of Moray, he looks 'a braw gallant'. Since his own evidence has proved unreliable and he has been overlooked by previous biographers it is necessary to read between the lines of his and others' memoirs to understand the course of Elizabeth's life over the next three years.

Early in 1920, in Stuart's own words, 'my whole life changed. I was asked by Louis Greig to come to London to see him. Prince Albert had gone to Cambridge after the war and the suggestion was that I should join him there about a month before he came down and started his official career. I was to be his first equerry. Such a thought had never entered my head.'[12] If Stuart did join Bertie at Cambridge he forgets to mention it in his autobiography. By the beginning of May, cross and lonely and not a little homesick, he was installed on the schoolroom floor of Buckingham Palace along with Mary, Harry, and his new 'master'.

It must have been a compensation that Elizabeth was in London that May – the Bowes-Lyons and Stuarts were neighbours and old friends. On the twentieth Lord and Lady Farquhar gave a ball at 7 Grosvenor Square to which Prince Albert and his equerry were invited. Among the other guests were Lord and Lady Annaly, chaperoning 'the youngest Strathmore girl'. Perhaps Major Stuart and Elizabeth danced together sufficiently often for Bertie to take notice. He told Lady Airlie long afterwards 'that he had fallen in love that evening, although he did not realise it until later.' There is no convincing evidence that he even asked Elizabeth for a foxtrot, with or without twinkle.*

At the beginning of June Prince Albert was made Baron Killarney, Earl of Inverness and Duke of York in the Birthday Honours List. ('I

---

*In his autobiography James Stuart claims that he introduced Elizabeth to Prince Albert at the Royal Air Force Ball at the Ritz in the summer of 1921. This is unlikely, since Bertie had already visited Glamis in October 1920; therefore I rely for my dates on John Wheeler Bennett's *George VI* and Elizabeth Longford's *Queen Mother*.

must write and thank you again ever so very much for having made me Duke of York,' he wrote to his father, '. . . and I hope I shall live up to it in every way.'[13]) Almost more encouraging, he and Louis Greig won the finals of the RAF Doubles Competition at Wimbledon. Bertie must have been in a sunny mood. Quite suddenly, with no reasonable explanation, we find him visiting St Paul's Walden Bury and 'basking' in Elizabeth's 'radiant vitality'.[14]

The theory seems to be either that Prince Albert unaccountably remembered that he was 'a friend of her many brothers'[15] or that Elizabeth's 'close friendship' with his sister Mary somehow brought these visits about. Bertie's friendship with the Bowes-Lyon brothers has not been mentioned anywhere else. He never went to school; none of them were up at Cambridge with him; their careers had been totally different; of the three surviving Strathmore sons only Michael was an approximate contemporary. As for Princess Mary, while she and Elizabeth were certainly acquainted on a basis of juvenile *thé dansants*, society weddings and a mutual enthusiasm for the Girl Guides, there is no evidence that either as children or young women they ever visited each other's homes, and they certainly never went out alone together. Close friendships are not indulged in by the Royal Family. 'You are right to be civil & friendly to the young girls you may occasionally meet,' Queen Victoria wrote to her seventeen-year-old granddaughter, '& to see them sometimes – but never *make friendships*; girls' friendships and intimacies are very bad & often lead to great mischief . . . Besides . . . you are so many of yourselves that you *want no one else*.'[16]

Elizabeth's parents were in any case by no means enamoured of Royalty; Lord Strathmore had thoroughly disapproved of the Prince of Wales' dissipation back at the turn of the century and always swore that 'if there is one thing I have determined for my children, it is that they shall never have any post about the Court';[17] Lady Strathmore, disgusted by the rapaciousness of some society hostesses, had been heard to murmur, 'Some people, dear, have to be fed royalty like sea-lions with fish.'[18] They were not the sort to invite Prince Albert for the weekend on the strength of a brief meeting at the Farquhars' Ball.

James Stuart, on the other hand, was a friend. If Bertie had fancied Elizabeth at the Farquhars' and learned that his equerry was going to stay with her parents, what would be more natural than to take advantage of it? An equerry cannot refuse a command, however reluctant he may be. That Bertie 'basked' at St Paul's Walden Bury may be true. What Major Stuart and Lady Elizabeth thought about it is another matter.

The exodus to Scotland took place as usual, the Strathmores to Glamis, Bertie to the Ancasters at Drummond Castle. By the end of August all the Royals were at Balmoral except David, steaming towards Honolulu on HMS *Renown*, and Mary, who was staying with Lady Airlie at Cortachy Castle. Stuart rather enjoyed Balmoral, even if he did have to dance with the Queen at the Ghillies Ball and play golf on a course that more closely resembled a hayfield.[19] He frequently went over to Glamis; the now eager Duke inevitably went with him. Elizabeth made the best of it. One evening the Strathmores gave a dance and their youngest daughter wore 'a rose brocade Van Dyke dress with pearls in her hair.'[20] She may have been in love, but certainly not with Bertie.

Shortly after this the Duke of York and his brother Harry went south for the required round of country house visits, which consisted of shooting a great many birds and inspecting the indigenous débutantes. They were entertained by Miss Edwina Ashley at her grandfather's shoot near Newbury and by the Pembrokes at Wilton, where 'the lovely Bath girl, Lady Mary Thynne, *and* the youngest and only unmarried Cadogan girl'[21] were among the guests. James Stuart kicked his heels at Balmoral and visited Glamis as much as he could. The *Tatler* of 27 October 1920 contains a picture taken during the lunch interval at a Glamis Shoot: Elizabeth, wearing a baggy tweed coat and skirt, embroidered jumper and sensible felt hat, looks demure; Major James Stuart stalwart and even tweedier; Miss Elizabeth Cator of Woodbiswick (a friend of Elizabeth's from the distant Birtwhistle days) is engulfed in a kind of blown-up bowler and Lady Strathmore wears a magnificently unsuitable black feathered toque. The rest, Captain and Miss Malcolm, Mary and Lord Elphinstone and Lord Strathmore, have the uneasy look of people unaccustomed to the camera. For some reason, perhaps to be on the safe side, there is an individual snap of Major Stuart smiling behind his pipe, his flat cap giving him a comfortably squirarchal air: a man who finds everything going his way and is enjoying it.

With the migration of those wild geese that had survived the season's slaughter everyone moved south. The castles and country houses were left empty except for servants and factors and major-domos. Armies of carpenters, plumbers, masons, painters and upholsterers moved in to repair the damage; gunsmiths oiled and polished; poachers set about stocking up their cottage larders with the 'rubbish' – exhausted stags, wounded rabbits – that remained. The lease of 20 St James's Square having expired, the Strathmores took possession of 17 Bruton Street, off Berkeley Square. The Prince of Wales was home again, which added a *frisson* to dances and dinners. The Twenties were in their infancy, but there was change in the wind: new sounds, new experiences, with any luck a new life. The *jeunesse dorée* glittered by Royal Command.

The more decorous aristocratic circles, to which the Strathmores belonged, followed the prescribed circuit of charity lunches, charity balls and sales of needlework. 'There are, it seems,' wrote *The Lady* with a sob in her throat, '4,600 little souls (Waifs and Strays) being cared for at the moment and what do you think it would cost to buy them two handkerchiefs each? I am sure you would never guess! £115! But it just gives one some little idea of what it must cost to keep the tiny folk in other things.' Handkerchiefs for the Waifs and Strays was a good enough cause for a fancy dress party or a smallish dance, or for girlfriends to get together and eat prodigious amounts of trifle and cream cakes, when the gossip would concern the Duke of Westminster's new bride – 'My dear, you know what she was wearing? *Brown* spats!' – and the extraordinary case of Miss Radclyffe Hall appearing in court in men's clothes – 'He said she'd come between him and his wife. I don't see *how*, do you? She does look very odd, but after all. . .' – and the latest rumours of marriage plans, which concerned them greatly. The humiliation of going through one's second season unmarried was too dreadful to contemplate; at the third one would be forced to flee to India, or worse. The heady business of being adored by the few surviving young men was all the more intoxicating for being so brief. They were butterflies preening themselves in the last patch of sunlight, anxious to be caught before dark.

A plausible reason for Elizabeth's rejection of all the suitors who clamoured to bestow on her their considerable worldly goods was that she was already in love. Why didn't she say so? Perhaps there were unusual complications. Perhaps Lady Strathmore had begun to have different ideas. Elizabeth seems to have lacked all the normal instincts for rebellion, or for expressing them anyway. She resorted to passive resistance, which in a few years would take the form of minor illnesses whenever a crisis loomed. This was made much easier if she refused to recognise that anything difficult or unpleasant was happening. With luck things would sort themselves out without involving her. So they did, though not in the way she expected.

Bertie had now seen enough of her to be catastrophically in love and unable to keep quiet about it. Queen Mary was delighted, though cautious. While they were taking a drive one afternoon she said to Mabell Airlie, 'I have discovered that he is very much attracted to Lady Elizabeth Bowes-Lyon. He's always talking about her. She seems a charming girl, but I don't know her very well.' Mabell understood immediately. She replied that she had known Elizabeth all her life, and could say nothing but good of her.[22] No more was needed. The two ladies drove on, bright-eyed and smiling under their toques.

# Chapter Six

Christmas at St Paul's Walden Bury was the usual riot of innocent fun – brothers and sisters and in-laws, nephews and nieces, unattached guests with no home to go to and guests who hoped to consider the Bury as home. Elizabeth entertained by singing popular songs with the words adapted to suit the personalities and idiosyncracies of the company.[1] She could do a lot with 'And her mother came too', 'Ma, he's making eyes at me' and 'Look for the silver lining', but her favourites came from music-hall and a spirited rendering of 'My old man said follow that van' would be the high spot of the evening. James Stuart also had a weakness for these songs and knew most of them by heart.[2] He looked as though he had a fine baritone.

Meanwhile at Sandringham the slow, costive festivities plodded through their usual routine, the young men restive, archbishops and dowagers discreetly breaking wind on their hard upright chairs, Queen Mary planning a little chat with her second son when the appropriate occasion arose. As for him, he had been unsettled by his glimpses of life at Glamis and St Paul's Walden Bury and had actually been heard to grumble about things at home: 'No new blood is ever introduced . . . no originality in the talk – nothing but a dreary acquiescence . . . No one has the exciting feeling that if they shine they will be asked again . . . they know they will be automatically, as long as they're alive. Traditionalism is all very well, but too much of it leads to dry rot.'[3] Strong words for a young man whose reflex action to his very existence seemed to be to thank his father. His youngest brother, Georgie, was equally glum. He hated the Navy and found the endless anecdotes about shooting, which he hated just as much, intolerably boring. David couldn't wait to get back to London. Only Harry's giggle broke the hush. He enjoyed a state of semi-concussion most of the time and didn't notice much. On Christmas morning he was the only one to sing 'God rest you merry, gentlemen' with any kind of verve.

Bertie had his chat with Mama and was greatly relieved. She approved of Elizabeth with the proviso that she would of course have to meet the girl properly before anything could be decided. Bertie, knowing his mother's eagerness to get her sons settled and what a powerful ally she was, said he was going to propose anyway. Either because he believed in Elizabeth's superiority or because he had such a low opinion of his son, his father growled 'You'll be a lucky fellow if she accepts you.'[4]

Prince Albert had at last found a job he liked doing and perhaps it was this, as much as the conduciveness of the season, that made him wait until spring before confronting Elizabeth. In May 1919 he had been asked to become President of the Boys' Welfare Association, soon to be renamed the Industrial Welfare Society, 'an organisation through which industry itself might be responsible for . . . the betterment of working conditions, the setting up of works' committees, the provision of health centres and canteens in factories, and of proper facilities for the maximum of enjoyment in the workers' free time.'[5] In the early 1920s this idea was revolutionary and soon commanded 'the interest, respect and commendation of over a hundred firms',[6] though certain elements in management bellowed Bolshevism and some Trades Unionists deplored the idea of Labour lying down with Capital.

In spite of his serious intentions Bertie was like a small boy on a spree. He went down coal mines, clambered up scaffolding, drove locomotives and trucks and, once, a tram through the crowded streets of Glasgow. He poured molten metal from crucibles, pressed a button to blast thousands of tons of rock, walked unflinchingly through glue factories. For the first time in his life he talked to working-class men and although the conversations were necessarily brief and one-sided, he learned more than he had done in the whole of his twenty-five years about the way that ninety-nine per cent of his countrymen looked, spoke and survived. Because he was enjoying himself they saw him at his best. 'Of all the many visitors we had here,' one manager said, 'I never met one who asked more sensible questions or showed greater understanding of our fundamental problems. He does like getting to the bottom of things.'[7] Margaret Bondfield, the Labour politician, once remarked that Queen Mary would have made an excellent factory inspector.[8] Her second son, who was invariably regarded as a replica of his father, inherited much more from his mother than is generally recognised.

Apart from the fact that he was relatively busy, Bertie was in no tearing hurry to propose, now that he had his parents' qualified blessing. He had no doubt of the result. The prospect of leaving his awful home after all these years might, illogically, have been a little daunting. There would be such a fuss over the wedding and what if he couldn't get the words out? This is the sort of thing that worries anyone on a sleepless night. Come the first crocus Bertie made his proposal. And was refused.

Elizabeth didn't want to marry Prince Albert. Because such a self-evident fact is too embarrassing to consider, all her biographers have relied on some fiction about her being nervous of everything such a marriage would entail – the public life, the responsibility of being royal, and so on. Elizabeth had been training herself for public life since she was nine years old, if not longer. Performing to an audience – the smiles, the waves, the applause – was second nature to her. She was confident of her ability to enchant, entertain, be adored. The role of Duchess of York, though one step down from Princess of Wales, would suit her admirably. There were only two convincing explanations – that she wanted to marry someone else, or the Duke himself.

Apart from his extreme moodiness, Bertie was not of a strong constitution and he was disconcertingly nervous. He had a serious speech impediment and numerous twitches, sometimes blinking his eyes with too much frequency and unable to control the muscles around his mouth. In addition, his drinking problem, though thought to be kept secret, had grown worse.[9] Far from Elizabeth's ideal hero and a poor alternative to some of his competitors.

She had not yet realised the cynicism and ruthlessness of Royalty's attitude to marriage. Prince Albert's great-grandmother firmly believed that 'if two eligible young people were pushed into a double bedroom, love would be sure to follow,' and if it didn't, any well-brought-up gal would be happy to make the best of it. King George did not intend his doubts about his son's acceptability to be taken seriously. It was nice that Bertie was so much in love, but the important thing was that Elizabeth seemed a suitable mare and mares did not have opinions. It was unthinkable that the girl should refuse such a catch.

Wanting to please everyone and more than a little flattered, Elizabeth could hardly tell Bertie that he didn't live up to her standards of the perfect husband. She may even have liked him by now – it is hard, though by no means impossible, to dislike someone who adores you and Bertie certainly had likeable qualities, once you got to know him. What did she say? Sorry, but I hope we can be friends – the classic put-down? Even that must have needed considerable courage. She had said it often enough before, but those occasions hadn't involved royal disapproval and turning down a good part. Unless she had a better alternative Bertie must have been exceptionally undesirable.

In spite of everyone's sympathy the Duke of York was desolate. 'I do hope he will find a nice wife who will make him happy,' Lady Strathmore wrote to Mabell Airlie. 'I like him so much and he is a man who will be made or marred by his wife.'[10] Prescient, but little comfort. Neither were the high spirits of his equerry.

Bertie was too familiar with failure to take it lightly. A gossip columnist's description of a reception given for him that spring presents a sad picture: 'The Duke of York seemed, perhaps, the least enthusiastic . . . Poor dear, it can't be really very amusing to be continually surrounded with pomp and ceremony.'[11] He not only had to contend with his own humiliation, his father's jokes and his mother's outrage, but he was being pitied by the Press.

Dutifully, he soldiered on. He hunted with the Quorn and appeared at Grafton Hunt 'Chases' with his two younger brothers, all identical in grey herringbone tweed; he climbed ladders and inspected nuts and bolts. Then it was Cowes Week with the Barings and Edwina Ashley and his cousin Louis Mountbatten, and Greig snapping 'Behave yourself, Sir!'[12] when he lost his temper on the tennis court. 'Such a collection of youth and beauty at Nubia House,' *The Tatler* enthused, 'Lady Crewe . . . Sir Harry and Lady Mainwaring, Captain James Stuart, Lord Moray's youngest son, who is generally with the Duke of York . . .'*[13] Now known to gossip columnists as 'the pretty Strathmore girl', Elizabeth had been seen at Lady Astor's, the Caledonian Ball and the requisite number of country houses. At Ascot she might have bobbed to the Royal brothers in their toppers and tails and noticed James Stuart's undue interest in the Cavendish girl, Rachel, just back from Canada.[14]

Major Stuart is not mentioned in any of the versions of subsequent events. In August 1921 Queen Mary descended on Lady Airlie at Cortachy Castle, accompanied by Princess Mary, a gentleman-in-waiting, his servant, two dressers, a detective, a footman, a chauffeur and an under-chauffeur. It was a small castle. The Queen's excuse

---

*James Stuart in his autobiography places this meeting in 1920. He overlooks the year 1921 except for the inaccurately dated episode already mentioned.

was that she could no longer go abroad to stay with the old Grand Duchess of Mecklenburg-Strelitz as she used to do, and needed a 'real holiday'.[15] In fact her objective was to inspect the Strathmore girl who had been causing Bertie such trouble. Bertie escorted his mother in her two-chauffeured motor car. When they arrived at Glamis they found Lady Strathmore ill in bed and Elizabeth acting as hostess. If it had been planned it couldn't have been more successful. Bertie's mother or not, this was Queen Mary. Elizabeth soared to the occasion, charming, exquisitely polite, properly humble; she smiled the whole time, asked the right questions and showed considerable knowledge of the history of her draughty castle. The Queen departed with a glint in her eye. She had decided this was 'the one girl who could make Bertie happy'. Perhaps it would be as well if something were done about that surly young man lurking in the background. 'But,' the old hypocrite added swiftly, 'I shall say nothing to either of them. Mothers should never meddle in their children's love affairs.'

Even when she was in her mid-eighties many otherwise rational people were disgusted by the idea that the Queen Mother as a young woman had been in love with anyone but her husband. In 1922, when it looked as though Lady Elizabeth Bowes-Lyon might become the Duchess of York, it never occurred to the public or the media that she could have other plans.* Women's magazines and the popular Press wrote respectfully about her high standards and the seriousness with which she regarded the marriage vows: she would only commit herself to a man who was kind and brave, unswervingly loyal and honest, unimpeachably virtuous and deeply religious. 'There was one immensely attractive man, the son of a neighbour, who kept on trying. But he also had flirtations in between, and she wouldn't have that . . . more than all her friends she knew what she really wanted, and that was absolute purity.'[16] Any man, short of the Prince Consort of blessed memory, would have a hard time living up to such expectations. Major Stuart, though kind and brave and unswervingly loyal (a virtue which only occasionally detracted from his honesty) did not.

When I was researching for this book I knew that if I was going

---

* There were exceptions. A column about Lady Elizabeth in an issue of *The Lady* early in 1923 adds this curious postscript: 'Marriage the happiest bond of love might be / If hands were only joined where hearts agree' says the poet. Then, on the other hand, an old proverb tells us that we should 'Marry first and love will follow.'

to write about James Stuart, I must ask the – very few – people close to the Queen Mother who agreed to talk to me whether my suppositions were valid. Sir Martin Gilliatt, her Private Secretary, muttered, 'I wouldn't know anything about it at all,' and hurriedly drew my attention to her engagement book.[17] (He said that he didn't know anything about Glamis either – 'It's out of my orbit, frankly.') Lady Rachel Bowes-Lyon, the Queen Mother's sister-in-law, was discreet but not, apparently, outraged. James Stuart was 'sent away', she said, 'because he was after the Same Thing.'[18] Sir Harold Macmillan, staring blindly at the ceiling in search of distant memories, quavered, 'Jamie Stuart was in love with her, of course . . .'[19] A distinguished publisher, who must remain anonymous, heard the story from Stuart himself on a convivial overnight train journey to Scotland. Rather less convincingly, a Royal butler, Ernest King, confided in his book *The Green Baize Door* that Queen Mary 'made quite certain of her second son's marriage to Queen Elizabeth the Queen Mother when she was Lady Elizabeth Bowes-Lyon. A possible rival had quickly found himself appointed to the Governor-General's staff in Canada.' Eavesdropping through a green baize door can be unreliable . The Governor-General of Canada was Lord Cavendish, James Stuart's future father-in-law.

If there are any more facts about this affair they remain as uncertain as the whereabouts of the Queen Mother's birth. The only one that has any real relevance to this story is that in the New Year of 1922, Major James Stuart left England for the oil-fields of Oklahoma.

# Chapter Seven

London: The paper 'London Gossip' printed . . . this morning
. . . that the Duke of York . . . was engaged to Lady Elizabeth
Bowes-Lyon, daughter of the Earl of Strathmore. It is stated on
authority here that the report is entirely without foundation. Gossip
on this matter was prevalent in London a month or so ago, when
it was also said that the Duke of York's wishes to enter upon the
engagement had brought him into conflict with his father. Inquiries
at the time failed to obtain any information tending to corroborate
these reports . . .

*New York Times, 4 February 1920*

Once he had made up his mind, Prince Albert was doggedly persis-
tent. Elizabeth continued to turn him down but it was beyond her
to refuse Queen Mary. Bewildered and unhappy, she did everything
she was told except give in to marriage. Holding hands in a boat was
Bertie's idea of courtship.[1] Elizabeth pulled her hand away and kept
him waiting when he came to call.[2] This could have been her flirtatious nature, but it seems unlikely. In the photographs of that period
she looks wan, almost bedraggled. Who did she confide in, apart
from close friends now dead and eternally discreet? Helen Hardinge,
sister-in-law of Elizabeth's young confidante Diamond and herself a
lady who would play a significant role in later years, tells the usual
tale: 'Lady Elizabeth had nothing against the Duke himself; but . . .
having been so happy in her own family, it was hard for her to have
to face a situation in which privacy would have to take second place
to her husband's work for the nation.'[3] In fact Elizabeth knew that the
temptation to gossip was irresistible, and that unless you happened to
be a Strathmore secrets were hard to keep. Because the Royal Family
was involved, an official explanation for the delay was necessary. It
would hardly have been possible to excuse her reluctance on the
grounds that she was waiting for another man.

In the meanwhile Queen Mary, being no fool, understood the

situation and arranged for the gal to be seen with the rig
A photograph taken in the autumn of 1921 at Brechin Castle
Elizabeth for the first time in a group surrounding the majestic figu
of her would-be mother-in-law.[4] The next step was to include her
among the bridesmaids for Mary's wedding to Viscount Lascelles
on 28 February 1922. Among the other seven blue-blooded misses
was Lady Rachel Cavendish.

In spite of much public rejoicing, this sounds a gloomy occasion.
Mary's bridegroom was fifteen years older than herself, and not the
most immediately desirable of men. King George, though he put on
a brave face at the ceremony, had 'quite broken down' when he went
to her room to take leave of his virgin child before escorting her to the
Abbey. David, who might have provided the necessary light relief,
was in India. The bridesmaids were decked out in silver roses worn
at hip-level and tied with lovers' knots, diadems of silver rose leaves.
In the wedding picture they look sullen and dowdy, with a hint of
acne here and there. Elizabeth came off worst, being almost hidden
in the back row, her expression, as seen by one of her biographers,
'pensive, if not anxious'.[5] Her expression as seen by everybody else
was one of wretchedness and fury. When the official portrait of the
wedding group was painted she got left out altogether. The excuse was
that there was no room on the canvas, but it seems more likely that
the painter felt he could do nothing to make her look even tolerably
joyful.

Describing the festivities to her eldest son, Queen Mary might
have been telling him about a funeral: 'Mary is married & has
flown from her home leaving a terrible blank behind her as you
can well imagine. Papa & I are feeling very low & sad without her,
especially as Georgie had to return to Malta yesterday while Harry
has at last joined the 10th Hussars at Canterbury & Bertie has gone
hunting for a few days . . . Papa & I felt miserable at parting, poor
Papa broke down, but I mercifully managed to keep up as I so much
feared Mary would break down. However she was very brave. . .'[6]
The gloom deepened. Three weeks later she was writing 'There has
been a perfect epidemic of deaths. Ly Farquahar's, Col: Erskine's
mother Ly Horatia Erskine, Dow: Ly Derby, Bertha's Aunt, Wigram's
brother-in-law, then Leopold & then Ly Stamfordham who as you
know has been ill since last July – It is all rather sad & depressing
& this added to the most odious cold dull rainy weather makes life
almost intolerable.'[7]

Insensitive to the depression settled over Windsor and Glamis,

rs-on were meddling under the guise of
ot a question of taking sides, since apart
obstinacy Elizabeth was unimportant, but
were in at the kill, whoever the victim might
by now a pillar of Belgravia Establishment,
with stringent dinner parties during the course of
pass a note to her butler with DCSC scribbled on
Second Chicken.[8] Generous hospitality was provided
by          ie Greville, another well-preserved and powerful relic
of Edw.     ın days and one of the greatest snobs of the century.
With the Prince of Wales away, the Duke of York held the stage
for a while, finding himself surrounded by sympathy and concern
to counteract the odious cold dull rainy weather and his parents'
low spirits. Those close to him were alarmed at these times at how
much whisky he drank. His stuttering was worse than ever.[9]

After the Lascelles wedding, Elizabeth disappears from the records
for over six months. Bertie staggered on. He deputised for his father
at the wedding of Princess Marie of Romania to King Alexander of
the Serbs, Croats and Slovenes, riding an 'excessively restive horse'
through the streets of Belgrade and scattering handfuls of coins to
children who had been taught to chant, 'O Koom, your purse
is burning.'[10] He was a great success, but it didn't relieve his
misery. Hardly was he home, but the *Daily Chronicle* announced
his engagement to Lady May Cambridge, basing this information
on the fact that the King, accompanied by the Duke of York and
Lady May, had galloped for an hour in Windsor Great Park. Earlier
in the year, he had been married off in the Press to Mary Ashley,
Edwina's sister. It was all getting too much. Louis Greig, once more
responsible for Prince Albert's welfare, was at his wits' end. Before
the Duke set off for Dunkirk on 25 July to lay the foundation stone
for a War Memorial, Greig telephoned Viscount Davidson, a young
man of whom King George apparently approved, asking him to make
a point of attending the ceremony.

Davidson, Conservative MP for Hemel Hempstead, was only six
years older than Bertie but extremely staid and a great respecter of
all royalty except the Prince of Wales, whom he thought 'an obstinate,
but really a weak man, in whose pastimes I could have taken no share,
and whose friends, male and female, I would not wish to have known
intimately.'[11] A more suitable influence, perhaps, than James Stuart.
Davidson duly arranged to sail in the specially chartered ship which
was to take members of both Houses of Parliament from Harwich to

Dunkirk. After the ceremony he loitered by the gangway until Greig turned up to take him on board the royal destroyer for the return journey; directly she cast off he was taken down to the wardroom and presented to His Royal Highness. They then remained alone for nearly three hours.[12]

As they chugged homeward, the Duke of York bared his soul. 'He seemed to have reached a crisis in his life, and wanted someone to whom he could unburden himself without reserve. He dwelt upon the difficulties which surrounded a King's son in contrast with men like myself who had always had greater freedom at school and university to make their own friends... We discussed friendship, and the relative value of brains and character, and all the sort of things that young men do talk about in the abstract... I sensed that he was working up to something important. I felt moved with a great desire to help him if I could, he was so simple and frank and forthcoming. Then out it came. He declared that he was desperately in love, but that he was in despair for it seemed quite certain that he had lost the only woman he would ever marry.'[13]

Davidson replied, man to man, that however black the situation he mustn't give up hope; his own wife had constantly refused him before she finally said yes. This irritated Bertie. Whatever Davidson's troubles had been, the situation was quite different. 'The King's son,' the Duke explained, 'cannot propose to the girl he loves, since custom requires that he must not place himself in the position of being refused, and to that ancient custom the King, his father, firmly adhered. Worse still, I gathered that an emissary had already been sent to ascertain whether the girl was prepared to marry him, and that it had failed. The question was, what was he to do?'[14]

The advice Davidson ventured to give him was simple: 'I suggested that in the Year of Grace 1922 no high-spirited girl of character was likely to accept a proposal made at second hand; if she was as fond of him as he thought she was he must propose to her himself. . His mood when we parted was much brighter and more buoyant than at the beginning of our talk.'[15]

Had the Duke of York in fact been relying on a third party to do his proposing for him? The Prince of Wales is quoted as telling Elizabeth 'You'd better take him, and go in the end to Buck House',[16] but this sounds no more than a wry dig at a girl who was, after all, a commoner. If he did act as his brother's emissary the idea is so bizarre in view of their subsequent relationship that it defies any attempt to see them as normal human beings. We know that the Prince of Wales found the formality of his father's Court intolerable and was bored by the stodginess of family life; that he thought Elizabeth provided 'a lively and refreshing spirit'.[17] We know that Elizabeth had strong reservations about marrying Bertie and that in her old age she wistfully remembered that David had been 'such fun'.[18] Marriage into the Royal Family would be a great deal more bearable if the King's heir was around; if he didn't marry – a possibility, even then – she would be the first lady in the land after Queen Mary's death. Such an arrangement, though second best, must surely have something to recommend it.

*Daily News*, Friday, 5 January 1923:
### SCOTTISH BRIDE FOR PRINCE OF WALES
### HEIR TO THRONE TO WED PEER'S DAUGHTER
AN OFFICIAL ANNOUNCEMENT IMMINENT

HAPPY CHOICE

ONE OF THE CLOSEST FRIENDS OF PRINCESS MARY

The formal announcement of the engagement of the Prince of Wales to a young Scottish lady of noble birth will be made within the next two or three months.

The future Queen of England is the daughter of a well-known Scottish peer, who is the owner of castles both north and south of the Tweed ... a happy feature of the engagement is that the girl of the Prince's choice is one of the closest friends of his sister, Princess Mary.

Elizabeth was staying with her old friend George Gage in Sussex. Among the guests was the ubiquitous Chips Channon, who wrote post-haste in his diary: 'The evening papers have announced her engagement to the Prince of Wales. So we all bowed and bobbed and teased her, calling her "Ma'am": I am not sure that she enjoyed it. It couldn't be true, but how delighted everyone would be! She certainly has something on her mind ... She is more gentle, lovely and exquisite than any woman alive, but this evening I thought her unhappy and distraite. I longed to tell her I would die for her, although I am not in love with her. Poor Gage is desperately fond of her – in vain, but he is far too heavy, too Tudor and squirarchal for so rare and patrician a creature as Elizabeth.'[19]

If this had been the first shock of Lady Elizabeth's New Year she would surely have laughed it off – almost everyone, after all, had been marked down as the Prince of Wales' intended at one time or another. She may have been worried by Bertie's persistence and pressure from both their mothers, but 'unhappy and distraite' indicates something that had nothing to do with threats and blandishments from Windsor and Sandringham and which, in the ordinary course of events, would have been of little interest to the newspapers. Perhaps Elizabeth herself had been turned down and had already lost heart by the time she made her first headline.

The Duke of York was staying with the Drummonds at Pitsford Hall and his fury caused a difficult weekend. It was one thing to excite sympathy for his unjust predicament, quite another to be ousted from the scene altogether in favour of his eldest brother. If they wanted to print their damnable lies why not at least pick on the right man? The reaction from Windsor was stern and to the point: the unfortunate situation had hitherto been managed with a certain decorum, but now the tiresome girl had got herself into the gutter press something had to be done, and quickly. In the Royal backwaters there were peremptory commands for action. Elizabeth Bowes-Lyon had met her Waterloo.

The Prince of Wales contented himself with a patient, slightly ironical denial. 'A few days ago the *Daily News* announced the forthcoming engagement of the Prince of Wales to an Italian Princess. Today the same journal states on what is claimed to be unquestionable authority that the formal announcement of His Royal Highness's engagement to a daughter of a Scottish peer will be made within the next two or three months. We are officially authorized to say that this report is as devoid of foundation as was the previous . . .' The papers quickly turned over their headlines to Tutankhamun's tomb and the imminent execution of Frederick Bywaters and Edith Thompson.

The following week Elizabeth went to tea with Lady Airlie. The Countess had known her since she was a baby and was the confidante of all the royal children; in the preceding months both Elizabeth and Bertie had used her as a sounding-board. Out of affection for the small boy who had made her an Easter card and perhaps, too, out of loyalty to her old friend Queen Mary, Mabell had gently been pleading Bertie's cause. This had shown no effect, and after the unfortunate publicity of the weekend she 'meant to make a final effort'.[20] Elizabeth, however, was already expert at deflecting conversation from unpleasant topics: Lady Airlie found herself talking about her own marriage instead.

Mabell, the girl who loved to spend days alone on the Irish moors with her sketch book, who was 'not a success' at the children's parties at Marlborough House and quite sure she would never get married,

married David William Stanley, sixth Earl of Airlie on 19 January 1886. He was a cavalry officer, 'essentially a product of the soldiering, Empire-building Britain. . . He might have been a prototype of Rider Haggard's Englishman, brave, honourable, chivalrous, with a simple faith in God and the infallibility of British rule' – and he adored her. Finding herself reduced to a nobody by her mother-in-law, Mabell was miserable. When they got away to Aldershot it was nothing but exercises and manoeuvres and polo. Lonely and self-pitying, she felt excluded from army life, and detested getting pregnant: she was almost continuously pregnant. She wrote a pamphlet entitled *The Real Rights of Women* which, as far as her social world was concerned, was a mistake. 'It was an unsettled phase for both of us,' she told Elizabeth, 'and one that I imagine a great many young couples must pass through. But in my youth there were no easy divorces – even a separation was considered a terrible disgrace.' Mabell and David were forced to have patience with each other. After the early quarrels 'resulting from the clash of two undisciplined personalities' they found a *modus vivendi*, which turned into a mutually rewarding, loving partnership. And that, Mabell implied, was worth all the agitation and inevitable disillusion of being 'in love'.[21]

It is unlikely that she also told Elizabeth it was the birth of a son after three girls, and her decision to 'follow the drum' – galloping in a cavalry charge across Salisbury Plain, wearing a straw boater or, in bad weather, a fetching billy-cock – that solved the problem. She simply said how much she had hated the life at first, and how she had grown to enjoy it. 'After she had gone,' Mabell remembered, 'I feared I might have bored her by bringing up a chapter of my past which had closed before she was born, and wished that I had talked more of the Duke.'[22]

In Elizabeth's world people so seldom talked about their feelings that Lady Airlie's story was something of a revelation. Lady Strathmore, surely, had never admitted to a moment's unhappiness in her marriage. One simply didn't. It wouldn't be helpful. The idea that someone of her mother's generation, a woman she had been brought up to admire and respect, could cheerfully confess to having been discontented with her husband was both shocking and oddly encouraging. At least two apparently disconnected arguments were beginning to weigh the scales in Bertie's favour.

At the end of that week the Duke of York arrived at St Paul's Walden Bury, jaw bones pumping and a glint in his eye. On Saturday he proposed once more. Elizabeth accepted. The Press concocted an unconvincing version of the scene. 'If you are going to keep it up for ever,' she is reputed to have said, laughing merrily, 'I might as well say "Yes" now.' She was twenty-two years old, her future prescribed until her dying day.

# Chapter Eight

Nobody marries one person. Even an orphaned bridegroom or bride carries a huge lump of history which is dumped, sooner or later, in their spouse's lap. When Elizabeth Bowes-Lyon accepted Albert, Duke of York she took on an entire species.

Although in this last decade of the twentieth century it is hard to believe that one group of people can be considered genetically superior to the rest, the Houses of Windsor, Saxe-Coburg and Gotha, Denmark and Wurttemburg were certainly distinctive. King George V, Elizabeth's prospective father-in-law, was the thirty-seventh British monarch since the Norman Conquest and eighth in descent from the Electress Sophia of Hanover, mother of George I, who had been presented with the British throne as a sort of self-assembly package by the Act of Settlement. To placate those who might consider the Hanovers mere upstarts, he could also claim to be twenty-ninth in line from William the Conqueror (the bastard son of Robert the Devil of Normandy and a tanner's daughter from Falaise) and thirty-sixth from Alfred the Great, who was born in Wantage. According to the genealogists, Charlemagne, Barbarossa, Rodrigo the Cid, Egbert King of Wessex, Cadwaller, Vortigern, Neill of the Nine Hostages, the High Kings of Erin and even Mahomet had contributed drops of variously coloured blood to this choleric Norfolk squire and his barely literate children.

Elizabeth would not have to take these remote ancestors into account very often. They just hovered in case of trouble. It was when Bertie's great-great-grandfather on the distaff side married his, Bertie's, great-grandfather's sister that the complications really began. Their only child was Alexandrina Victoria, a very fecund Queen.

Of the nine children she bore to Prince Albert of Saxe-Coburg-Gotha, seven married into the royal houses of Europe and one, after marrying Princess Alexandra of Denmark, became King Edward VII of England. Among George's more familiar relatives were Aunt Vicky and Uncle Frederick, Empress and Emperor of Germany; Aunt Alice and Uncle Louis of Hesse and the Rhine; Uncle Alfred Edinburgh and Saxe-Coburg-Gotha (who died, you may remember, at the end of the 1900 heatwave); Aunt Helena and Uncle Christian Schleswig-Holstein; Aunt Louise and Uncle John Argyll; Uncle Arthur Connaught and Aunt Louise Prussia; Uncle Leopold and Aunt Helen Waldeck and Aunt Beatrice and Uncle Harry Battenberg. Those who were not actually reigning sovereigns were Princes or Princesses or Grand Dukes or Duchesses.

On his mother's side there was Uncle Frederick VIII Denmark and Aunt Louise Sweden; Uncle Willy (who became George) and Aunt Olga Greece; Aunt Dagmar (alias Marie Feodorovna) and Uncle Alex Russia; Aunt Thyra and Uncle Ernest Cumberland and Hanover; Uncle Valdemar Denmark and his Roman Catholic wife.

This little lot – 'little', that is, compared with the rest of the population – ran Europe as though it was a group of country estates, constantly visiting each other, writing letters to each other, marrying each other, involving themselves in each other's weddings and christenings and funerals, easing the way for their politicians by family chat over brandy and cigars, getting dreadfully upset when the politicians imposed squabbles on them or gave one of them the sack. The catastrophic row of the Great War had been a family disaster. Queen Mary's sister-in-law, Princess Alice Countess of Athlone (*née* Princess of Albany) found that most of her mother's relations, and many of her father's, were on the German side. So, of course, was her husband's family, the Wurttemburgs. The confused Princess Alice's affections, though never her loyalty, were split between these close German relatives and her cousins King George of England and the Empress Alexandra of Russia, not to mention the cousins who, at the start of the disagreement, professed themselves neutral – Queen Ena of Spain, Queen Maud of Norway, Queen Sophie of the Hellenes and Crown Princess Marie of Romania. 'Overnight, close, dearly-loved relatives had to be treated as enemies; princes who had grown up together faced each other across the firing line.'[1] And why? 'To have to go to war on account of tiresome Serbia beggars belief!' wrote Queen Mary, whose family connections were similarly complicated, in a moment of exasperated honesty.[2] When it was all over those who had survived the shock, knowing the old dynastic blood was running thin, pulled themselves together and started looking about for young members of the aristocracy to breed from.

Even so, in 1923 Bertie's cousins, either directly or by marriage, still included six operational or semi-operational Kings – Greece, Sweden, Denmark, Norway, Romania and Yugoslavia; five Queens – Spain, Sweden, Yugoslavia, Greece and Romania; the Prince of Monaco, the Prince of Liechtenstein, Princess Marina of Greece, various Counts, Hereditary Grand Dukes, Marquesses, Viscounts, Earls and Dukes; and Louis Mountbatten who would become Burma, to name but a few. Most of them were a little younger than Bertie and some of them had already started having children. The one word that never passed their lips was ominously similar in all their languages: Republic.

In spite of their divine right, their ceremonial and rigmarole, their unshakeable belief in themselves, this vast, homogenous family had lived for years in increasing fear. They were sitting ducks for the *battue* conducted by unsportsmanlike anarchists, Bolshevists, lunatics of all kinds. 'These are among the little uncertainties of our profession,' King Humbert of Italy had said before he was shot through the head at Monza. That may have been so, but when the entire Russian contingent was wiped out overnight Buckingham Palace was shaken to its foundations. 'The news were confirmed of poor Nicky of Russia having been shot by those brutes of Bolsheviks last week,' Queen Mary wrote in her diary. 'It is too horrible and heartless – Mama and Toria came to tea, terribly upset. . .'

Their stoicism, however, was amazing. When poor Ena and Alfonso were blown up – fortunately not fatally – at their wedding, everyone was naturally a little *distrait*, but Aunt Marie Edinburgh-Coburg had been heard to murmur disdainfully, 'Moi, je suis tellement accoutumée à ces sortes de chose.' They were all used to it. Only the other day, on 29 January 1923, a small man with a club foot tried to strike King George with his crutch at St Pancras and the King remarked bravely that he supposed the poor fellow was suffering from shell-shock. People must be deranged to attack the monarch: it was the only explanation. One had to pity them, dispose of them, and rise above it.

King Edward VII, more worldly than most sovereigns, once introduced his son George as 'the future last King of England'. Such an idea was unthinkable to George himself. He benefited from a total lack of imagination. A simpleton in some ways, his honesty and straightforwardness were natural characteristics rather than acquired virtues. He had no inner censor, no protective mechanism to prevent him from speaking his mind. 'He was sometimes too outspoken,' his wife said ruefully. 'I remember that I once had a lady-in-waiting who was a fool and used to ask indiscreet questions of my husband in the motor car. He always answered exactly what he thought. I had to get rid of the woman.'[3] In politics, too, he was unable to dissemble. When Lloyd George talked him into giving secret guarantees to create new peers if the Parliament Bill were vetoed in the Lords, he was horribly uncomfortable. 'I have never in my life done anything I was ashamed to confess,' he grumbled. 'And I have never been accustomed to concealing things.'[4] This was not boasting; it was more of a statement of fact, like being allergic to cats. The King 'never liked going round and round'[5] and Lloyd George was particularly circuitous. When the King was still Prince of Wales he had leaned across the dinner table one night and bellowed at the Permanent Secretary of the Treasury, 'I can't think . . . how you can go on serving that damned fellow Lloyd George!' and some years later, forgetting that the lady he was addressing was the wife of an eminent Cabinet Minister, he 'poured into her astonished ear terrific denunciations of Lloyd George on the subject of pheasants and mangold-worzels,'[6] a subject about which the King knew a good deal and his Chancellor of the Exchequer patently nothing.

If it is normal to be circumspect and approach the truth with care, George was an eccentric. When he came to the throne he had dealt with rumours of his drunkenness by instructing the Dean of Norwich publicly to refute them. The Dean, in all good conscience, did so. The rumours stopped. He never made any bones about the fact that as a young man he had kept a girl in Southsea and another, whom he shared with his brother, in St John's Wood. He cheerfully admitted that he had been much taken with a Miss Julie Stonor and would have married her if he could, and that his cousin 'Missy' had also been the object of his affections for a while. But when he was accused of bigamy by a republican called E F Mylius (dam' foreigner, naturally) George did not issue an official denial or pretend it wasn't happening. He sued the man and sent a statement to Court saying that Mylius' story was a load of rubbish and that he would have given evidence himself had not the Law Officers advised him that it was unconstitutional for a sovereign to appear in the witness-box.[7] That such naïvety could remain intact in the centre of diplomatic subterfuge, political manoeuvre and family pressure is remarkable.

Though it would have astonished him if he had known it, George Windsor was a good man.

His goodness, unfortunately, paved much of the hell of his sons' childhoods. There was something about them – indeed, about all growing boys – that he found irresistibly contemptible and he lost no opportunity to guffaw at their weaknesses and bellow at their shortcomings. During an inspection of the fleet he caused agonies of shame to the future Lord Mountbatten by loudly inquiring about a rag doll which the young midshipman had dearly loved in childhood.[8] There must have been a sexual element in this, a need to emasculate young male competition, for once his sons had proved themselves capable of providing him with legitimate grandchildren the baiting stopped and they all got on quite amicably.

Queen Mary was a very different proposition. She was fifty-eight when Elizabeth entered the family, 'her appearance . . . formidable, her manner – well, it was like talking to St Paul's Cathedral. . .'[9] Her grandfather, Alexander, Duke of Wurttemburg, had made a morganatic marriage, thereby tainting the Wurttemburg blood and adding considerably to their intelligence. Perhaps Mary was compensating for this slip-up with her all-consuming passion for the Monarchy and its families – there was nothing she didn't know about the genealogy of Europe's aristocracy. Minor off-shoots, like the Strathmores, were immediately investigated. In Elizabeth's case, when the Queen spotted Robert Bruce (also a distant ancestor of her husband's) she was reasonably satisfied.

Like the iceberg she frequently resembled, the greater part of the Queen's personality was submerged in the chill waters of duty. She had 'sacrificed everything to [George's] needs and to the preservation of his peace of mind, thinking of him before she thought of anyone else, her children and, of course, herself, included.'[10] Her appearance was created from top to toe by her husband; she felt this to be proper, however much his dreary taste might be regretted. George wished his wife to grow old looking exactly as she had done when they had first become engaged;[11] and so, with the addition of a few million pounds' worth of diamonds, she did. Lady Airlie recalls one brave effort to keep up with the times: having been gifted with perfect legs, the Queen once tentatively suggested to her in the 1920s that they might both shorten their skirts by a modest two or three inches, Mabell to be the guinea pig in this experiment. It was not a success. Mabell let down her hem again with all speed and Mary's legs remained the exclusive property of the Crown.[12] Around the same time the Queen shyly asked Sir Frederick Ponsonby to teach her some of the new dance steps. The lesson was interrupted by the entry of the King, who expressed himself so violently that she never ventured to repeat it.[13]

One of those ubiquitous 'members of the household' once commented that 'the Royal Family were not given to talking things out, even *en famille*. If anything was wrong, the subject was carefully avoided. They would talk about shooting, the weather, a friend's marriage, the shocking behaviour of the French – but never a word about the subject gnawing at their souls.'[14] At the age of twenty-five, unmarried and apparently overwhelmed by her ebullient mother, Mary had written to her much-loved governess, Helene Bricka; 'Sometimes I grumble at my life, at the waste of time, at the *petitesse de la vie* when one feels capable of greater things.'[15] Fifteen years later, as Princess of Wales: 'So many things appear futile, frivolous, waste of time & energy, yet they must be done as long as the world is as civilisation has made it, of course one often rebels, *mais que faire?*'[16] Her complaints and her rebellion had to be packed away, 'Not Wanted On The Voyage' on which, as fiancée to Prince Albert Frederick and wife to his brother, she had embarked. If she had not opened them up from time to time for Helene Bricka, no one would ever have known they were there. Her natural high spirits suffered the same fate. 'In youth she was gay and amusing and would often be in fits of laughter,' her sister-in-law Princess Alice remembered. 'As Queen she was so sedate, so *posée*'[17]. She did add that after the King's death his wife 'blossomed out once more and all her great worth was revealed', but no one was to know this in 1923, least of all Queen Mary.

Could she honestly, and without reservation, encourage her daughter-in-law to follow such an example? *Mais que faire?* Queen Mary's 'real world' was what James Pope-Hennessy describes as 'the calm, doomed world of privilege' and she knew no other. Her husband was also her King. Whatever drawbacks he may have had as a man, the fact remained that according to her beliefs he could do no wrong. That this ceaseless juggling with square pegs and round holes required 'a constant and dramatic exercise of imagination, foresight and control' was something she might have admitted to Helene Bricka (unfortunately dead by now) but not – at least not explicitly, to Elizabeth. The girl had a good pedigree, she had been well reared and her sense of duty, if not love, would find a way to placate and manage Bertie. She was not, after all, going to be Queen (or did the old lady have a shrewd suspicion, even then?) and the job of Duchess of York was not particularly onerous. Once she had satisfied herself that those little signs of obstinacy and wilfulness had been ironed out and that Elizabeth had received proper instruction in protocol and family history, the Queen probably did little more than keep a watchful eye. Emotionally, she had no resources left to deal with other people's problems.

Of all Elizabeth's contemporaries in the Royal Family, Princess Mary is the most shadowy. At the age of six, according to Mr Hansell, her disposition had been 'mercurial; one can enforce discipline and order of a sort but the fact remains that, so long as she is in the room, her brothers cannot concentrate their attention on any serious work.'[18] She was soon removed from the schoolroom and put under the stricter supervision of a Mlle José Dussau. What happened to her between then and her emergence as a keen enthusiast in the activities of Brown and Tawny Owls is obscure. Lady Airlie writes that as the girl was her father's favourite, she was 'the least inhibited' of the children,[19] but by the time she was twenty-two there were signs that even this relatively tolerable home life left a lot to be desired. Her father was possessive and jealous, her mother incapable of communicating except in the most oblique way. 'I don't feel she's happy,' the Prince of Wales told Mabell. 'If she'd confide in me I might be able to do something. But she never complains. The trouble is that she's far too unselfish and conscientious. That's why she was so overworked at her lessons. When my brothers and I wanted her to play tennis she used to refuse because she had her French translation to do, or she hadn't read *The Times* for the day. Is that normal for a girl?'[20]

Not, certainly, for a daughter of King George V. Perhaps Mary would have been charming, and might have been extremely happy, if the misfortune of her birth had not condemned her to the severe and miserable existence of being a princess. She occupied herself laying foundation stones and opening memorial clubs and being President of charitable institutions until she married the elderly, but at least reasonably cultivated, Lord Lascelles. Then, with time off for giving birth to two sons, she seems to have gone on being President of charitable institutions and opening memorial clubs and laying foundation stones. Apart from one long out-of-print biography[21] there is very little record of her life and little, apart from the admirable Lord George Harewood, to commemorate it.

When David, Prince of Wales was twelve years old, Lord Esher remarked that he could not trace 'the look of Weltschmerz' in the boy's eyes to any ancestor of the House of Hanover.[22] To his mother, he was not only 'winning, intelligent and handsome, he had . . . the further and supreme merit of looking like "the old Royal Family".'[23] Whether his Uncle Frank, one of Queen Mary's three brothers, had this particular characteristic or not, there is at least more superficial similarity between him and his nephew than there is between David and the Guelphs. Frank had been handsome, irreverent, a glamorous ne'er-do-well loved by his family against their better judgement. He kept an elderly married mistress and died, himself unmarried, in 1910. The obvious difference between them is that Frank seems to have been born a black sheep, whereas it took David over half his life to become one.

In 1923, when Elizabeth joined the family, he had hardly begun. On the contrary, apart from a certain carelessness over his dress and an engaging informality in public, he was a star royal performer, combining duty and spontaneity with unprecedented success. His war record had shown just the right amount of bravado. He had traipsed, apparently indefatigable, through one-horse towns in Canada and Australia, he had been caressed black and blue in Melbourne and practically stripped in Quebec; he had driven through Bombay in a horse-drawn carriage with a Kitmatgar holding a gold-embroidered umbrella over his head and won the lightweight hog-hunter's race at Lucknow. 'Statesmanlike . . . gracious . . . tactful . . . courageous . . . a true leader of men' were some of the accolades bestowed on him by the Press and the Government. Even his father expressed qualified approval.

Nevertheless, it was 'the look of Weltschmerz' that gave him his charisma. He came and left unpredictably, lonely, excited, nervous, melancholy, jaunty, a pint-sized Prince or elderly *gamin* but never, in his father's terms anyway, a man. Some people, Noël Coward among them, believed he was homosexual,[24] but while David himself wrote that he was 'full of curiosity, and there were few experiences open to a young man of my day that I did not savour'[25] it seems improbable that homosexuality was among them. There were 'moments of tenderness, even enchantment, without which a Princely existence would have been almost intolerable',[26] but like most 'rebels' of his day, he was basically conservative, a protestant against manners rather than morals. On the other hand, what Lady Donaldson terms his 'special affinity of tastes'[27] with his younger brother George might be taken to indicate some sort of deviation from the accepted norm. Isolated from all contacts outside the family, poorly educated and yet plagued with unattainable standards of virtue and nobility, it is surprising that the royal brothers were normal in any way. It must have been frustrating for girls to find the Prince of Wales impervious to their strenuously cultivated charms. 'I danced with a man who danced with a girl who danced with the Prince of Wales' was the nearest most of them could get to him, even in bed.

David himself considered that he was 'a product of the war',[28] Lady Donaldson thinks that he was 'a genuine product of his period . . . bereaved and uprooted and emotionally exhausted but with an entirely new freedom from convention.'[29] If this is so, would it not apply equally to Bertie, only a year his junior ? Neither of them had been bereaved or uprooted. Emotional exhaustion, particularly in a family noted for the lassitude and apathy of its young men, can be caused by having insufficient emotion to draw on, as well as by excessive use of it. David at twenty-nine and Bertie at twenty-eight were the dissimilar products of something much older and more powerful than the post-war mood, to which Elizabeth, incidentally, though a contemporary of Poppy Baring, Audrey James and all the other Bright Young Things, seems to have been immune.

David's fidelity to Freda Dudley Ward made her accepted as another Alice Keppel by everyone except his parents. As he lived at York House in the genial company of Captain 'Fruity' Metcalfe and the slightly suspect Brigadier-General Trotter, their disapproval could not have worried him unduly. Elizabeth was just right for his rather dull brother. She was sweet and appealing, amusing and decorative. Between them they might liven the old place up a bit. David himself was unmoved.

When told of Bertie's engagement to Lady Elizabeth Bowes-Lyon, Prince Henry was 'a little slow to appreciate his brother's good fortune.'[30] It is hard to believe that he had any perceptive criticism or reason to dislike the girl. Perhaps it simply means that Prince Henry was a little slow. In a large family there is often one member who gets lumbered with the prefix 'poor', and poor Harry certainly earned it. He had a worse temper than Bertie, was more stupid and, almost incredibly, even more sickly. Having weak legs as well as knock-knees, he also spent much of his childhood in splints and suffered from what his mother called the 'tiresome nervous habit' of bursting into tears on the slightest provocation. He was also subject to uncontrollable fits of giggling for which, since his fancy was tickled by disaster, there was plenty of cause.

Theoretically, at least, he had an advantage over his elder brothers in being sent to school, though with one thing and another he hardly led the life of a normal schoolboy. At Eton he had endless colds ('You always seem to have one which is tiresome,' wrote Queen Mary[31]) and spent many of his holidays in rented houses with his old tutor, Hansell, knitting comforts for the troops. From Eton he did a stint at Sandhurst and at Trinity College, Cambridge, before becoming a cavalry officer attached to the 13th Hussars. To those who could appreciate his good intentions he was endearing. 'Prince Henry,' Diana Cooper, a fellow guest at Belvoir Castle, wrote to her husband in the winter of 1919, 'is not half bad. I sat next to him at deenah. The Prince arrived sans equerry, sans clothes, sans valet, sans everything . . . I am favourably impressed with him.'[32]

There remains George, the only son who has never had, or never been allowed to have, a biographer. He, too, had been sent to school where, unlike poor Harry, he was an immediate success. 'Superficially much more charming than Prince Henry, he was also intellectually far more gifted; in fact, academically, musically and culturally in general he was streets ahead of anyone else in the family circle.'[33] Queen Mary found him a great comfort. She could 'talk to him openly and with ease, the 2 other sons – Bertie and Harry – are *boutonnés*.'[34]

George was twenty-one when Elizabeth became engaged to his brother, and already in the Navy he hated. In the future he would pass under various clouds and emerge married to the stylish Marina of Greece to become one of the leaders of a social set far removed from Elizabeth and Bertie's orbit. He had recently joined his brother David at York House, after Louis Mountbatten moved out on his marriage to Edwina Ashley. Georgie probably seemed to Elizabeth a nice boy, only a year younger than herself but, as women tend to believe, aeons away in wisdom and experience.

# Chapter Nine

COURT CIRCULAR
YORK COTTAGE, Sandringham
15 January: The Duke of York, attended by Wing Commander
Louis Greig, has arrived at York Cottage. It is with the greatest
pleasure that the King and Queen announce the betrothal of their
beloved son the Duke of York to the Lady Elizabeth Bowes-Lyon,
daughter of the Earl and Countess of Strathmore, to which union
the King has gladly given his consent.

'I was so startled and almost fell out of bed when I read the Court
Circular. We have all hoped, waited, so long for this romance to pros-
per, that we had begun to despair that she would ever accept him. . .
He is the luckiest of men, and there's not a man in England today who
doesn't envy him. The clubs are in gloom.'[1] Chips Channon wrote his
diary with both ears cocked for posterity, and it is hard to believe that
people genuinely devoted to Elizabeth felt such whole-hearted delight
at the match. As for the entire male population of England nursing
its broken heart, that was simply the beginning of the hyperbole that
would obscure Elizabeth from view for the rest of her life.

At first the papers couldn't think of much to say. There had
been brief interest in the girl at the beginning of the month, but
after the Prince of Wales' denial she had been dropped and nobody
seemed to know much about her. 'She has been described as one of
the most beautiful and popular young women at Court,' the *Daily News*
hazarded hopefully. Glamis was a help: a sixteenth-century ancestor
had been burned as a witch, Macbeth was vaguely associated with
the castle (might as well say he owned it) and the Monster was
good for a few lines. The front-page photograph in the *Daily News*
looked as though they were both direct descendants of the egg-shaped
Earl. Headlines in the *Daily Sketch* announced that the Duke of York
had fought at Jutland and was a fluent speaker. By the following

day, Wednesday, reporters were queuing outside 17 Bruton Street. Elizabeth happily gave the first and last personal interview of her life:

*Lady Elizabeth is seated at a little writing desk, pen in hand, a pile of letters and telegrams before her. She is wearing a morning frock of greyish blue edged with fur, and round her neck is a double string of pearls. The bride-elect is very petite and has a magnetic personality.*

| | |
|---|---|
| Elizabeth: | How very kind of you to come. And I am so happy – as you can see for yourself. You ask where is the Duke? Well, Bertie – you know everybody calls him Prince Bertie – has gone out hunting and he won't be back until this evening, when I've no doubt (*with a smile*) I shall see him. |
| Interviewer: | You are fond of hunting, too? |
| Elizabeth: | Oh yes, but I have done little lately. I play golf – badly – and I am fond of lawn tennis. |
| Interviewer: | And so many people know what a beautiful dancer you are. |
| Elizabeth: | That is kind of you to say that … You see how busy I am trying to answer all these! I had no idea our engagement meant so much hard work. I think telegrams have come either here or to Buckingham Palace from all parts of the world. I had not the remotest idea everybody would be so interested or so extraordinarily kind. Edinburgh and Glasgow lead the public bodies in sending congratulations: it is altogether impossible to give anything like a list. |
| Interviewer: | Has the Prime Minister sent a message? |
| Elizabeth: | Not yet. |
| Interviewer: | You are not wearing your engagement ring? |
| Elizabeth: (*laughing*) | No. It is to be made of sapphires. |
| Interviewer: | And what are your immediate plans? |
| Elizabeth: | First of all, I'm staying indoors today to deal with this correspondence. Of course, no wedding date has been fixed or where we are to live. I think we shall go down to Sandringham this coming weekend when all the wedding plans will be discussed. The visit to Sandringham is for that express purpose. |
| Interviewer: | What were the circumstances surrounding the Duke's proposal? |

| | |
|---|---|
| Elizabeth: | Yes, it is true that he proposed in the garden at Welwyn on Sunday. But the (*with great composure*) story that he proposed or had to propose three times – well, it amused me, and it was news to me. |
| Interviewer: | Princess Mary and Viscount Lascelles drove through the West End the afternoon after their engagement was announced. Do the Duke and yourself contemplate following that example? |
| Elizabeth: | I don't know, but perhaps not just yet. He has a banquet at the Savoy tomorrow night. I am not [*with another merry laugh*] going to that. |

*Enter further telegrams and a message to say that the photographers are ready upstairs.*

| | |
|---|---|
| Elizabeth: | Thank you so much. I am sorry there is so little I can tell you.[2] |

Fleet Street was captivated. Such candour, such radiant charm. No one was going to point out that Lady Elizabeth's account of Bertie's proposal was unrelated to the facts, which were that Bertie had proposed for the umpteenth time on Saturday. No one except her parents knew that her birth certificate, already lodged with the appropriate authorities, could have been considered a felonius document. 'ALL THE WORLD LOVES A LOVER' the *Daily Sketch* declared, eagerly recording its share of the prattle:

> 'It's so very embarrassing,' said Lady Elizabeth, with a captivating smile. 'I've never been in such demand before, and it takes a little while to get used to it . . . Do people really want to know about my ring? . . . I can't realise that what is being written in the newspapers refers to me. I read it all quite impersonally as though it were about somebody I do not even know. I simply can't accustom myself to being the centre of such enormous public interest . . . Do they want to photograph me?' – she broke off in a surprised tone, glancing out of the window at a score of photographers who had been waiting outside the house for an hour or more - 'That's an ordeal I shrink from, especially indoors. I hate flashlight photographs. Wouldn't it do if just one of them took me?'[3]

Friends and relations also had their say. 'Oh, she didn't bother about it,' her sister Rose remarked when asked about the reputed engagement to the Prince of Wales. 'I don't think she paid the slightest attention to it.'[4] Lord Strathmore, 'laughing happily' (perhaps the most bizarre notion of all), said that his daughter's friendship with the Duke dated from early childhood: 'As to when and where the wedding will take place, I can tell you nothing. You must go to the womenfolk for that.'5

This naïve garrulity was short lived.

> The interviews granted to the Press, for which, let me add, both Press and public are duly grateful, by Lady Elizabeth Bowes-Lyon are surely without precedent. Never before has the bride-to-be of a prince of the blood-royal established such a link between the teeming millions and the private affairs of the exalted few. But I shouldn't be at all surprised to find a complete cessation of these interviews in the very near future.6

They were right. The King and Queen had difficulty in surviving the shock of such outrageous publicity and Elizabeth's innocent prattle was cut short by an edict from Sandringham. Her talents in future would be restricted to mime.

Perhaps it was just as well. Her enterprising attitude to the truth, and the gullibility of the popular Press, led to one of the few public reprimands she would ever receive. 'One may be pardoned for imagining that Lady Elizabeth Bowes-Lyon was, when her engagement was first made public, quite a novice in the art of being interviewed,' wrote the *Illustrated London News*. 'Intent on being nice to everyone, she agreed to all that was suggested, even to the Duke of York being "quite as surprised as she was when he proposed!" This is assuredly not at all what she meant. Smiles were almost audible at the naïve statement that the Countess of Strathmore came into the room and the interview closed. I should say it did!'

On the other hand, when she had been effectively silenced and forced to rely entirely on the smile, the cheekily cocked head, the fluent wave, she wasn't at first entirely successful, 'people averring that it was impossible for her to be so permanently good natured as she would lead them to believe by her everlasting smile, which must surely be put on for the benefit of the public, and that when she got home it fell from her like a mask, to be replaced by a perfectly vile temper, and the unkindest behaviour to all around her. Her pink and white complexion was also made the target for unkind remarks. . .'7 Elizabeth, in short, was still considered a human being.

No doubt she continued to be one. It becomes increasingly difficult to sympathise and identify with her as she moves from place to place wearing this or that, waving from trains, opening a Sale of Work in aid of the National Orthopaedic Hospital, supporting the

Duchess of Portland's 'At Home' to benefit the Nottingham lace industry, attending a performance of *Elijah* at Eton to patronise the St George's Chapel Restoration Fund, showing no preferences, expressing no dislikes, always predictable even in the moments of calculated spontaneity. This is royalty's job, as digging holes is a road-mender's; they are equally tedious, though the holes may be more necessary.

It wasn't all work, however. Lady Elizabeth was seen dancing at Claridges, 'charmingly dressed in ivory laces [sic], the low waist finished on one side with a shower posy of blush roses.' She was photographed choosing the wedding cake at McVitie and Price, Bakers and Confectioners and Purveyors By Appointment to His Majesty the King in Edinburgh, a firm whose latest biscuit tin was decorated with a portrait of her future father-in-law and a cheery verse:

> Prince of sportsmen
> Peerless shot
> But happiest
> Aboard his yacht.

She stood for hours while the Convocation of Canterbury, the City Corporation, the Convocation of York, London University, Cambridge University, the representative Ministers of the General Body of Protestant Dissenting Ministers of the Three Denominations and the Deputies of Protestant Dissenters presented their Loyal Addresses to the King on the occasion of his son's engagement, and the King answered them all one by one. And always, whatever she was doing, there was Bertie by her side, looking grateful.

Much though he wanted his sons to settle down, King George had not looked forward to having a daughter-in-law. 'He disapproved of . . . painted fingernails, women who smoked in public, cocktails, frivolous hats, American jazz, and the growing habit of going away for weekends.'[8] Most young women nowadays seemed inclined towards all those things. It was a great relief to find that Mabell Airlie's description of Bertie's girl as 'a born homemaker' was less than adequate. She was soft and cuddly, tractable and yet the tiniest bit naughty, 'a perfect little duck,' chortled Admiral Beatty.[9] The King fell slightly in love with her himself. He made excuses for her unpunctuality, kept his temper in her company and patted her affectionately whenever the opportunity offered. Queen Mary, well satisfied with the outcome of all her hard work, wrote primly to her brother, 'Elizabeth is with us now, perfectly charming, so well brought-up, a great addition to the family.'[10]

'The cat is now completely out of the bag and there is no possibility of stuffing him back,' Elizabeth said in a letter to a friend a few weeks earlier:[11] an image which the Queen, had she known of it, would have found out of character. No point crying over spilt milk. The future Duchess of York set about learning her new job.

Life at St Paul's Walden Bury, Glamis and Bruton Street was Bohemian compared with the clockwork ceremonial of Windsor and Sandringham. Elizabeth hoped that Helen Hardinge, now married to the King's assistant private secretary, would show her the ropes, but Helen was inexplicably distant. The newcomer was unaware at first that 'one or two of the older members of Queen Mary's entourage had said that it was thought wise that Lady Elizabeth should not see too much of her old friends. . .'[12] A Duchess must learn that royalty did not have friends.

No rebel, Elizabeth did not tell the old ladies to mind their own business. The important thing, now as always, was to stay with the winning side. Like Helen Hardinge, she quickly learned that 'to feel reasonably secure, one just had to learn the rules – it was rather like . . . keeping out of trouble in the army.'[13] She noted that the King liked the ladies to remove their long white gloves at dinner rather than poking their hands through the wrists, as was the usual custom. Perhaps the cumbersome unrolling and unravelling was a nostalgic reminder of that nice little gal in Southsea, though the arms revealed were hardly as graceful. At the end of the meal they would all get dressed again, led by Queen Mary. As the gloves reached up to their armpits it must have taken a considerable time. For these elaborate dinners, the King and the Prince of Wales wore the Windsor uniform designed by George III – dark blue tail coat with red collar and cuffs, breeches, and a white tie and white waistcoat. The meal was accompanied by selections from such works as *The Merry Widow* and *No, No, Nanette* played by a string orchestra hidden behind a grille of fine wire gauze – a humane innovation since Queen Mary had discovered that for years the musicians had been crammed into an airless cupboard, with the result that many of them collapsed unconscious over their violins.

Precisely one hour after they had all sat down the Queen would rise, followed by the women, each of whom curtsied to the King as they backed out of the room. Then they would proceed to the Green

Drawing Room, where the Queen sat bolt upright on her sofa and received the ladies, one by one, for a brief chat while the rest stood about swallowing their yawns. The King and his gentlemen appeared exactly twenty minutes later. Then there might be a short gramophone concert – Caruso singing Handel's *Largo*, followed by the *Hallelujah Chorus* and ending with a record of the Aldershot Military Tattoo, or perhaps the King's favourite, 'a sentimental yet stirring piece, entitled "The Departure of the Troopship." '[14] The recital ended with the National Anthem, during which everybody, including the King and Queen, stood to attention. On the stroke of eleven Their Majesties and members of their family said goodnight to their guests – another lengthy ceremony – and went to bed.[15]

Night after night of this absurd and joyless ceremonial led to digestive complaints and, in the younger generation, a desperate longing for depravity. One evening David, Bertie, Harry and Georgie told the orchestra to wait for them after the old people had gone to bed; after lights-out they crept back to the Green Drawing Room, rolled back the rugs and tried to have a party. The musicians, more familiar with classical music and martial airs, made an earnest attempt to cope with outmoded foxtrots, which were as close as they could come to jazz, but it was a hopeless failure. 'The ancient walls seemed to exude disapproval,' David recalled sadly. 'We never tried it again.'[16]

The wedding was announced for Thursday, 26 April 1923. James Stuart returned from America that month. Whatever Elizabeth was feeling – regretful, relieved, optimistic, doubtful – she looked much perkier than the year before. Her new *café-au-lait* brown duvetyn skirt, loose 'Russian-shaped' coat to match and big black straw hat trimmed with soft black and gold ribbon were most becoming – presumably the Russian in question had been very short and plump, while 'soft black' became the rage overnight. Van-loads of presents were arriving at 17 Bruton Street and the Palace. At the Archbishop of Canterbury's Faculty Office the veteran clerk, a Mr Bull, spent three days in a locked room engrossing the marriage licence on a roll of parchment nearly a yard square, using twenty quill pens of various thicknesses.[17] Court officials were working night and day on sensitive problems of protocol and precedence. Invitations were sent out to 3,000 guests, among whom were thirty 'factory boys', all of whom had to be provided with new suits.[18] Scores of seamstresses were snipping and stitching; hundreds more women and men were employed preparing the Abbey, rehearsing the procession, polishing buttons and harness, baking, decorating, cleaning up the streets, hurrying purposefully from place to place with sacks of letters, packages, flowers, buckets, ladders, potted palms, bandboxes. When she wasn't on call at the Palace or Windsor, Elizabeth spent hours with Madame Handley Seymour and her girls, being fitted for the wedding dress and trousseau.

On 24 April the King and Queen gave an after-dinner party for 600 guests at Buckingham Palace. Most of the evening was spent taking an obligatory tour of the wedding presents. Herbert Asquith was there in his knee breeches and medals. 'There were huge glass cases like you see in Bond Street shops, filled with jewels and every kind of gilt and silver ware: not a thing did I see that I would have cared to have or give. The poor little bride, everyone says, is full of charm and stood in a row with the King and Queen and the bridegroom, and was completely overshadowed.'[19] She may have been wondering what on earth she could do with a thousand gold-eyed needles from the Livery Company of Needlemakers, not to mention the English oak chest stacked with twenty-four pairs of Wellington boots and galoshes from the Pattenmakers ('I look forward to an opportunity of putting to a practical test the contents of this beautiful chest which you have so generously given me,' she said).

The day before the Royal Wedding *The Times* announced the engagement of Captain the Hon. James Gray Stuart, MVO, MC, formerly Equerry to the Duke of York, third and youngest son of the Earl and Countess of Moray, to Lady Rachel Cavendish, fourth daughter of the Duke and Duchess of Devonshire. Photographs of the couple shared a page with Elizabeth's wedding presents: a pearl necklace with heart-shaped pendant of amethyst set in brilliants from Queen Alexandra, two hideous vases, no doubt of great worth, from the Prince Regent of Japan, a necklace of diamonds and sapphires with bracelet, ring and pendant to match from Queen Mary, a diamond necklace and pendant from the bridegroom and a diamond bandeau from Lord Strathmore. To fill up the page there was J S Helier's winsome portrait of the Prince of Wales which was about to be exhibited at the Paris Salon, and a photograph of Signor Mussolini and General Diaz, Italian Minister for War, taking the salute at a *Fascisti* procession to celebrate the founding of Rome in 753 BC.

The great news in the world of charity was Pencil Week, the

object of which was to sell a million pencils to raise funds for 'welfare work with mothers and babies'. A concert in aid of this estimable cause was held at the Mountbatten residence, Brook House, in Park Lane. Everybody bought a pencil and Miss Violet Vanbrugh recited Shelley's *Arethusa*.[20] On the same day, 25 April, *Tatler* ran a full-plate colour portrait of Elizabeth looking infinitely wistful.

Lady Elizabeth Bowes-Lyon and Prince Albert, Duke of York, were married next day in Westminster Abbey by Randall Davidson, Archbishop of Canterbury, and Cosmo Gordon Lang, Archbishop of York, assisted by Bishop Herbert Edward Ryle, Dean of Westminster, and the Most Reverend Walter John Forbes Robberds, Bishop of Brechin and Primus of the Scottish Episcopal Church.

# PART TWO
## DUCHESS OF YORK

# Chapter Ten

The York-Bowes-Lyon wedding was not broadcast because the Arch-bishop of Canterbury feared that men in pubs might listen to it with their hats on. In every other way it was much like any Royal wedding in living memory. Traffic in the West End was disrupted. Fifty different 'bus routes were diverted and it was estimated that the Underground would have to carry over one million more than its daily number of passengers. Arrangements were made for both 'buses and trains to run 50,000 miles in excess of their normal day. 'Fabulously large crowds . . . assembled, or tried to assemble, in Whitehall. There, perhaps, the soldiers . . . and the police had to be more genially firm, or rather firmly genial, than anywhere. . . . It was fortunate, too, that the weather was no more than fitfully fine, or the stream of ambulances in and out of Scotland Yard might have been really embarrassing.'

Superior journalism of those days reads as though reporters were eager young graduates anxious to exploit the latest literary fashion. The historic present was much in favour. Inside the Abbey there 'is the ceaseless clank of swords and tinkle of spurs, the rustle of silks and chink of medal on medal; sailors stiff with gold lace, soldiers in scarlet and green and gold, divines in their robes, great men of law in wigs and gowns; orders, ribbons . . .' When the bride arrives on the arm of her father 'an immense beadle, or other officer, garbed in a huge, scarlet gown, comes softly up to her. From his great hand dangles a little, white, very feminine object – a handkerchief bag, we judge it – which the bride has left in her carriage. . .' Elizabeth takes the bag with a grateful smile, then steps forward and, sensibly solving the problem of holding two things at once, lays her bouquet on the tomb of the Unknown Warrior.

The bride is dressed in fine chiffon moiré the colour of old ivory, embroidered in silver thread and pearls, with long medieval sleeves of fine Nottingham lace. Her train, lent by her mother-in-law, is made of point de Flandres lace mounted on tulle and her shoes are ivory moiré embroidered with silver roses. She is attended by eight bridesmaids – the Ladies May and Mary Cambridge, Katharine Hamilton, Mary Thynne, the Misses Diamond Hardinge, Betty Cator and her two nieces, Elizabeth Elphinstone and Cecilia Bowes-Lyon. The bridegroom is in the uniform of a Group Captain of the RAF with the Garter Riband and Star and his recently acquired Thistle Star; the gold aiguillettes over his right shoulder show that he is a Personal Aide-de-Camp to the Sovereign and his single row of medals include his Service Medals from the Great War. His best man, or supporter, the Prince of Wales, wears the scarlet uniform of the Grenadier Guards. King George is impeccable as Admiral of the Fleet, Harry trussed into the uniform of the Tenth Hussars and Georgie miserably got up as a naval cadet. The mother of the bride is wearing a handsome gown of black marocain and georgette embroidered in jet and blue paillettes, with a cloak of black lace and marocain, the collar composed of shaded blue roses; the mother of the bridegroom is in aquamarine blue and silver, to which an iridescent effect has been added by showers of aquamarine blue crystals that sparkle on the skirt and corsage. Queen Alexandra wears purple velvet trimmed with gold lace. The Marchioness of Lansdowne is in pearl grey embroidered in cut steel; she wears badges which include the Royal Order of Victoria and Albert, the Imperial Order of the Crown of India, the Companion of Honour, the Lady of Justice of the Order of St John of Jerusalem in England and the ribbon and star of the Order of the British Empire, as well as a quantity of diamond and pearl knick-knacks.

There are dark tortoishell paillettes and cabochans over heavy self-coloured satin beauté, draped bleu de soir chiffon velvet and crêpe marocain with old Carrickmatcross lace, oxidised and lie-du-vin woven drape d'argent bouclé with embroideries in claire de lune colourings, shot green and brown taffeta giving the effect of beetle wings, Persian designs in multi-silks and metal thread. There are picture hats of cream-coloured lace straw trimmed with large cockades of gardenias and foliage, hats of fine crinoline with shaded ostrich feathers falling at one side, small hats of auburn-hued velvet decorated with sweeping aquamarine feathers, turban hats of almond green embossed satin adorned with bunches of green feathers. There are *gris fumé* fox collars and sable wraps, diamonds, amethysts, sapphires, emeralds and the Lesser Star of Africa. Dr Lang, in his customary inspiring manner, told the couple, 'You will not think so much of enjoyment as of achievement . . . it is to yourselves, as simple man and maid . . . that our heart turns as you go forth to meet the years that are to come. On behalf of a nation happy in your joy, we bid you Godspeed.'

The only recorded mishap was when a cleric in the bride's procession fainted, though the two smaller bridesmaids had a few awkward moments when Queen Alexandra and Queen Mary converged for a chat on either side of the bride's train and the children, holding the end of it, were left stranded. However they gallantly fought their way through the purple velvet and showers of aquamarine crystals to emerge, still clasping the train, triumphant. Apart from these minor crises the production went smoothly, accompanied by Elgar, Parry, Stanford and Mendelssohn, and even the Registers were correctly signed and witnessed. 'There is but one wedding,' the *Times* pronounced solemnly, 'to which [the public] look forward with still deeper interest – the wedding which will give a wife to the Heir to the Throne, and, in the course of nature, a future Queen to England to the British people.'

As Elizabeth had been a commoner up to this point (i.e. below the rank of peeress), she had driven to the Abbey in an ordinary State landau, escorted only by four mounted police and the troops lining the route had not been required to present arms as she passed. So much for the common people. On her return as Duchess of York she rode with her husband in a scarlet and gold coach escorted by cavalry, followed by the King and Queen, the Princes, the Princess and the Viscount, Queen Alexandra, the Strathmores, and carriages full of royal relics. Behind them came six ambassadors, thirteen foreign ministers, six chargés d'affaires, the Prime Minister, the Baldwins, the Neville Chamberlains, the Lloyd Georges, the Asquiths, the Winston Churchills, the Clyneses and Mr Ramsay Macdonald MP. The troops saluted as she passed and the common people yelled delight at her elevation. She looked, not surprisingly, radiant.

When the procession finally disappeared into the inner quadrangle the troops were withdrawn and the crowds made a concerted rush on the Palace. The sun came out, well-polished tubas and bassoons and trumpets hooted and tooted merrily across the Park, people swarmed over the Victoria Memorial and clung to the Palace railings. At 1.15pm the windows of the Balcony Room opened and the bridal couple appeared in front of the red velvet drapes, followed by the King and Queen, Queen Alexandra and the Strathmores. Cheering resounded down the Mall, across Green Park and St James's Park and Constitution Hill. After five minutes, Alexandra 'stole away' and the parents stepped back. The Duke of York stood stiffly, looking a little dazed, but his new Duchess gave her benediction again and again, north, south, east and west, repeating 'Thank you . . . thank you!' The audience roared. Paradoxically, the act that isolated her from them made them feel that they owned her; the gesticulating, inaudible little figure on the balcony suddenly 'belonged'. If she had been down there among them, a twenty-two-year old girl hanging on her husband's arm, she would have been a stranger.

The menu for the eight-course wedding breakfast included Consommé à la Windsor, Supreme de saumon Reine Mary, Cotelettes d'agneau Prince Albert, Chapons à la Strathmore and, very suitably, Fraises Duchesse Elizabeth. There were no speeches but the bride prettily mimed cutting one of the pre-sliced wedding cakes. Meanwhile the rain had started again, a worry for those who were responsible for the next procession but surely no great matter of concern to the Royal party. The wedding pictures, nevertheless, are joyless. The newly-weds look stuffed, the bridesmaids like ghoulish wax-works. Recklessly contradicting the evidence, the papers asserted that the Duchess's 'happiness infected everyone, and happiest of all was the bridegroom'. Their appearance of gloomy fortitude must have been caused by the restraint of the occasion or the incompetence of the photographers.

Luckily the rain stopped by the time they climbed into the open landau which was to take them to Waterloo. They were pelted instead with 'favours' hurled by the three mischievous royal brothers, one of whom – Harry? – moulded confetti and bag into a lethal ball which he aimed at the bridegroom. For a split second it looked as though there might be a nasty scene. Fortunately Queen Mary, Princess Mary and Aunt Vicky began wafting rose petals – made by blind workers for the occasion – from the balcony; Elizabeth bowed and waved and smiled, Bertie was distracted and the onlookers howled their approval. No sooner had the landau and its four greys trotted off down the Mall than the Prince of Wales bundled into his car and was gone, with only a peremptory salute to the crowd.

At Waterloo the couple were received by Sir Herbert Walker, an official of the Southern Railway, Mr Szlumper, chief engineer, and Mr Bushrod, acting superintendent of the line. The platform barrier, normally jammed with commuters, was decorated with palms, hydrangeas and rhododendrons. The newly-weds were conducted to their special train by Sir Herbert, Mr Szlumper and Mr Bushrod, who no doubt informed them that they were due at Bookham, slightly north-east of Guildford, at 17.10 or, as they said in those days, ten minutes past five. Their saloon carriage was upholstered in old gold brocade and decked with white roses, white heather, white carnations and lilies of the valley. Mr Szlumper or Mr Bushrod blew the whistle, the signals came down and Driver Wiggs, with a celebratory blast on the hooter, steamed off in the direction of Surrey. Holding hands in a boat may suddenly have seemed inadequate preparation for the immediate future.

Arrived at Bookham, they were received by the Chief Constable of Surrey and a posse of officials. After the usual speeches of welcome, they drove out of the station yard through a modest crowd of cheering natives, proceeded a couple of hundred yards and stopped for the Duchess to be presented with a bouquet by the daughter of a works manager, a child who was apparently unable to toddle as far as the station. Then they drove on to the church, where three hundred schoolchildren and smartly polished Girl Guides and Boy Scouts were lined up together with the Chairman of the Parish Council and his fellow Councillors. The Chairman presented a short but painstakingly rehearsed speech of welcome and stood back, humbly expectant. The Duke summoned the spirit of Jutland. Politely but firmly he thanked the Chairman, pointed out that it had been a tiring day, and propelled Elizabeth towards the car. After a moment's dismay, fifteen-year-old Jean McFarlane pelted after them with a bouquet of red roses tied up in a long streamer of Strathmore tartan. The Duchess thanked her for the bouquet. At last they were free to drive the mile and a half to Polesden Lacey, lent for their honeymoon by the ecstatically flattered Mrs Ronnie Greville.

On 28 April the London Gazette announced:

> In accordance with the settled general rule that a wife takes the status of her husband, Lady Elizabeth Bowes-Lyon on her marriage has become HRH Duchess of York, with the status of a Princess.

# Chapter Eleven

Polesden Lacey had none of the comforts of home as Bertie and Elizabeth understood them. There were seven self-contained guest suites, each with its own bathroom, 'an unobtrusive luxury' that even Osbert Sitwell said he had never encountered elsewhere. Apart from this opportunity for indulgence it is hard to know how the Yorks could put up with Mrs Greville, though in years to come she would say, 'I was so happy in the days when they used to run in and out of my house as if they were my own children.'[1] Her only admirers were royalty, which by its very exclusiveness must be naïve and ignorant of normal behaviour, and Sir Osbert. Harold Nicolson, no mean snob himself, called her 'nothing more than a fat slug filled with venom', Sacheverell Sitwell thought she was 'sheer hell', Lady Leslie said she would rather have an open sewer in her drawing room than Maggie Greville. The young Yorks, revelling in the unaccustomed fleshpots, were her prize protégés. When she died in 1942, leaving an estate of around £2 million, she bequeathed Marie Antoinette's priceless jewels to Elizabeth, £20,000 to Princess Margaret and £25,000 to the Queen of Spain. Having no heirs, she left Polesden Lacey to the National Trust.

Mrs Greville's two unreliable butlers, Boles and Bacon, may or may not have remained to attend on the honeymoon couple. If they did, there must have been some hilarious meals. Both retainers were constantly as drunk as the lords they waited on, but oblivious to reprimand and never, for some curious reason, sacked. Boles, who claimed to be a communist, had been known to eat the entire dish he was about to serve; Bacon, on receiving a furious note from Mrs Greville saying 'You're drunk. Leave the room at once', placed it on a silver salver and carried it unsteadily down the table to Sir Austen Chamberlain,[2] who was astounded. On later visits, anyway, this raffish pair became very attached to Elizabeth. 'All the butlers were drunk,' Osbert Sitwell wrote of one dinner party, '. . . bobbing up every minute during dinner to offer the Duchess of York whisky.'[3] It would be nice to think that the first ten days of the Yorks' honeymoon passed in a state of innocent inebriation.

Next they went to Glamis. After the luxuries of Polesden Lacey the Duke was unimpressed by the new bathroom installed in their honour and Elizabeth caught whooping cough. In spite of his own experience of the complaint, her husband was unsympathetic. Honeymoon or no, daily letters to the family were written and received and Bertie vented his feelings on his mother: 'So unromantic to catch whooping cough on your honeymoon,' he wrote bitterly. King George wrote to Bertie: 'It must have been with a pang that you left your home after 27 years. I miss you very much & regret your having left us. . .'[4]

A fortnight later they travelled south again, to Frogmore House in Windsor Great Park. In spite of the glum connection between his birthday and 'Mausoleum Day' and the close proximity of his dead great-grandparents, Bertie was happy at Frogmore. In his childhood there had been a single bathroom on the ground floor, poor lighting, bad drainage, inadequate plumbing and very little heat; it was crammed with commemorative statuettes, miniatures, gold lockets containing strands of hair from the dear departed, letter-weights of bronze hands modelled after death.[5] Nobody had actually lived there since George V came to the throne, though Queen Mary often came across from the Castle to spend summer afternoons in the garden and it was sometimes lent to exiled royal relatives, which Her Majesty found 'a decided bore'.[6] Elizabeth was familiar with ghosts, but hers were a disreputable lot compared with the stodgy Hanovers and their memorabilia. It was like spending your honeymoon in a cross between a furniture repository and a necropolis.

Not, however, to the Duke of York. The further he got from his childhood, the more golden it seemed. He was delighted to find the schoolroom just the same, even to the ink stains on the table. This is where he and David and sister Mary drilled with midget bayonets; that's the statue of great-great-Grandpa – we had a footman called Smithson who looked just like him – and I'll never forget when poor old Hua took his first mouthful of tadpoles on toast, we'd caught them in the lake and got the kitchen to serve them up – he thought they were frogs' legs, we nearly died laughing.[7] Smiling, exclaiming, asking questions, taking it all in for future reference, Elizabeth was the perfect companion.

At the beginning of June, the honeymoon over, they moved into

White Lodge in Richmond Park, 'a shallow and impermanent-feeling house'[8] built as a hunting lodge by George II and much enlarged by his daughter Amelia. It had been given to Queen Mary's parents when she was two years old, her father and mother had died there and it was where her eldest son had been born – the Queen wanted to keep it in the family. Forgetting how upset she had been to find York Cottage fully furnished when she moved in as a young bride (George, with the best intentions, had given the whole place over to a 'Maple's man' without consulting her), she had happily supervised the decoration and furnishing of White Lodge while her son and daughter-in-law were away. Elizabeth, the 'born home-maker', found precious little to do apart from rearranging the knick-knacks and making room for twenty-four pairs of Wellington boots.

Alone at last, apart from cooks, butlers, footmen, parlourmaids, house-maids, kitchen maids, ladies maids, valets, bootboys, chauffeurs, grooms, gardeners, ladies-in-waiting and equerries, the newly-weds made themselves as cosy as possible in their eighteen reception rooms, only one of which was large enough to receive in, and their warren of bedrooms, only one of which was large enough for the ducal bed. Their estate was a miserable five acres and on holidays and at weekends they were peered at by sightseers. Although the Duchess of Teck had found it 'quite possible to conduct a social life from Richmond if one had plenty of good horses and carriages', the Yorks in their Daimler found it exhausting. The climate in Richmond Park seemed particularly inclement and the central heating broke down.

On 9 June, two days after the Yorks moved in, Princess Christian of Schleswig-Holstein-Sonderburg-Augustenburg (known as 'Lenchen', to which her mother usually added the prefix 'poor') died in London. Nobody had any great reason to mourn her. The third daughter of Queen Victoria, she had behaved very badly back in the 1890s when Mary of Teck became engaged to the Prince of Wales, apparently thinking that her own daughters, Marie Louise ('Louie') or Helena Victoria ('The Snipe') had a greater claim to Prince Eddy's affections. Royal memories are long and Queen Mary never forgave her for this indiscretion. Nevertheless, the Court plunged into its familiar black and the Yorks' holiday was extended for a further month. When it was all over Elizabeth found that the bulk of poor Lenchen's official duties had been bequeathed to her.

Lady Cynthia Asquith summed up this amorphous employment: 'Each day she was asked to become Patroness of several societies, to

84

visit hospitals, to lay foundation stones. Every sort of appeal poured in, and each one had to be seriously considered and answered. The daily post became a very formidable factor in her life. Then there were Court Functions to attend, and visits to be paid with her husband to Industrial Centres, visits that sometimes involved a stay of two days.'[9] The first of these, described as 'a round of duties', was to Liverpool at the end of July.

They did not actually stay in Liverpool, but as guests of Lord Derby at Knowstey. The Duchess smeared a blob of cement on the foundation stone of the new Nurses' Home at the Royal Infirmary and was warmly applauded. She then stood on the balcony of the Town Hall and watched the inspection of the Guard of Honour. The Duke gave a bronze medallion to an X-ray pioneer and unveiled some frescos in the Memorial Hall. Next day they boarded the tender *Galatea* and chugged up the Mersey. Elizabeth stayed in the saloon, since it was raining, but later joined her husband on deck to wave and bow to the damp crowds lining the banks. Then they took a brisk look at the excavations at Gladstone Dock, drove to Aintree to watch the racing and returned to London.

Elizabeth was now 'very tired' and in need of a break, so Bertie took her to Balmoral. She was marched up a nearby mountain by Princess Alice, Countess of Athlone, reputed to be the only woman in history who could knit and mountaineer at the same time.[10] Since they got stuck in a snowstorm Alice may have finished a sock or two. In September they moved on to Holwick Hall, one of the Strathmore properties in County Durham, for the shooting, but had barely settled down when the Duke received a telegram ordering him to go to Belgrade in October to stand godfather at the baptism of Peter, the infant son of King Alexander, King of Serbia, Croatia and Slavonia, and to represent King George at the wedding of Alexander's cousin, Prince Paul, to Princess Olga of Greece. His instructions were that both ceremonies were intended to demonstrate that the House of Karageorgevitch was securely in possession of the Yugoslav throne and strengthen the dynastic ties between Britain and the Balkan royal families.

Bertie was furious. He was a married man now, with responsibilities. They were having a well-earned rest and he was fed up with the bloody Balkans anyway. 'Curzon should be drowned for giving me such short notice,' he raged to the long-suffering Greig, '. . . he must know things are different now.'[11] The culpable Foreign Secretary being unavailable, the house-party, which included most of the Strathmore family, went through a short period of stress. Perhaps this was the first of the many times Elizabeth had to use all her wiles to restore order. She must have managed it, as on 27 September Bertie had 'a very nice day' – three rabbits, one snipe, two black game and 354 grouse hit the heather.[12] Three weeks later they set off to attend one of the final performances of European monarchy.

On August 6th 1900, when Elizabeth was two days old, the *Times* published the following leader:

> The marriage of King Alexander of Servia and Mme Draga Maschlin was solemnized yesterday at Belgrade with much ceremony' we are told. On the more personal aspects of this marriage to which grave exception has been taken in Servia, not merely on account of the great disparity of age between the young bridegroom and his matronly bride, we do not propose to dwell. The Obkenovitch family is neither of such ancient nor of such illustrious origin that the term *mesalliance* must necessarily be applied to the union of the King with one of his subjects, were there no other objection to the choice which he has made but that of the lady's social standing. From that point of view King Alexander might appeal with no little force to the example set to him by his father when he raised the daughter of an army contractor to the throne. Rightly or wrongly, however, the announcement that Mme Maschlin's notorious influence over the young sovereign was to be tightened by a matrimonial alliance provoked at the outset such widespread disapproval as to threaten serious consequences for the tranquillity of Servia and even for the peace of the Balkan peninsular.
>
> King Milan, in whom his son could hardly have expected to find so stern a censor, marked his paternal displeasure by throwing up ostentatiously the post of Commander-in-chief of the Servian army; the Servian Cabinet handed in its resignation, and the Pretender, Prince Peter Karageorgevitch, son-in-law of the Prince of Montenegro, was reported to be holding himself in readiness on the frontier for any opportunity which popular disturbance might offer. . .

On 10 June 1903 King Alexander and Queen Draga were assassinated in Belgrade – 'Iynched' is more accurate, it was a nasty killing – and Peter Karageorgevitch unanimously elected King of the Serbs, Croats and Slovenes. His eldest son, George, abdicated his right of succession owing to a report that he had mortally wounded his valet in a fit of passion, therefore it was the younger son, Alexander, three years the Duke of York's junior, who was appointed Prince-Regent when his father became too ill for the job in 1918. In 1921 he succeeded to the throne of the new kingdom of Yugoslavia, a country divided between Serbs of various political persuasions, Croats, Moslems and Communists. A year later Alexander married Princess Marie of Rumania (known as 'Mignon'), daughter of King Ferdinand and Queen Marie of Romania (known as 'Missy'), who was herself the daughter of Grand Duchess Marie Alexandrovna of Russia (known as 'Aunt Marie') and Queen Victoria's son Alfred, Duke of Edinburgh and Saxe-Coburg-Gotha, who died on the first page of this book in the summer of 1900.

As for Prince Paul, he was King Alexander's cousin, the son of Prince Arsene Karageorgevitch; his bride, Princess Olga, the granddaughter of Queen Alexandra's brother King George 1st of Greece (known as 'Uncle Willy') – the one who was assassinated in 1913 while taking his morning stroll in Salonika – and the sister of Marina, who would later rescue Bertie's youngest brother from 'an errant love'.[13] Prince Paul had been up at Oxford with the Prince of Wales and was part of what Chips Channon liked to consider the Channon-Elizabeth-Gage clique in Elizabeth's débutante days

The entire cast of Balkan royalty, regnant and exiled, was lined up on the platform when the Yorks' special train pulled in at Belgrade on the evening of 20 October. 'They were all enchanted with Elizabeth, especially Cousin Missie,' Bertie wrote proudly to his parents. 'She was wonderful with all of them & they were all strangers except two, Paul and Olga.'[14] The Palace was overcrowded, there was no hot water, Kings and Queens, Archdukes and Grand Duchesses, scurried about on a hopeless search for a lavatory, a hot water bottle, someone to sew on a button. At the christening the ancient Patriarch lost his grip on the Crown Prince who sank, bubbling, to the bottom of the font. Bertie scooped him out just as the whole of the infant's short life was passing before his eyes and the House of Karageorgevitch, temporarily saved from extinction, breathed again. Blue in the face and bawling murder, the child was then placed on a cushion and carried three times round the altar by his godfather, preceded by a deacon with a thurible emitting clouds of incense. The chapel, unlike the Palace, was as hot as a sauna. Sweating under their gold braid and ribbons and orders and hardware, choked by the fumes and deafened by the Crown Prince's protests, the nobility of Europe survived the ordeal.

The following day they all watched while Princess Olga stepped over a strip of cloth, symbolising the moat of her husband's house, scattered corn and kissed a boy baby.[15] As things turned out she would have been wiser to slip away incognito. Except for Elizabeth and Bertie, they were all doomed.

Five years later King Alexander proclaimed a royal dictatorship and the Kingdom of Serbs, Croats and Slovenes became Yugoslavia. In 1934 he was assassinated by a Macedonian terrorist in Marseilles. Prince Paul was appointed Regent on behalf of nine-year-old Peter and desperately tried to reconcile Serbs and Croats until the outbreak of World War II. After Germany's invasion of Yugoslavia in 1940 Germany and Italy divided Slovenia between them, Bulgaria annexed most of Macedonia, Hungary chose the western half of Vojvodina and a few minor bits of the Croatian border and the Axis powers presented Ante Pavelic, an exiled Quisling, with the control of Bosnia. In 1941 Prince Paul, distrusted by the Germans as an Anglophile, fled to England with his wife. The British Government dispatched them in disgrace to South Africa. Eighteen-year-old Peter, left to cope as best as he could, was rescued by the RAF and eventually brought to England. Early in 1945 he transferred his powers to a regency appointed by Tito, ex-guerilla fighter and Croatian leader of the Yugoslav Communists. Fifty years later the states that were once Yugoslavia are still involved in senseless fratricide. Belgrade is in Serbia again; Sarajevo, where the First World War began, in Herzagovina, just over the Bosnian border. The occasional assassination of Kings and Princes seems tame stuff now that children can be slaughtered with impunity.

The royal guests at Paul's christening in 1923 had lost a good deal of confidence since the end of the Great War but still had no idea of their fate. By 1947 fourteen of the twenty-four representatives of European royalty to attend Princess Elizabeth's wedding would be exiles, their titles meaningless as the Emperor's new clothes. Today many descendants of that vast imperial family live peacefully in the suburbs, selling secondhand cars or running boutiques. The Scandinavian countries still have monarchies of a sort, as have the Netherlands and Belgium. Spain, a fascist republic for a number of years, is on the rebound. There is a Grand Duke of Luxembourg, a Prince of Lichtenstein, and Prince Rainier is constant in Monaco but only a Queen Mary could believe in their possession of divine right.

It is almost incredible that there is someone alive who took part in all that ceremonial glitter, felt the discomfort, smelled the reek of incense, sweaty imperial uniforms, Balkan tobacco; someone who knows what the weather was like and which Queen was offended with which Archduchess. Apart from her 93-year-old sister-in-law Princess

Alice of Gloucester, and 93-year-old Princess Olga inching through her last days in an Old People's Home in France, Elizabeth *née* Bowes-Lyon is one of the very few people who can vouch for that long, elaborate tragi-comedy.

# Chapter Twelve

It was hard to settle down to the rigours of White Lodge and the staid English Court. Fortunately there was the wedding of Louise Mountbatten and Crown Prince Gustav of Sweden to look forward to – with two working kings, four queens, six princes and ten princesses among the guests it was almost as good as the Balkans. A week later the Yorks were off to the Guards Chapel for the marriage of Bertie's cousin Maud to Lord Carnegie. Maud's uncle, King George, was not present at this relatively homely affair; he was trying to persuade Stanley Baldwin not to dissolve Parliament and call a General Election, but failed. Baldwin was heavily defeated at the polls on 8 December. 'The result of the General Election must be very worrying to Papa now,' Bertie wrote nervously to his mother. 'I wonder what is going to happen.'[1] On 22 January 1924 King George handed over the government of his country and Empire to the Labour Party for the first time in history.

Socialism was the beginning of the end to royalty, and a very nasty end at that. Every creak in the corridors, every rustle in the rhododendrons might mean their hour had come. Fog lay heavily over Windsor and Richmond Parks; they appeared to be empty, but who knew what was lurking out there? The mob had already sung the Red Flag in the Albert Hall, of all places. In the dripping silence the family waited for the sound of tumbrils.

But it seemed that the only people who believed in the consequences of socialism were those who, theoretically, should have been its first victims. Nothing happened. These regicides and rabblerousers were, thank God, British. 'As we stood waiting for His Majesty amid the gold and crimson magnificence of the Palace,' the new Lord Privy Seal recalled in his memoirs, 'I could not help marvelling at the strange turn of Fortune's wheel, which had brought Macdonald the starvelling clerk, Thomas the engine driver, Henderson the foundry labourer and Clynes the mill-hand to this pinnacle beside the man whose forbears had been Kings for so many splendid generations.'[2]

The contrast between a thriving aristocracy and the men in bowler hats who now governed them gave a curious twist to British snobbery at both ends of the scale. It was rumoured that Co-op vans were delivering provisions to 10 Downing Street. The Dowager Countess of Warwick threw open her stately home, Easton Lodge, as a rest home for Labour Members of Parliament. There was a brief scandal about Ramsay Macdonald holding 30,000 £1 shares in McVitie and Price. The first State ball at the Palace started disastrously, all the guests standing about as though at a village hop. 'At last,' Chips Channon recorded, 'the Prince of Wales opened the ball with the Duchess of York and soon everyone was dancing.'[3] No other couple in the family, or in the Court, could have saved the situation.

The Government lasted for nine months, during which time the only new legislation that had anything to do with socialism was Wheatley's Housing Act. King George liked Mr Wheatley: 'He is an extreme Socialist and comes from Glasgow. I had a very interesting conversation with him.'[4] He admired Ramsay Macdonald with reservations, but the Bolshevik he became most attached to was Jim Thomas, the engine driver, who was invited to stay every year at Balmoral: 'Well, it's a bloody dull 'ouse, of course, and I told the King so. 'E was regretting that the young Princes didn't like the place. So I said, "I don't wonder at that, Sir. It's a bloody dull 'ouse. . ."'[5]

In spite of its welcome moderation, the government did recognise the Soviet Union. The King confined himself to hoping that Russia's representative would be a Minister he could ignore rather than an Ambassador who would have to be asked to dinner. Would the starvelling clerk and the foundry labourer agree to wear Court dress? The King was meticulously fussy about correct *equipage*. Of course they would. But could they afford it? Tactful inquiries were made and Moss Bros. offered to provide regulation trousers, coat, cocked-hat and sword for a mere £30 the set. It soon became difficult to distinguish between Conservatives and Socialists until they opened their mouths: Baldwin would have been at home leading the Labour Party, and Macdonald, with his romantic cast of mind, was well suited to lead the Conservatives.[6] It all came to the same thing in the end.

The point was that although Socialism undoubtedly had most worthy aims it simply wasn't *necessary* in Britain. Everyone, after all, was deeply concerned with welfare and improving the lot of the poor. The young Yorks, in spite of their gruelling round of official duties and the inconveniences of their domestic life, found time just before Christmas to attend a Banquet for Little Londoners and a distribution of Hampers to Crippled Children. An orchestra played while the children enjoyed their roast beef and potatoes and after that there was community singing. The Duke and Duchess watched from the gallery. Later they talked to the children, who had each been given a packet of food to which the Duke and Duchess had contributed biscuits.

As for all the nonsense about privilege, the Family was feeling the pinch as much as anyone. £360,000 of the King's annual income was spent on maintaining the functions of monarchy, leaving him only 110,000 for his personal use. Even with the additional revenue from the Duchy of Lancaster – a mere £44,000 – it didn't go very far. The Queen, it's true, received £10,000 a year, but surely she earned it? The Queen Dowager, they had to admit, was a liability. The country gave her an annual £70,000, but even with the interest on the fortune bequeathed by her husband she couldn't seem to make ends meet – generous to a fault, that was Motherdear's trouble. Her affairs were investigated by the Treasury and to everyone's horror it was discovered that the old lady had been paying tax. That was soon put right. The State could surely afford to pay its widows 10/- a week without robbing the Queen Dowager. As for the younger generation, they worked hard for their living. The Prince of Wales received nothing at all except the revenue from the Duchy of Cornwall and the Duke of York certainly earned every penny of his £25,000 a year.

Complacently, but not without a certain amused sympathy, the Royal Family watched the Labour Government's ineffectual attempts to undermine British capitalism. By the end of October it had admitted defeat. On 7 November Stanley Baldwin, Lord Curzon, Viscount Cave, Lord Salisbury and Lord Birkenhead, together with an assortment of knights and distinguished Members, put on their own Court dress once more and set out for the familiar Palace. The Yorks, badly in need of a holiday after such a nerve-wracking year, left for four months' big-game shooting in Africa. 'I don't think I really thanked you properly for allowing Elizabeth & me to go,' Bertie wrote hurriedly to his father.[7]

They ate in the open and slept under canvas, watched tribal dances ('some of which were very weird,' Bertie thought[8]), were taken on safari by a Portuguese white hunter known as 'The Hoot' and offered a farm, which the King told them not to accept – 'What would you do if the farm didn't pay?'9 Elizabeth wore an untypical but fetching costume of breeches, belted shirt and felt bush-hat. With her 0.275 Rigby rifle she bagged a rhinoceros, a buffalo, a waterbuck, an oryx, a Grant's gazelle, an antelope, a Kenya hartebeest, a steinbuck, a water-hog and a jackal. In Uganda, Bertie, intrepidly hunting on foot, shot an elephant whose tusks weighed 90lb each: 'It was very lucky as there are not many very big ones left.' He killed a smaller one two days later, 'so we did well in the home of the elephant.'10 It didn't compare, of course, with his father's and brother's hauls in India – thirty-nine tigers in one day, not to mention panthers, bears, and most of the remaining lions – but it was a pretty respectable score.

They returned home on 19 April to face a major ordeal. The British Empire Exhibition at Wembley had been opened by the King the previous summer, an historic occasion, as it was the first time the Emperor's voice had been broadcast, the apparatus and microphones cunningly concealed among cinerarias on the Royal Dais. This year the Duke of York succeeded the Prince of Wales as President of the Exhibition, which was due to re-open on 10 May. The most popular exhibits on the 220-acre showground were Queen Mary's dolls-house, the tomb of Tutankhamun and an effigy of the Prince of Wales made out of butter. There was a coal mine with real pit ponies, a reproduction of Niagara Falls, an entire Maori village, complete with authentic Maoris, and a Palace of Engineering six-and-a-half times the size of Trafalgar Square. 'The British Empire Exhibition aims to complete in 1925 the educational work for Empire unity and Empire trade so well begun in 1924,' Bertie's official announcement read. Saying it through a microphone in front of his father and thousands of spectators, not to mention the unseen millions of listeners, was a different matter. 'I do hope I shall do it well,' he wrote to the King. 'But I shall be very frightened as you have never heard me speak & the loud speakers are apt to put one off as well. So I hope you will understand that I am bound to be more nervous than I usually am.'11

It was an agonising experience. Elizabeth might smile and smile at the inarticulate, struggling man on the dais, but it was no use. 'Bertie got through his speech all right, but there were some rather long pauses,' the King wrote gloomily to Georgie the following day.12 There was grave disquiet in the family circle. Could Bertie really be counted on? He was inadequate in public and even his private abilities seemed open to doubt. He had been married for two and a half years and not a sign of an heir. Had they been mistaken in Elizabeth? Backed the wrong horse? One didn't discuss such things, but there was an aura of failure round the Duke of York which nobody cared for, least of all his wife.

Somehow, between unveiling a stained glass window in York Minster, attending the Railways Centenary celebrations in Darlington, dining with the African Society and touring the Kodak works at Wealdstone, something was done. By the time they left for Glamis and Balmoral in August Elizabeth was pregnant. 'Alge and I are thrilled over your news of Elizabeth's hopes; thank God,' Alice Athlone wrote fervently to Queen Mary, adding rather wildly, 'Kenya is famous for having that effect on people, I hear!'[13]

# Chapter Thirteen

In November 1925 Queen Alexandra died at Sandringham. The decorative, silly, kind-hearted old lady, no deafer now than she had been in life, was stowed away in the Memorial Chapel at Windsor. The King was downcast, experiencing at the age of sixty 'that stark moment of abandonment when a man realises that he is no longer a son.'[1] He felt lonely. Some damn scribblers were criticising the Prince of Wales. Goodwood had been spoiled by a threatened coal strike. He had protested to Baldwin about the Prime Minister's flippancy and disregard of parliamentary decorum, which had brought a sharp reminder 'that one of the earliest historical objects of the House of Commons was to exclude the Crown from interfering in its proceedings.'[2] There had been nothing like that under the Labour chaps. He missed Jim Thomas. He didn't feel well. Elizabeth's pregnancy was the only bright spot on the horizon.

The Yorks were now living in Curzon House, Curzon Street. During that winter Elizabeth helped her mother-in-law sort out Queen Alexandra's vast accumulation of treasures and junk in Marlborough House. Neither Queen Mary nor King George could understand what she had against White Lodge. It was quite obviously the place for Bertie's heir to be born and they refused to consider any alternative. But Elizabeth didn't want to live in White Lodge. She wanted to live in Carlton House Terrace, but nobody died in Carlton House Terrace, nobody was even hopefully poorly, and eviction was out of the question. She considered Norfolk House in Norfolk Street, Mayfair, but it wasn't right. In desperation Bertie arranged to rent a house in Grosvenor Square from a Mrs Hoffmann, at which Lady Strathmore offered them the Strathmore residence in Bruton Street. Elizabeth at last seemed satisfied, and Bertie moved in with his in-laws. It was clearly a temporary arrangement. People were beginning to think it odd that the Yorks had been married for nearly three years and still had no place of their own.

Then Elizabeth heard about 145 Piccadilly, an imposing but dilapidated Crown Property backing onto Hyde Park. The estate agent's advertisement ran:

> This important mansion ... which is approached by a carriage drive used jointly with No. 144 Piccadilly, contains spacious and well-lighted accommodation, including entrance hall, principal staircase hall, a secondary staircase with electric passenger lift, drawing room, dining room, ballroom, study, library, about 25 bedrooms, conservatory etc. . .

It was still empty in 1926 and Elizabeth set her heart on it. Anxious to keep his pregnant darling happy – though not without some misgivings, since he was a practical man – the Duke entered into protracted negotiations with the Crown Estates Office and Buckingham Palace and finally obtained a yearly lease on the property. The Crown Estates Office would pay for the renovation, adding a fire escape to the nursery floor, carrying out 'various necessary and overdue repairs' and decorating the whole place in the new, fashionable pastel shades. Bertie generously offered to pay for the construction of an extra bedroom. With a growing family approximately twenty-five bedrooms was scarcely enough. Although it was termed a 'grace-and-favour residence' he also promised to contribute to the rent. Any sacrifice was worth the chance to get out of White Lodge.

Once that was settled the Duchess of York could turn her attention to the matter in hand. Clara Knight was summoned to report back for duty in time to take over the royal heir. Her latest charge, Elizabeth's niece, was only nine months old and there were some ineffectual protests. 'She was mine first!' the Duchess declared, stamping her size three-and-a-half foot. For a short while it looked as though sawdust Clara might be torn limb from limb.

Although tiny and dainty and all the rest, Elizabeth was a healthy Scottish lass who seemed to survive most physical rigours without much fuss. Presumably the doctors discovered the child was a breech when it was too late to turn the foetus.[3] After she had been in labour all day it was decided to perform a Caesarian section. To undergo such an operation in a private house appears extraordinary to us, but in 1926 it was still considered *infra dig* for a royal person to attend hospital in anything but a charitable capacity. If there was the slightest likelihood of dying, the correct thing was to do it in the room, preferably the bed, in which one had been born; failing this, then at least in familiar surroundings where proper provision could be made for mourners and necessary officials. Even without such gloomy forebodings a royal birth needed the presence of the Home Secretary and a whole gaggle of relations. To facilitate matters the surgeon, Sir Henry Simpson, and the obstetrician, Walter Jagger, Consultant at the Samaritan Hospital for Women, were installed in the house. Their first mystifying bulletin announced they were going to follow 'a certain line of treatment'; their next that 'Her Royal Highness the Duchess of York was safely delivered of a Princess at 2.40am this morning, 21 April.' For some reason it sounds more painful than having a daughter.

Ten days later a national coal strike began and the following evening a General Strike was proclaimed. Thick, drizzling fog and bitter cold must have added to the misery, but no, all the Court's accounts are of courage, ingenuity, and a good time had by all. 'Our old country can well be proud of itself,' the King wrote in his diary when the crisis was officially over, 'as during the last nine days there has been a strike in which 4 million men have been affected; not a shot has been fired & no one killed; it shows what a wonderful people we are. . .'[4] The miners held out for another six months before they were driven by starvation to accept longer hours and lower wages. The Archbishop of Canterbury, preaching at St Martin in the Fields, took his timely text from Ephesians iv 1: *Walk worthy of the vocation wherewith ye are called.*

Elizabeth had provided a third successor to the throne: everyone else moved down a peg. The next thing on the agenda was her husband's stammer. They were due to go on a World Tour in January 1927 and knew that the Australian Premier, Stanley Bruce, had forcibly expressed his doubts about what was known as the Duke of York's 'affliction'. The King, too, was uneasy and Bertie even more so. They were told that an Australian called Lionel Logue, an ex-engineer with no medical qualifications but a remarkably successful record in faith-healing, was practising in Harley Street. The Duke was sceptical – there had been too many 'cures', too many failures – but the Duchess insisted he should at least try. 'The Duke of York entered my consulting room at three o'clock in the afternoon,' Logue recalled, 'A slim, quiet man, with tired eyes and all the symptoms of the man upon whom habitual speech defect had begun to set the sign. When he left at five o'clock, you could see that there was hope once more in his heart.'[5]

Hope was half the battle. The actual treatment consisted of

being taught to breathe correctly, to develop the lungs and control the rhythm of the diaphragm. There was no instant miracle but Bertie's new optimism and Elizabeth's determination had a considerable effect. For two-and-a-half months they visited Harley Street almost daily and by 6 January, when they sailed for New Zealand en route for Australia, the Duke of York could claim that he was 'full of confidence'. The Duchess, on the other hand, was in tears. Princess Elizabeth, known as Lilibet, was nine months old and they would be away until June. '*Mais que faire?*' as her mother-in-law had so frequently asked. Australia needed her more.

The World Tour, like every other World Tour, was accounted a great success. There was some bad feeling in Melbourne about the fact that they had chosen to go to New Zealand first, but that was ignored. Two Labour MPs, Mr Ammon and Mr David Kirkwood, tactlessly suggested in the House of Commons that 'a pleasure trip of this kind' should not have been undertaken at a time of industrial depression: 'in spite of the country's distress it can afford to vote £7,000 to send out their Royal Highnesses to the uttermost parts of the earth, and it would not matter one iota to the welfare of the country supposing they never returned!'[6] Baldwin regarded this as a joke. The King was not amused: 'His Majesty takes a graver view of these flippant, discourteous, if not insulting allusions to his Family. . .' Mr Ammon and Mr Kirkwood clearly had no conception of the 'almost terrifying schedule of dinners, receptions, garden-parties, balls and other official duties relieved by brief fishing excursions'[7] which the Duke and Duchess were enduring. Cantankerous letters from his father didn't make Bertie's task any easier: 'I send you a picture of you inspecting the Gd of Honour (I don't think much of their dressing) with yr Equerry walking on yr right side next to the Gd & you ignoring the Officer entirely. Yr Equerry should be outside & behind, it certainly doesn't look well.' 'I had finished inspecting the guard of honour,' his son explained laboriously, '& was walking back to join Elizabeth. . . It was an unfortunate moment for the photograph to be taken. . .'[8]

However, the new Parliament at Canberra was duly opened – the purpose of the trip – and Australia conquered. Although Bertie endured a terrible ten days alone while Elizabeth withdrew with tonsillitis, she achieved 'the responsibility of having a continent in love with her',[9] and probably the Governor as well. She also accumulated three tons of toys and twenty live parrots for the Princess.[10] At Portsmouth on 27 June they were met by David, Harry, George and instructions from the King regarding their reunion at Victoria:

'We will not embrace at the station before so many people. When you kiss Mama take yr hat off.'[11]

Lilibet was now over a year old. It was a bewildering day, what with the hugs and kisses and being held up on the balcony like a football cup, the crowd roaring below. Eventually the reunited family drove through more crowds to 145 Piccadilly, where they were welcomed by Captain Basil Brooke, their Comptroller, Mr Ainslie, the butler, Mrs Macdonald, the cook and Mrs Evans, the housekeeper. In addition were an under-butler, two footmen, an odd man, a steward's room boy, three housemaids, three kitchen maids, a nursery maid, a dresser, a valet, an RAF orderly, a night watchman, and a Boy Scout to operate the telephone.[12]

The glowing accounts of the Yorks' World Tour, their connubial bliss, impeccable morals and sense of duty provided a happy contrast to the increasing flightiness of the bachelor brothers. While the Duke and Duchess of York were slogging round New Zealand in the rain Prince George had been enjoying a relatively trouble-free affair with Poppy Baring, a notoriously flighty débutante. So far every effort he had made to follow his own inclinations had ended in squalor and scandal. His more unacceptable girlfriends were chased out of the country by Scotland Yard and the few who passed muster at Cowes or Ascot had been turned down flat by his parents. The progress of his affair with Poppy was watched with keen interest by his friend Duff Cooper: '8 January 1927: Poppy sleeping peacefully in the arms of Prince George . . . 14 January: there is talk of marriage. I hope it comes off . . . [Poppy] says she couldn't bear the Royal Family. I said it wasn't much worse than other families . . . 29 January: the great news was that Prince George had been to see his parents and told them he wanted to marry Poppy. They had taken it wonderfully and raised hardly any objection . . . 8 February: [Prince George] was afraid it was all off. Unfavourable reports about poor Poppy appear to have reached His Majesty's ears . . . So the girl's sunk.'[13] If it is going too far to say that Georgie's parents drove him to homosexuality and drugs, they certainly didn't allow him any satisfactory alternative until they produced Princess Marina of Greece six years later.

London's Bright Young Things, led by the thirty-four-year-old Prince of Wales, were dancing the Charleston dressed up as babies or tramps or Japanese cookies, careering about on paper chases and treasure hunts, drinking quantities of Manhattans and Sidecars and Bronxes and doing their utmost to give the decade a bad name. Unlike their Sixties grand-children they really believed, with a delicious frisson of guilt, that they were damned. Evelyn Waugh was their Savonarola, Noël Coward their St Paul:

> *Poor little rich girl,*
> *You're a bewitched girl*
> *Better beware!*

That summer the unpredictable Prince of Wales spent a bucket-and-spade holiday at Sandwich with Freda Dudley Ward and her two young daughters. A few weeks later Stanley Baldwin accompanied him and the Duke of Kent to Canada for the Diamond Jubilee celebrations and regretted it because both Princes behaved so badly. The York star rose ever higher in the firmament. Little Lilibet was wheeled around Hamilton Gardens in the royal perambulator every afternoon unless a royal carriage drawn by a pair of bay horses, a coachman and footman on the box, arrived to take her for a drive. When her mother was not on view accepting brooches from her Regiments or dolls from institutions like the Sunshine Guild or Streatham Hospital for Incurables, she occupied herself like any other housewife with routine desk work and general household decisions. 'The Duchess was most interested in the well-being of her staff and had taken the trouble to learn all their names.'[14] It seems odd that the events of 1936 were not a foregone conclusion.

Late at night on 22 October 1928, in total darkness, the remains of eight unidentified members of the Royal Family were removed from the Royal Vault of St George's Chapel and re-interred at Frogmore. It was rumoured that one of the coffins had exploded during evensong, but the official explanation for the move – though not for the bizarre way it was conducted – was that in future only Sovereigns would be buried at Windsor. Four weeks later Queen Mary was writing in her diary: 'George had a chill & had to go to bed – too tiresome.'[15] A week later the Prince of Wales, big-game hunting in East Africa with Thelma Furness and brother Harry, received a cable telling him to return home immediately. With assistance from Mussolini, who sent his own train to meet the ship at Brindisi and ordered the tracks to be cleared at the Swiss frontier, David made the 7,000-mile journey in nine days. He found his father barely conscious. Bertie did not sound unduly concerned: 'There is a lovely story going about which emanated from the East End,' he told his brother, 'that the reason of your rushing home is that in the event of anything happening to

Papa I am going to bag the Throne in your absence!!! Just like the Middle Ages. . .'[16] He had been appointed a Counsellor of State and was perhaps a little intoxicated by his new authority.

The King had acute septicaemia; his heart was growing weaker. He was operated on. Licensing hours for prayer were relaxed and the churches stayed open twenty-four hours a day. Christmas was gloomy. The old man battled through and by February 1929 was well enough to be moved for his convalescence to a house near Bognor. In March Lilibet visited her grandfather while her parents went to the wedding of Crown Prince Olav of Norway (the only child of King Haakon and their Aunt Maud, known as Harry) to Princess Martha of Sweden. On their way home the Yorks stayed at the British Embassy in Berlin and were taken to lunch at the golf club by Harold Nicolson. The Duchess's perception astounded him. Not only had she read his book *Some People*, but she understood it. 'You choose your colours so carefully,' she told him. '"That bit about the Palace in Madrid was done in grey and chalk-white, the Constantinople bits in blue and green, the desert bits in blue and orange." What an amazing woman!' If he was over-estimating her intellect, he could not exaggerate her charm. It was overwhelming. 'The Duke's,' he added laconically, 'was less evident.'[17]

They returned home to find that the King had been much amused by his granddaughter. He was rapidly losing faith in the Prince of Wales and already beginning to think what he would so vehemently say in a few years' time: 'I pray to God that my eldest son will never marry and have children, and that nothing will come between Bertie and Lilibet and the throne!' Bertie was praying equally fervently for the opposite.

That summer the Labour Party scraped in again with a bare majority, but no one was unduly alarmed. The King, wearing a Chinese dressing gown, received his old friend Jim Thomas and the rest in his bedroom at Windsor. Jim went to Canada and came back announcing he had found 'the complete cure' for unemployment. Unemployment rose by eight per cent. A Thanksgiving Service was held for the King's recovery on 7 July but a few days later he laughed so heartily at one of Jim's ribald jokes that he had a relapse and was operated on for the removal of a rib. As for the Yorks, Elizabeth had every reason to congratulate herself, and did. Lilibet was a success and Bertie's stammer under control: 'Through all this nervous strain my speech has not been affected one atom,' he wrote proudly to Lionel Logue.[19]

# Chapter Fourteen

For the past four years Bertie had slogged on conscientiously through his assignments as his father's representative and his elder brother's understudy. When his photograph appeared in the Press it either showed him inspecting a factory, playing games with the boys at his camps or, more often, playing second fiddle to his wife and daughter.[1] He had played second fiddle all his life, and was good at it. The trouble arose on the rare occasions when he had to perform a solo.

In January 1930 the Crown Prince of Italy, young Umberto, was to marry Princess Marie-Jose of Belgium in the Pauline Chapel of the Palace of the Quirinal in Rome. Like the Belgrade wedding seven years before, this was an important political alliance, intended to demonstrate the reconciliation of the House of the Savoy and the Italian State – Benito Mussolini, Knight Grand Cross of the Order of the Bath (1923)[2] – with the Vatican. The Yorks, as usual, had been told to attend; but the Duchess was feeling poorly. The Duke, with growling reluctance, had to go alone.

He was helpless without her, and on top of that he had a terrible cold. In Rome he stayed with Ambassador Sir Ronald and Lady Sybil Graham, to whom he 'appeared to be in a perpetual state of discontent and ill-humour'. When Lady Sybil's small dog snuffled under the breakfast table one morning, the Duke 'touched it with his foot, perhaps more forcibly than he had intended'. The dog yelped. Lady Sybil turned pale. 'How republican one feels near certain royals!'[3] she was heard to mutter as she cradled her innocent pooch.

At the wedding itself the *placements* had been arranged by the Grand Master of Ceremonies, Duke Borea d'Olmo, who was approaching his hundredth birthday and no longer seemed able to distinguish between black and white. The Duke of York was placed after ex-King

Amanullah of Afghanistan, a nice enough fellow (he had visited Windsor the year before and given the Princess Royal a massive gramophone in a mahogany case)[4] but to him a 'nigger' nevertheless. The final insult was being offered the Grand Cross of San Maurizio e Lazzare instead of the Ordine dell' Annunziata, or Italian equivalent of the Garter: brother David had already been given the Ordine dell' Annunziata, and no two members of the same family were permitted to wear it.[5] If Elizabeth had been with him none of this would have happened. No wonder he kicked the dog.

Soon after his return from this calamitous visit the Duchess's secret was out – another little successor to the throne was on the way. In spite of her first experience she was determined to have this baby at Glamis, at extreme inconvenience to everybody, particularly the Home Secretary and the Ceremonial Secretary at the Home Office, both of whom had to be present. As always, the 'Little Duchess' got her way. The baby was due between 6 and 12 August. On the morning of 5 August the Home Secretary, Mr Clynes, and the Ceremonial Secretary, Mr Boyd, arrived as Lady Airlie's guests at Cortachy Castle.

Lady Airlie wrote an hilarious account of this visit in her memoirs. Mr Boyd was 'a small anxious-looking man, meticulously neat in his dress and movements, who had spent many years of his life in China.' It had been suggested to him that he and the Home Secretary might book into a hotel in Perth and that two sleepers should be reserved for them on every night train from London until the event was over, but the implications horrified him. 'What if the birth should take place in the early hours of the morning and the Home Secretary could not get to Glamis in time?' (In his agitation he sprang out of his chair and paced up and down Lady Airlie's sitting room.) 'If the birth was not properly witnessed its legal right might be questioned. The child would be in direct succession to the Throne. Look at what had happened at the birth of the son of James II and Mary of Modena,' (He had brought the book with him, the relevant passages underlined in red ink.) By offering her hospitality, Lady Airlie saved the throne of England from dishonour.

Mr Clynes, a small man, was quiet and shy, dressed in a rather ill-fitting suit and a grey Homburg hat. He talked very little, in contrast to Mr Boyd, who fidgeted incessantly and still seemed preoccupied with the fear of some plot. 'I could not help feeling,' remarks Lady Airlie, 'that his long residence in China was inclining him to view the situation in too oriental a light.' A single telephone wire had been installed from Airlie to Glamis and a dispatch rider was available at Glamis day and night in case the wire broke down. They could only wait.

Mr Clynes went for walks and admired the scenery. Mr Boyd's anxiety developed into frenzy. On hearing from Sir Henry Simpson that the event could not be later than 11 August they sat up all night, 'sustained by frequent cups of coffee'. Not a word. By 4 August Mr Boyd was in a panic and lost his temper with Mr Clynes when the latter was on the point of going out for a tranquil drive with Lady Airlie. On the following day Mr Clynes and Lady Airlie resumed their pleasant excursions. Mr Clynes even made an impromptu speech at the Airlie Flower Show. On the morning of 21 August Boyd, 'wild-eyed and haggard after sitting up all night', telephoned Glamis. No news. He dashed out into the garden and kicked a few stones.

That evening, as Lady Airlie was dressing for dinner, Admiral Brooke phoned asking in an agitated voice for Mr Boyd. Mabell bundled into her dressing gown and banged on Mr Boyd's door. 'Telephone! From Glamis!' she shouted.

There was the sound of frantic opening and shutting of wardrobes, then a wail of anguish: 'I can't go downstairs, I'm not dressed and I can't find my suit!'

'Never mind!' bawled the noble lady, 'Take the call in my room! I'm not dressed either but it doesn't matter!'

Mr Boyd rushed out of his bedroom wearing a dark blue kimono and into Lady Airlie's. 'What? In an hour? . . . We must start at once!' He renewed the desperate search for his suit. Lady Airlie ordered sandwiches. When they got downstairs Mr Clynes was calmly waiting at the door in his big coat and Homburg hat. He pointed to the sunset. 'Just look at that, Boyd,' he said. *'In such a night did Dido from the walls of Carthage . . .'* Mr Boyd pushed Mr Clynes into the car. They arrived at Glamis with half an hour to spare. So was the birth of Princess Margaret honourably, if euphemistically, witnessed and passed into history. Mr Clynes returned to recoup what he could of his interrupted holiday in Brighton with his wife and children. No one cared much what happened to Mr Boyd.

On 7 March that year Mrs Ronald Armstrong-Jones gave birth to a boy, Anthony, in Eaton Terrace, Belgravia. The biggest hit of the theatre season was Noël Coward's *Private Lives*, a play demonstrating that even the Elyots and Amandas of this world have hearts of gold. There was a craze for midget golf; everyone owned a yo-yo; a motor yacht for a Greek millionaire was the only ship being built in the Clyde shipyards and the dole queues lengthened by half a million. The Prince of Wales, perhaps a little envious of the Yorks' domesticity, asked his father to give him 'a castellated conglomeration' called Fort Belvedere near Sunningdale. 'What could you possibly want that queer old place for?' the King asked. 'Those dam' weekends, I suppose.'[6] Freda helped with the alterations and decorations while David worked in the garden. In November, while staying with Thelma Furness and her husband at Melton Mowbray, he met Mrs Wallis Simpson.

# Chapter Fifteen

Those who are shocked by the idea that the Queen Mother as a girl was in love with someone other than her future husband are even more outraged by the suggestion that sexuality has been her most formidable characteristic. I am not suggesting that either as Duchess of York or as Queen she invited lovers to bed. On the contrary. Rigid moral principles often leave huge reserves of excess energy available for other purposes, as many saints, martyrs and philanthropists demonstrate. All I suggest is that the power which transformed Prince Albert from an inarticulate nobody into a man of some stature, hypnotised the media and eventually reinstated the throne in the public's fantasy was essentially – if the term is preferable – female.* She appealed to the little boys lurking in the hearts of hearty extroverts: sportsmen, politicians and tycoons were bowled over by the hint of being 'in the know' that spiced her delicate femininity. Men permanently yearning for an accessible mother found her irresistible – 'the great mother figure and nannie to us all, through the warmth of her sympathy bathes us and wraps us in a counterpane by the fire-side. . .' 'Regal, yet maternal, hers is the constitutional bosom upon which weary millions would gladly rest their heads.' This is certainly the reason why her closest friends and greatest admirers, as well as the members of her personal staff, have nearly always been bachelors disinclined for marriage. She may have capitalised on 'the drowsy caressing voice, the slow sweet smile, the delicious gurgle of laughter, the soft eyes glowing etc.' and cultivated her reputation as a charming flirt, but without the sexual dynamo churning behind all that the present Queen Mother would have been a nonentity.

* Those who cite the current Princess of Wales as the Royal Family's greatest sex symbol don't appreciate my point: Diana is 'sexy', an ephemeral and less significant quality.

By 1931 she had put on a good deal of weight; her face was rounder, her eyes smaller; she was no longer a wistful waif, a Barrie heroine, but a pneumatic mother of two with a roguish twinkle. That summer she accompanied her husband to Paris to open 'British week'. While they were there they visited the Colonial Exhibition, presided over by the brilliant old colonial administrator Marshal Lyautey who, according to Rebecca West, 'was sustained by male vanity in its most benificent form. It was not that he looked down on anybody; he looked up at the sun and congratulated it on having an object like himself who was worthy to be shone on by its rays'[1]: a challenge to any woman.

The old man seemed tired and sombre as he showed them round. The Duchess suggested they should stop for a cup of tea in one of the cafés; then, turning the full battery of her charm on the Marshal, she asked, 'Monsieur le Marechal, you are so powerful – you created the beautiful country of Morocco and you have made this fine exhibition – would you do something for me?'

'For you, Madame? But what can I do for Your Royal Highness?'

'Why, this. The sun is in my eyes. Will you make it disappear?'

The sun immediately disappeared behind a cloud. 'Thank you, Monsieur le Marechal. I *knew* you could do anything!' Her expression of admiring gratitude unchanged, she murmured to Bertie 'I saw the cloud coming.'[2]

Perhaps the story would be better without the final line, but the point is that the magic worked and Lyautey was vanquished. The whole thing depended on a collusion between hoaxer and hoaxed. Elizabeth's youngest daughter would attempt to emulate her mother's performance and fail. The eldest never even tried.

The Prince of Wales and his brother George spent the early months of 1931 on a semi-official tour of South America, 'poking around department stores and wholesale mercantile establishments',[3] addressing Chambers of Commerce, inspecting factories and avoiding revolutions. A suggestion was made that the Duke of York should become Governor-General of Canada; before the Duchess could make up her mind about the idea Jim Thomas vetoed it on the untenable grounds that the Canadians didn't like royalty. Lord and Lady Strathmore celebrated their Golden Wedding at Glamis, the two little York girls footnotes to the family photograph, and Mrs Wallis Simpson was presented at Court wearing Thelma Furness' train, feathers and fan. An apparently insignificant bank, the Credit Anstaldt in Vienna, locked its doors and the entire Western economy toppled. By August the crisis was so acute that on reaching Balmoral the King had to turn straight round and go back to London. 'I will *not* be left sitting on a mountain!' exclaimed Queen Mary furiously.[4] Gandhi arrived in London for the second Round Table Conference. The King and Queen gave a tea party for the delegates, at which the Mahatma in his loin-cloth failed to remind them of the splendours of the Durbar.

The crisis escalated. America refused to help. Ramsay Macdonald flung out of the Cabinet Room in a state of extreme agitation: 'I am off to the Palace,' he shouted, 'to throw in my hand!' He found himself heading a National Government instead. The King worked hard that day. After seeing Macdonald he had King George of the Hellenes to lunch, his aunt Princess Louise to tea and Lord Cromer to dinner, visited Harry in hospital, worked on his boxes and spent some time on his stamp collection. 'Our Captain played one of his best innings with a very straight bat,' said his Private Secretary. 'He stopped the rot and saved his side. He was not-out at the end and had hardly turned a hair or shown any signs of fatigue.'[5] There were two identical sides to the British coin of fortune: triumph and Triumph. Whichever way it spun, the result was always a certainty.

Not that things weren't a little unstable. Direct taxes were increased by £51½ million, beer, tobacco and petrol by £24 million. Teachers' salaries were reduced by fifteen per cent, unemployment rates cut by ten per cent and the rate of contribution increased. Then there was a minor mutiny in the British Navy, which shook the faith of foreign investors – £33 million in gold was withdrawn from the Bank of England in one week. On 21 September Britain went off the Gold Standard. King George gave up £50,000 from his annual Civil List for as long as the emergency lasted. The Prince of Wales contributed £50,000 from the Duchy of Cornwall to the National Exchequer. The Duke of York, with a wife and two daughters to keep, gave up hunting with the Pytchley and sold his six hunters for a miserable 965 guineas. 'This is the worst part of all,' he wrote to the Master, 'and the parting with them will be terrible.'[6]

Even as all this stringent tightening of belts was going on the King offered the Yorks a grace-and-favour country house, the Royal Lodge, in Windsor Park. David, after all, had Fort Belvedere and perhaps it would compensate for the loss of the hunters. The place was, of course, uninhabitable. Concerned as they were about the financial crisis, the Yorks restricted themselves to begin with by restoring the great Wyatville Saloon, building a new wing and putting in a few bathrooms.

By the spring of 1932 the Yorks were installed in the Royal Lodge. Just before Easter the children's first governess, Marion Crawford, arrived, a 22-year-old Eton-cropped graduate of the Moray House Training College in Edinburgh. Her ambition was to be a child psychologist, but as it turned out she devoted the next seventeen years of her life to Lilibet and Margaret, providing hearty, cheerful good sense in a household that was rapidly coming to resemble its public image. The Duchess 'had a definite idea of the sort of training she wished her daughters to receive, and pursued her course untroubled by other people's doubts. She wanted them to spend as much time as possible in the open air, to acquire good manners and perfect deportment, to cultivate all the distinctively feminine graces. While she agreed that the Princesses should "gain as much reasonable book-learning as might prove to be within their capacity", she insisted this was kept "in proper proportion with the rest and in subordination to the whole." '7 When it became clear that Lilibet's capacity for mathematics was extremely limited it was Miss Crawford who worried, not the Duchess. There were hilarious bath-times and hopscotch and hide-and-seek, endless grooming of ponies and mucking out of stables, but nobody had any ideas or bothered to make any mundane decisions. Queen Mary was the only person – if such a term is not *lése-majesté* – to give the governess any practical support. The bankrupt and mostly unemployed Welsh gave Lilibet a house for her sixth birthday. It was, of course, child-sized. Her grandmother insisted on inspecting it on her hands and knees, a regal Alice whose toque alone was as high as the chimney. She satisfied herself that the plumbing was in good order and the kitchen well stocked.

Meanwhile Uncle George was involved in a blackmail scandal – something to do with letters to a young man in Paris,8 but of course it was never mentioned. David's new friends the Simpsons spent their first weekend at nearby Fort Belvedere. Thelma Furness seemed to have supplanted Freda in David's affections and Elizabeth much enjoyed visiting the Fort. One evening they had great fun hurling David's new unbreakable plastic records across the Terrace. 'Come on, David, let's see if these are really unbreakable, as the label says,' Bertie cried. The women ducked and dodged like rabbits and finally fled indoors. Roaring with laughter, the brothers followed and continued the game in the drawing room until one of the Prince's most treasured lamps was bowled over by a direct hit.[9]

Then there was the weekend when Virginia Water froze and they all went skating, Thelma and Elizabeth hanging on to a couple of old kitchen chairs and both 'in gales of laughter. If ever I had to live in a bungalow in a small town,' Thelma thought, 'this is the woman I would most like to have as a next-door neighbour to gossip with while hanging out the washing in our backyards.'[10] Thelma put up a Christmas tree at the Fort, with ornaments from Selfridges and all the trimmings.

King George made his first broadcast from Sandringham on Christmas afternoon, the script written by his friend Rudyard Kipling. 'I speak now from my home and from my heart to you all; to men and women so cut off by the snows, the desert, or the sea, that only voices out of the air can reach them. . .' Monarchy's Prospero, the old man touched the most cynical of listeners.

'1933,' according to Lady Longford, 'was the year of the corgi.'[11] There were a few secondary events, such as Hitler becoming Reich Chancellor, the Reichstag Fire, a demonstration by 30,000 Jews from Stepney and the Oxford Union's decision that it would in no circumstances fight for King and Country, but it was 'Dookie' which made the news at the Royal Lodge. Unfortunately the animal emulated the less pleasing aspects of the royal temperament. Members of the Household gallantly hid their bleeding hands while passing the time of day with the Princesses; the staff went in constant fear of hydrophobia. This angry animal was soon joined by Jane, Mimsy, Stiffy, Scrummy and Choo Choo. The last four were were golden labradors and a Tibetan lion dog, not corgis.

In November 1934 Prince George, recently made Duke of Kent, married Marina of Greece, the granddaughter of Queen Alexandra's brother George ('Uncle Willy') and first cousin to thirteen-year-old Prince Philip of Greece. The story went that she had been brought over to England the previous year in the hope that she would do for the Prince of Wales who was, as usual, stubbornly uninterested. Aristocratic, chic, with no pretensions to cleverness, she was the ideal wife for George, if he had to have one at all. Queen Mary's high hopes of her, were somewhat dashed when the Princess turned up at the Palace with red fingernails.

'I'm afraid the King doesn't like painted nails,' the Queen said icily. 'Can you do something about it?'

'Your George may not,' Marina replied, equally regal. 'But mine does.'[12]

Such *hauteur* did not endear her to the Duchess of York, who was referred to by Marina as 'that common little Scottish girl'. An added irritant was that King George, always appreciating a pretty gal whatever the colour of her fingernails, was much taken by his new daughter-in-law, cheerfully overlooking the fact that she had spent most of her adult life as an itinerant exile and had no money. Marina complained that 'the Duchess of York's serene professionalism was so far ahead of everybody else that instead of helping by its example she set a standard that seemed almost impossible to reach.'[13] The royal amateur and the impeccable commoner did not, in short, feel warmly towards each other.

Two days before the Kent wedding a State reception was held at Buckingham Palace. The Prince of Wales invited Ernest and Wallis Simpson who were, after all, close friends of Marina's sister Olga and her brother-in-law Prince Paul. Even so, their presence raised a few courtly eyebrows. Wallis, small, flat as a board, with her big head, labourer's hands and noisy chatter, wore a violet lamé dress with a vivid green sash – 'the most striking gown in the room,' said Prince Paul sincerely.

1935 was the year of King George's Silver Jubilee and for the first few months there wasn't a cloud in the sky. Elizabeth wore pink at Lady Astor's ball and danced with Anthony Eden, George Gage and Duff Cooper. The Prince of Wales went skiing in Kitzbuhl with a group of friends, including Mrs Simpson. On 6 May the Yorks rode in an open landau to St Paul's for the Jubilee Thanksgiving Service, 'the two tiny pink children waving more energetically than their parents'.[14] 'Wonderful service,' the King told the Dean. 'Just one thing wrong with it – too many parsons getting in the way. I didn't know there were so many dam' parsons in England.'[15] There were processions and fireworks and brass bands every day; the crowds, dazzled under the illuminations, sang and cheered all night.

On Jubilee Day itself Lady Alice Montagu-Douglas-Scott, daughter of the 7th Duke of Buccleuch, left Mombasa for England. Prince Henry had decided to marry her and she had gone to Kenya 'for a last taste of freedom before abandoning a truly private life for ever.'[16] Alice was thirty-four years old and in the future would sound a small, calm note of sanity whenever she made an appearance in the royal drama. Two of her bridesmaids were the York princesses wearing truncated Kate Greenaway gowns. 'I want to see their pretty little knees,' the

King explained to designer Norman Hartnell.[17] His wife may have wryly recalled the fuss there was when she thought of showing her pretty little ankles. 'May God bless the dear couple,' she wrote in her diary on the Gloucesters' wedding night. As far as she could see, He was certainly not blessing the Prince of Wales.

There was no good reason for David to invite the Simpsons to the first State ball of the Jubilee season, but there they were. Everyone knew by now that Ernest had not accompanied his wife to Kitzbuhl and that she and the Prince had gone on together to waltz in Vienna and *csárdás* in Budapest. Foxtrotting in Buckingham Palace, in front of the family, was going too far. Wallis has not recorded what she wore – something a little more restrained, I suspect – but we know what she felt: 'As David and I danced past [the King and Queen], I thought I felt the King's eyes rest searchingly on me. Something in his look made me feel that all this graciousness and pageantry were but the glittering tip of an iceberg that extended down into unseen depths . . . depths filled with an icy menace for such as me.'[18] She might have seen the same look in the Duchess of York's normally soft and sympathetic eyes if she had glanced round for a moment.

# Chapter Sixteen

On 16 January 1936 King George complained of a cold and stayed in his room all day. This time the Queen was worried. She sent for Bertie to help her with the Sandringham house-party and wrote a note to David saying 'I think you ought to know that Papa is not very well.'[1] Although Elizabeth's 'flu had turned to pneumonia, Bertie was at Sandringham by late afternoon. The Prince of Wales flew there next day in his new De Havilland Gypsy Moth. That night the old man wrote shakily in his diary, 'A little snow & wind. Dawson* arrived this evening. I saw him & feel rotten.'[2]

On Sunday 19 January the Archbishop of Canterbury, Cosmo Gordon Lang, arrived. Bertie and David flew to London and informed the Prime Minister that the King was not expected to live more than two or three days – grim news that apparently could not be mentioned over the telephone. Bertie stayed the night at 145 Piccadilly and saw his sick wife. The brothers flew back to Sandringham on Monday afternoon. A Privy Council had been held that morning to appoint Counsellors of State.

> We were summoned to the sick room ... The King was in his chair, looking pathetically weak and frail, but fully conscious ... The President read the Order in Council. With a clear voice the King gave the reply so familiar to him, 'Approved.' Then Dawson, kneeling at his feet and watching his face, said, 'Sir, do you wish to sign yourself?' 'Yes,' said the King, 'I have always signed in my own hand.' Dawson tried to put the pen in his fingers, but owing to the failure of circulation they could not hold it. Then the hands moved most pathetically over the paper in the effort to sign. This took some minutes. Then the King turned to his Counsellors and said, 'I am very sorry to keep you waiting so long', adding shortly after, 'You see, I can't concentrate.' Once again the hands moved

*Lord Dawson of Penn, the King's doctor.

113

impotently up and down. Then, with great adroitness, Dawson put the pen in his hand and guided it, saying, 'Make a mark, Sir, and you may sign afterwards.' So two marks, XX, were made. Then the King turned again to his Counsellors and dismissed them with the old kind, kingly smile.[3]

The family had tea together, the Prince of Wales full of vitality and touchingly attentive to the Queen.[4] After that they waited. At 11.15pm the Archbishop put on his cassock and went to the King's room. 'The Queen and Princess Mary were there, with the doctors and nurses. The sons were together downstairs. No one seemed to think of calling them, and for this I was sorry.' The Archbishop then read the Twenty Third Psalm, 'The Lord is my shepherd', and some passages from the Bible, 'and then, going to the King's side, I said the Commendatory Prayers – "Go forth, O Christian Soul" – with a final Benediction. As it was plain that the King's life could only last for a few minutes, I felt that I must leave the Queen and her family alone, and retired. I was told afterwards that the sons, especially the Prince of Wales, were painfully upset.'[5] King George V died at five minutes to midnight.

In 1921, when Louis Mountbatten's father died, the Prince of Wales told his cousin, 'I envy you a father whom you could love. If my father died, we should have felt nothing but relief.'[6] That was fifteen years ago. Now, wrote Helen Hardinge, 'his grief was frantic and unreasonable. In its outward manifestations, it far exceeded that of his mother and his three brothers, although they had loved King George V at least as much as he had.'[7] She did not say how much grief she considered 'reasonable' for a son to feel on the death of his father, or how she knew the relative amounts of grief felt by the family. In six months' time the Hardinges would be among the new King's most virulent enemies. Everything Lady Hardinge writes about the reign of Edward VIII is embittered by wifely loyalty and womanly outrage: it is not unreasonable to suppose that she had no qualms in sharing her hostility with her friend the Duchess of York.

On 21 January the Duke of York and King Edward VIII flew to London for the Accession meeting of the Privy Council at St James's Palace. '. . . I place my reliance upon the loyalty and affection of my peoples throughout the Empire, and upon the wisdom of their Parliaments, to support me in this heavy task,' the King told them, 'and I pray God will guide me to perform it.' Bertie went home and the King rushed to the Ritz to meet Wallis Simpson, who was ten minutes late; Lord Charles Montagu saw him 'stamping up and down the long corridor, looking angry and anxious till she came in and joined him.' The Yorks, who had never kept such an assignation in their lives, were horrified. That night, while Bertie and Elizabeth were discussing the mournful events of the week and speculating about the even more mournful events of the future, David dined with Wallis.

While the Accession was being proclaimed from St James's Palace the next day, mourning for King George V was temporarily suspended to allow for official jubilation:

> Whereas it has pleased almighty God ... We, therefore, the Lords Spiritual and Temporal of this Realm ... with one Voice and Consent of Tongue and Heart publish and proclaim that the High and Mighty Prince Edward Albert Christian George Andrew Patrick David is now, by the Death of our late Sovereign of Happy Memory ... God Save the King!

The crowds roared, trumpets blew, the band played the National Anthem, a salute of guns boomed out from Hyde Park and the Tower and the King himself, accompanied by Mrs Wallis Simpson and a group of friends, watched the ceremony from a room in the Palace overlooking Friary Court. 'It was all very moving,' Wallis told the King, 'but it has also made me realise how different your life is going to be.' To which he replied, 'Wallis, there will be a difference, of course. But nothing can ever change my feelings towards you.'[8]

The story was all round London in no time. 'We are all riveted by the position of Mrs S — ,' buzzed Chips Channon. 'No man has ever been so in love as the present King; but can she be another Mrs Fitzherbert? If he drops her she will fall – fall – into the nothingness from whence she came, but I hope he will not, for she is a good, kindly woman, who has had an excellent influence on the young Monarch.'[9] The *Times*, still maintaining that a King could do no wrong, surpassed itself for this occasion: 'The King's son was proclaimed ... with a glow of heraldic pageantry, like the light of dawn seen upon distant mountain tops from a valley still wrapped in the shadows.'[10]

The following day the King and the Duke and Duchess of York returned to Sandringham with the Gloucesters. On the morning of 23 January the body of King George was taken on a gun-carriage from Sandringham Church to Wolferton Station. The weather was fine and frosty, the procession moved at the quick-march pace of the contingent of Guards preceding the coffin. Behind the coffin walked the King, looking grim, and his three brothers and brother-in-law wearing identical black overcoats and carrying their silk hats. Behind them came a closed carriage containing Queen Mary, the Duchess of York and the Princess Royal; after that, a similar carriage with Alice, Duchess of Gloucester, Marina, Duchess of Kent and two ladies-in-waiting. Then, an imaginative touch, George's shooting pony, Jock, riderless, phlegmatic, followed by a group of sombre officials; behind them, the local dignitaries, mayors and mace-bearers, and then a trudging phalanx of tenants, servants, beaters, keepers – countrymen, well booted, wearing their tweeds and deer-stalkers and gaiters. The King's Piper, Forsyth, brought up the rear, the plaintive wheeze of 'Flowers of the Forest' accompanying the muffled clopping of horses, creaking carriages and hundreds of footsteps. 'Just as we topped the last hill above the station the stillness of the morning was broken by a wild, familiar sound – the crow of a cock pheasant . . . The thought occurred to all of us that . . . he would have chosen something like that: a pheasant travelling high and fast on the wind, the kind of shot he loved.'[11]

By five o'clock that evening the dead King was alone in Westminster Hall except for the four Yeomen guarding the coffin and the few officers charged with special duties. Over the next four days well over half a million people shuffled past the catafalque; some waited all night, equipped with camp stools and thermos flasks, others queued for hours in the rain. By Saturday, queues extended as far as St Thomas's Hospital and it was taking seven hours or more to cover the distance to Westminster Hall along both banks of the river. At 6 o'clock on the evening of Monday 27 January Queen Mary arrived with Lilibet, followed by the Yorks, Harry and Alice Gloucester, George Kent, the Princess Royal and her husband the Earl of Harewood, the King and Queen of Norway, Prince Olaf, the King of Denmark, the King of Belgium, the Crown Prince of Italy, Prince Axel of Denmark, the Comte de Flandres, Prince Ernest Augustus of Hanover, Prince Frederick of Prussia, Prince George and Prince Nicholas of Greece. 'The Royal party came in so unobtrusively that many then inside the hall did not realise that they were present,' the *Times* reported blandly. Just after the changing of the guard had taken place that night an officer saluted the Colour lying on the catafalque and removed it. From the entrance of the officers' quarters marched the King in the uniform of the Welsh Guards, the Duke of York in the uniform of the Scots Guards, the Duke of Gloucester in the uniform of the 10th Hussars and the Duke of Kent in naval uniform. The four brothers took up position between the Guards already on duty and remained motionless, resting on their swords, for about a quarter of an hour. It was,

Queen Mary said, 'a very touching thought'. She commissioned Mr E E Beresford to paint a picture of it called *The Vigil of the Princes* and the family gave it to David for his forty-second birthday in June.

The following day George V was taken to Windsor, via Paddington Station. The procession from Westminster Hall, miles long, included everyone from Mr T Tubb, the Sergeant Footman, to Commander Funpapzeanu of the Rumanian Army. The royal brothers walked behind the coffin, followed by twenty-eight royal foreign colleagues and the President of the French Republic. Among the former were the King of Romania, the King of the Bulgarians, HRH Prince Chakradongse, HRH Duke of Saxe-Coburg and Gotha, HRH The Hereditary Grand Duke of Hesse, HRH Duc de Nemours, HRH Prince of Said, Prince Frederick of Prussia, HRH Duke of Braganza, HRH the Infante Alfonso of Spain, HRH Prince Alvaro of Orleans-Bourbon, the Grand Duke Dmitri of Russia, and a Prince Salih: a procession of ghosts compared with the lively mourners in Norfolk, but it had become impossible to be too discriminating. Lord Louis Mountbatten KCVO and the Duke of Beaufort GCVO were among the more corporeal figures to attend them. Next came Queen Mary in a glass coach accompanied by her daughter-in-law Elizabeth, HM Queen Maud of Norway and HRH the Princess Royal. The procession stretched behind them in doleful splendour to a detachment from the London Fire Brigade as the whole cortège moved slowly and solemnly towards Paddington Station. Wallis Simpson watched it from a window in a room at St James's Palace that had, until recently, been occupied by Sir Frederick Ponsonby, Queen Victoria's Private Secretary. What 'affected her profoundly' was the sight of the heavily veiled royal women.[12]

Lilibet was waiting at Paddington with Marion Crawford. They occupied the time by playing 'endless games of noughts and crosses on GWR notepaper',[13] then she joined her strangely shrouded mother for the journey to Windsor. There, after more than a week of being bumped about and stared at, the old King was finally laid to rest. 'I had the uneasy sensation,' his successor wrote, 'of being left alone on a vast stage, a stage that was the British Empire, to play a part not yet written.'[14]

Elizabeth was now the wife of the Heir Presumptive and, until Queen Mary emerged from her mourning, effectively the first lady in the land.

# Chapter Seventeen

The Yorks had flourished under King George's benevolent autocracy; they had become his favourites, responsible for maintaining the high standards of mediocrity characteristic of his reign. His death was an appalling loss. Overnight they had been cut adrift, spiritually exiled. Elizabeth went into a temporary decline and the Press was informed that the strain of the funeral had been too much after her illness. 'I miss him dreadfully,' she wrote to Lord Lawson. 'Unlike his own children, I was never afraid of him, and in all the twelve years of having me as a daughter-in-law he never spoke one unkind or abrupt word to me.'[1] But that wasn't all. 'I am only suffering, I think, from the effects of a family break-up, which always happens when the head of a family goes. Outwardly one's life goes on the same, yet everything is different, especially mentally and spiritually. I don't know if it is the result of being ill but I mind things that I don't like more than before.' After this lapse she added briskly, 'But it will be very good for me to pull myself together and try to collect a little willpower.'[2]

Hearing gossip from well-meaning friends didn't help: at the Brownlows – Perry Brownlow was lord-in-waiting to the King – Mrs Simpson had rocked the room by declaring that until now she hadn't worn black stockings since she gave up the can-can.[3] The King, like any businessman, was stopping by at her flat in Bryanston Court for a cocktail on his way home from work; he had taken her to Windsor Castle and she was at Fort Belvedere every weekend. It was a relief for Elizabeth to talk to sympathetic people like Harold Nicolson who, although he was a friend of that dreadful Lady Cunard, had the right instincts about David and Mrs S. He did not, he said, feel at ease in such company.[4]

Bertie went off for a fortnight to Sandringham to conduct an inquiry into the economy of the 'voracious white elephant' that had been his father's favourite home. Putting aside his own fond memories of the place and resolutely refusing to listen to the old mole under the floorboards, he produced a report which in its 'clarity and common sense . . . would have done credit to his great-grandfather, the Prince Consort.'[5] As official mourning gave him six months off work, when he had finished his Sandringham survey he took the family to stay at one of the Duke of Devonshire's houses, Compton Place at Eastbourne, hoping the sea air would buck Elizabeth up a little.

Apart from two occasions at the Palace the Duchess of York had seen Wallis at the Fort and York House, but they had never spoken more than a few polite words. Their first informal and, to Elizabeth, unwelcome meeting was soon after her return from Eastbourne. The new King had bought an American station-wagon: 'Let's drive over to Royal Lodge,' he said to Wallis one afternoon. 'I want to show Bertie the car.'[6] Wallis, already knowing the Duchess's feelings towards her, was nervous. She was well aware of the bad manners many members of the aristocracy thought were their privilege. 'I had one friend who absolutely refused to shake hands with her,' Lady Hardinge recalled. ' "What did you do?" I asked her. "Oh," she replied, "it was quite easy. I dropped my handbag just as she got to me, so I had to stoop down to find it." '[7] However unappealing the Baltimore divorcée, she was never guilty of the incivility she received from others.

There are two eye-witness accounts of that afternoon. One comes directly from Wallis: 'Turning into the entrance of Royal Lodge, David made a complete swing round the circular driveway and drew up to the front door with a flourish . . . [He] insisted that they [the Yorks] inspect the station-wagon. It was amusing to observe the contrast between the two brothers, David all enthusiasm and volubility . . . the Duke of York quiet, shy, obviously dubious of this new-fangled American contrivance. It was not until David pointed out its advantages as a shooting brake that his younger brother showed any real interest. 'Come on, Bertie,' David urged, 'let's drive around a little, I'll show you how easy it is to handle.' It was quite a sight to see them drive off, the King at the wheel, his still sceptical brother sitting beside him. After a few minutes' (which seems improbable) 'they returned, and we all walked round the garden . . . [The Duchess of York's] justly famous charm was highly evident.'[8] They went in for tea and were joined by Lilibet, Margaret and Miss Crawford. The two children 'were both so blonde, so beautifully mannered, so brightly scrubbed that they might have stepped straight from the pages of a picture book . . . David and his sister-in-law carried on the conversation with his brother throwing in only an occasional word. It was a pleasant hour; but I was left with a distinct impression that while the Duke of York was sold on the American station-wagon, the Duchess was not sold on David's other American interest.'9

Anyone interested in Marion Crawford's version of the afternoon will not find it in the British edition of *The Little Princesses*, Crawfie's once notorious memoirs. In 1950, when the book was published, it was still considered improper for the Duke of Windsor's former subjects to read that Wallis 'appeared to be entirely at her ease; if anything, rather too much so' and that 'she had a distinctly proprietory way of speaking to the new King . . . she drew him to the window and suggested how certain trees might be moved and a part of the hill taken away to improve the view.' The Duchess tactfully suggested that she should take the children for a walk. As they were leaving the house Lilibet asked, 'Crawfie, who is she?' Miss Crawford describes the question as 'uneasy',10 but perhaps this was in hindsight. Crawfie 'never admired the Duke and Duchess more than on that afternoon. With quiet and charming dignity they made the best of this awkward situation and gave no sign whatever of their feelings, but the atmosphere was not a comfortable one . . . No one alluded to the visit when we met in the evening . . . Maybe the general hope was still that if nothing was said, the whole business would blow over.'11

Although the King's cronies thought the Duke of York 'uninteresting and unintellectual, but doubtless well-meaning,'12 Bertie at that time had a sneaking admiration for his brother's glamorous lifestyle. If it hadn't been for Elizabeth he would have enjoyed going over to the Fort, hearing the gossip, having a few drinks, admiring the new gadgets. Even Harry and Alice visited occasionally, and you couldn't find a more respectable couple than the Gloucesters. Alice said Mrs Simpson was always charming and friendly and, being American, a wonderful hostess. She said it was all very informal – they would play rummy or watch a film and David and Wallis were most loving together.13 He would never do anything to upset Elizabeth, but it was rather a pity she didn't see things the same way.

The King, unaware of anything except his all-consuming love affair, had no idea of the Yorks' feelings. On 9 July he invited them to a dinner party at York House in honour of Sir Samuel Hoare, the First Lord of the Admiralty. Among the guests were the Viceroy of

India, Lord Willingdon, Margot Asquith, the Winston Churchills, Sir Philip Sassoon, Alec and Helen Hardinge and Wallis Simpson. The fact that she was there without her husband was the cause of much disapproval among the ladies. Helen Hardinge reported the occasion with her usual prim venom: 'Winston Churchill was one of the few people around the dinner table that night who found Mrs Simpson acceptable. Curiously enough, he considered that she just did not matter and had no great significance; he believed that, in the ultimate analysis of the Monarchy, she simply did not count one way or the other.'[14] In so far as Churchill believed the doctrine that the King is an eternal concept and never dies, majesty being transferred to the heir the moment its previous embodiment ceases to live, he was right: Mrs Simpson could not disturb the Monarchy any more than she could disturb God. But she could, and did, disturb royalties and bishops.

Churchill was out to make mischief that night. After dinner he plumped himself down on a sofa next to the Duchess of York and embarked on a long diatribe about the Prince Regent and Maria Fitzherbert, a Roman Catholic widow whom the Prince had secretly married in defiance of the Act of Settlement and the Royal Marriage Act. 'Well,' Elizabeth said, 'that was a *long* time ago.' Churchill then started on the War of the Roses – red Lancaster at loggerheads with white York – to which she replied, 'That was a very, *very* long time ago.' The Duchess was in poor form that night. By contrast, Mrs Simpson, 'enthusiastically moving into the regal rôle into which she had cast herself', caused Sir Samuel Hoare to comment not only on her sparkling talk, but also her sparkling jewels with up-to-date Cartier settings. Wallis Simpson was, he said, 'very attractive and intelligent.'[15]

The next morning, to Bertie's distress, George V's much-loved *Britannia*, which in her forty-three years had sailed in 569 races and won 231 prizes for her Commander, was towed out to a point south of the Isle of Wight and scuttled in deep water.[16] Almost a week later some idiot threw a loaded revolver at the King's horse as he and the Duke of York were riding down Constitution Hill on their way back from presenting new Colours to the Brigade of Guards. 'Boy!' the King said, 'I don't know what that thing was, but if it had gone off it would have made a nasty mess of us.'[17] Mussolini telephoned and Hitler sent a telegram: 'I have just received news of the execrable attack on your Majesty. I beg to tender to your Majesty my heartiest congratulations on your escape from this danger.' For a few days the King could do

121

no wrong. Then it rained on an afternoon reception at Buckingham Palace and when only half of the six hundred or more ladies in 'decorative rainproofs' had sunk gracefully to the mud he ordered that 'those ladies . . . who were unable to pass the King's presence will be considered as having been officially presented at Court' and bolted into the Palace. Mothers raged, daughters wept. The Duchess of York, in a long black and white flowered dress, silver fox cape and large damp hat, did her best.

It was a relief when David set off with a group of friends and Wallis to cruise along the Dalmatian coast in Lady Yule's *Nahlin*. 'I am glad you have chartered a yacht,' Queen Mary wrote, '& I hope you will find sunshine & good weather abroad & be able to get out to Venice or wherever you join the yacht in comfort, I hope too that this autumn may be free from complications of which we have had more than our share for years. It was a nice day today & less cold & no rain for a wonder.'[18]

The Yorks went to stay with Mr J P Morgan, the American financier, at Cannochy for Elizabeth's thirty-sixth birthday, then moved eagerly on to Glamis.

Queen Mary's hopes were not fulfilled. The moment David returned from the *Nahlin* cruise complication followed complication. The Archbishop of Canterbury, who had already taken it on himself to give the King a paternal talking-to, did not receive the customary invitation to Balmoral. 'The kind Yorks' invited him to Birkhall, about eight miles away, instead. Their nearest neighbours were the ubiquitous Hardinges. While David and Wallis, tanned by the Mediterranean sun and in high spirits, entertained their friends at Balmoral – cocktails and three-decker sandwiches and 'These Foolish Things' playing on the gramophone – the Birkhall and Altnaguibhsach contingent 'walked over the hills, lit bonfires to keep the midges at bay, fished for trout and salmon, tended the kitchen garden . . . small things which made up a simple pleasant life.'[19] The Princesses performed action songs and the Archbishop refrained from putting Margaret on top of a pillar. The Sunday before the King and his entourage arrived at Balmoral the Minister of Craithie Church preached on the subject of Nero.[20]

David, predictably, didn't ease the situation. He had turned down a request to open new buildings at Aberdeen Royal Infirmary that September on the grounds that he would still be in mourning, though the official mourning period had ended in July. The Duke of York was asked to do the job for him, so on 23 September he and the Duchess traipsed to Aberdeen and did their duty. At the same time the King, in motoring goggles, was hanging about Aberdeen Station waiting for Wallis Simpson's train to arrive.[21] He was, of course, recognised, and 'although the news was neither broadcast nor published in the papers ... it spread all over Scotland within forty-eight hours.'[22] It was a silly risk to take, but did it really deserve such outrage? Would the medical treatment in the Infirmary have suffered if the buildings hadn't been 'opened' at all? The Establishment's priorities were just as unrealistic as the King's. When it hauled him up on the carpet and demanded, 'What would happen if everybody behaved like that?' the King, far from finding the question unanswerable, invariably replied, 'Everybody does.'

The Duchess of York was not the only one to think him a little mad. It seemed the only explanation. His behaviour was bizarre, even apart from his obsession with Mrs Simpson: he walked from Buckingham Palace to the office of the Duchy of Cornwall without telling his chauffeur; he insisted on making his own 'phone calls, which led to confusion and panic on the switchboard;[23] he wandered about playing his bagpipes; his clothes, off duty, were embarrassing; he was unpredictable in every way. Even Bertie, for all his loyalty, was becoming uneasy. David and 'that woman' between them had made changes in the running of Balmoral without consulting him and he was deeply hurt. Still unaware of their suspicions, the King once more invited the Yorks to dinner. This time, greeted by Mrs Simpson as hostess, Elizabeth 'openly showed her resentment'[24] and the evening was a dreadful failure.

The authorities seemed to think no one would notice when foreign newspapers and magazines arrived on the bookstalls with every reference to Wallis Simpson cut out. They also seemed to overlook the fact that such papers arrived in their hundreds through the post and that boatloads of indiscreet travellers returned every day, only too anxious to spread the news that the King of England was intending to marry an American divorcée. The British Press looked the other way. Still nobody would confront the King, least of all his brothers. 'I have been meaning to come and see you,' Bertie wrote plaintively to his mother, 'but I wanted to see David first. He is very difficult to see and when one does he wants to talk about other matters. It is all so worrying and I feel we live a life of conjecture; never knowing what will happen tomorrow, and then the unexpected comes . . .'[25]

Nothing, now, could have been unexpected to anyone of normal discernment. On 15 October the Press Association telephoned Alec Hardinge at the Palace and told him that Mrs Simpson's divorce case was to be heard at Ipswich Assizes on 27 October. It occurred to Hardinge – a bolt from the blue – that once Mrs Simpson was free, and in a position to marry the King, 'grave constitutional – and not only moral – issues might only too easily arise.'[26] He lost no time in writing to Stanley Baldwin, imploring the Prime Minister 'to see the King and ask if these proceedings could not be stopped, for the danger in which they placed him [HM] was becoming every day greater.'[27]

Baldwin, staying the weekend at Cumberland Lodge in Windsor Park, asked the Hardinges over to lunch. Major Hardinge arrived with a sheaf of carefully prepared notes, with the help of which he hoped to persuade the Prime Minister to advise the King to stop Mrs Simpson's divorce proceedings and to stop 'flaunting' Mrs Simpson in public, particularly in the Court Circular. Baldwin was dubious, but eventually agreed. But where *was* the King? His Majesty wasn't at the Fort: he wasn't at Sandringham. Major Hardinge's telephone calls became ever more frantic, his messages increasingly desperate until he remembered that Mrs Simpson had taken a house at Felixstowe, conveniently near the Ipswich Assizes. The King, obviously, was at Felixstowe and therefore *incommunicado*. He chafed until the King 'phoned him back from Sandringham at nine o'clock on Monday morning. Hardinge said his piece and was horrified to be told that Mrs Simpson's divorce was her own business; neither the King nor the Prime Minister nor the Archbishop of Canterbury nor anyone else had the right to intervene; if Baldwin wanted to see him the old boy must come to Sandringham. Impossible, Hardinge expostulated, the meeting must be in complete *privacy*, he must stress the importance of *secrecy*. Perplexed by all this drama, the King agreed to meet his Prime Minister at the Fort the following morning. 'Plainly a crisis of some kind was imminent in my personal affairs,' he commented laconically.[28]

The meeting was not a success. The King stubbornly refused to hide his relationship with Mrs Simpson or interfere in any way with her divorce. He was perturbed nevertheless: 'A friendship which so far had remained within the sheltered realm of my private solicitude' (a pretty phrase, but not quite accurate) 'was manifestly about to become an affair of State . . . along with the air estimates, the Polish corridor, the civil war in Spain and the value of the pound sterling.' It was absurd, but perhaps he needed advice. He decided to ask his old friend Walter Monckton, the former Attorney General, to lunch.

A few days later, while he and Monckton were strolling under the cedar trees at Fort Belvedere, the King suddenly stopped short. 'Listen, Walter, one doesn't know how things are going to turn out. I'm beginning to wonder whether I really am the kind of King they want . . . Well, there's my brother Bertie . . .'[29]

# Chapter Eighteen

Major Hardinge sped to 145 Piccadilly immediately he had heard Baldwin's account of his fruitless interview with the King. The divorce would go through; in the sad likelihood of there being no obstructions, Mrs Simpson would receive her decree absolute on 27 April, just in time for the King to marry her before the Coronation; such a disaster would necessitate the King's abdication; the Duke and Duchess of York must be prepared to take over. Having delivered this bombshell he dashed away to spread the feeling of impending disaster through Whitehall.

On the same day, after a satisfactorily gloomy meeting with the Archbishop of Canterbury, Major Hardinge received Geoffrey Dawson, Editor of the *Times*. Mr Dawson brought with him a long and pompous letter which he had received from a British resident in the United States who signed himself BRITANNICUS IN PARTIBUS INFIDELIUM. The letter was scurrilous and abusive, but the use to which it was put gives it some dubious historical importance. The presumptuous and impertinent expatriate concluded his diatribe:

> It may be presumptuous, and even impertinent, for a person far removed from the centre of events to suggest a remedy, but I cannot refrain from saying that nothing would please me more than to hear that Edward VIII had abdicated his rights in favour of the Heir Presumptive, who I am confident would be prepared to carry on in the sterling tradition established by his father. In my view it would be well to have such a change take place while it is still a matter of individuals, and before the disquiet has progressed to the point of calling in question the institution of monarchy itself.[1]

'For some months,' Lady Hardinge remembered with pride, 'my husband had . . . been forwarding to the King samples of similar letters from abroad . . . in order that the King should be under no illusion about public opinion overseas.' Of course it was Major

Hardinge's duty to keep the King informed, but this sort of thing could hardly be classed as 'information'. Hardinge eagerly agreed to Geoffrey Dawson's request that he should pass on 'Britannicus's' opinion. It would be untrue to say that a poison-pen letter decided the futures of at least six people, but it was effectively used to that end. The Yorks' worst fears were confirmed. On 27 October, Mrs Simpson received her decree nisi on the grounds of her husband's adultery with one Buttercup Kennedy at the Hotel de Paris, Bray, near Maidenhead.

On 3 November the King opened Parliament with several irregularities, as was expected. It was pouring with rain, so, 'to the disappointment of my children, among others' said Lady Hardinge, the King drove to the House of Lords in a closed Daimler instead of the customary State coach. As he had not yet been crowned he decided to wear the cocked hat of the Admiral of the Fleet instead of 'the massive bejewelled headgear of kingship' (his father used to say that he knew of few worse ordeals than being obliged to read somebody else's speech while at the same time balancing a 2½lb gold crown on his head). Since he was a bachelor there was only one throne under the canopy behind the Woolsack. His Private Secretary was not alone in visualising another beside it, occupied by the whore of Babylon.

That day's *New York Journal* ran an article under the headline 'KING WILL WED WALLY' in which it cited the example of the Duke of York marrying 'a commoner, so-called' and stated categorically that eight months after the divorce King Edward would marry Mrs Simpson after the Coronation. This puzzled Whitehall. The gist of it must be true because the owner of the *Journal*, William Randolph Hearst, was believed to have visited Fort Belvedere recently and heard it from the King himself. In their issue of 9 November *Time* magazine claimed that Mr J P Morgan, with whom the Yorks had stayed during the summer, was likely to intervene 'at the personal request of the Duke and Duchess of York' over American Press stories about the King and Mrs Simpson.[2] Was this, if true, a sign of hope? Of support? Of what? A month later the same magazine was to report that 'Her Royal Highness the Duchess of York, weekending with the Earl and Countess of Pembroke,' reacted with hard gaiety on Sunday to the cautious question by a titled guest as to whether the King is resolved to marry Mrs Simpson. ' "Everyone knows more than we do," replied the Duchess of York. "We know nothing. Nothing!" Her Royal Highness followed this by a brittle laugh.' When the 'delicious gurgle' that had enslaved Lord David Cecil could be described, even by hearsay, as 'brittle', it was clear something had gone very wrong.

The drama inched to its climax. Early on 12 November the King left for two days with the Home Fleet, far from domestic squabbles, the Prime Minister, the Archbishop and, he foolishly thought, the Hardinges. On the evening of 13 November he arrived back from Portland at the Fort, exhausted, cold, pleased with himself and longing for a hot bath. He was met by his butler, who told him there was an urgent letter from Major Hardinge; and there indeed it was, 'Urgent and Confidential', on top of the pile of dispatch boxes. He took it upstairs, ran his bath and opened the letter. 'An instant later I was confronted by the most serious crisis of my life.'³

The letter set out the situation as seen by Hardinge, Stanley Baldwin, the Lords Spiritual, their supporters, and his own family. It made three main points: 1) that the silence of the British Press would not be maintained much longer. 'It is probably only a matter of days before the outburst begins. Judging by the letters from British subjects living in foreign countries . . . the effect will be calamitous'; 2) that the Prime Minister and senior members of the Government 'are meeting today [13 November] to discuss what action should be taken.' The resignation of the Government – 'an eventuality which can by no means be excluded' – would mean that the King would have to find someone else capable of forming a government which the present House of Commons would support. Major Hardinge had 'reason to know that, in view of the feeling prevalent among members of the House of Commons of all parties, this is hardly within the bounds of possibility.' The alternative would be a dissolution and a General Election fought on the marriage issue, which would, in Major Hardinge's opinion, irreparably damage the Crown, 'the corner-stone on which the whole Empire rests'; 3) the only way of avoiding this tragedy was for Mrs Simpson to go abroad *without further delay*. Major Hardinge *begged* His Majesty to give this 'proposal his earnest consideration before the position became irretrievable, and had the honour etc. etc. of being . . .' This letter, Hardinge maintained, was 'a last bid to enable the King to remain on the throne.'⁴

The King, alone in his bathroom, suddenly felt like a king. How dared this upstart suggest that 'I should send from my land, my realm, the woman I intended to marry?' His first instinct was to seize the telephone. Then he thought better of it, and took his bath instead. When he joined Wallis and her Aunt Bessie downstairs Wallis knew something was seriously wrong, but during the evening he cheered up and they all played three-handed rummy.[5]

What the King did not know at this time – but Major Hardinge's confidantes undoubtedly did – was that Baldwin had been asking the opinions of Clement Attlee, Leader of the Opposition, and Sir Walter Citrine, the General Secretary of the TUC; both had agreed that the Labour votes in the country would not countenance Mrs Simpson becoming Queen. Neither did he know that representatives of the Civil Service had composed a draft ultimatum so harsh in its wording that Baldwin took it to Chequers and somehow mislaid it. Nor was he informed that Baldwin had sounded out the Dominions and that both Lord Tweedsmuir, the Governor-General of Canada, and Stanley Bruce, the High Commissioner for Australia, were dead set against any possibility of a Queen Wallis. On that very day, in fact – the ill-omened Friday the thirteenth – the King's indefatigable Private Secretary had lunched with the High Commissioner of Australia, as a result of which Bruce sent a stern memo to Baldwin itemising all the points the Prime Minister had failed to make in his meeting with the King three weeks before. If the King seriously intended marriage 'you would be compelled to advise him to abdicated, and unless he accepted such advice you would be unable to continue as his adviser and would tender the resignation of the Government.' As Hardinge mentioned none of this in his letter – though the implications of 'I have reason to know' might suggest something ominous – it was understandable that the single-minded King took it as a personal attack. He decided it would be impossible to continue negotiations with the Government through Hardinge and again contacted Walter Monckton.

This increased the bitterness in what was now called the 'Round-head' faction. The Duchess of York and Lady Hardinge spent much time on the telephone. Anonymous abuse arrived daily in the 'Cavaliers' ' mail. 'You old bitch,' Lady Cunard read with alarm, 'trying to make up to Mrs Simpson, in order to curry favour with the King . . .' Two affidavits were filed demanding the intervention of the King's Proctor in Simpson v. Simpson, on the grounds of collusion.[6] In the maelstrom of gossip, rumour and intrigue one thing that most certainly did not happen was the Duchess of York asking Wallis round for a chat, which might have saved everyone a great deal of anguish and expense.

On Sunday 15 November the King and Wallis were invited to tea by Marina and George at Coppins. He said he wanted to call by Windsor Castle on the way to re-hang some portraits, but admitted to Wallis later that the real reason was to meet Walter Monckton 'for a private talk about a serious matter'. On their return to the Fort David, presumably on Monckton's advice, showed her Hardinge's letter. Wallis was 'stunned'. Her first instinct was to leave the country immediately.

'You'll do no such thing,' the King said peremptorily. 'I won't have it. This letter is an impertinence.'

'To use a good American expression,' Wallis said, 'they're about to give me the works. They want me to give you up.'

'They can't stop me. On the throne or off, I'm going to marry you.'[7]

What had started as a challenging flirtation was now far beyond Wallis' control. She had inadvertently opened Pandora's box – bits of the ancient throne, shreds of the British Constitution, ghoulies and ghosties and long-legged beasties from dead Parliaments and deserted churches whirled into her trivial, well-ordered life. Most frightening of all was the unrecognisable animus of her funny little Prince, released from centuries of inhibition and frustration, deaf to reason, wild, formidable and grim. If she followed her instinct and bolted he would simply come after her. As an individual she no longer mattered. She had become a cause.

The following evening the King summoned Baldwin to the Palace and told him categorically that he intended to marry Wallis as soon as she was free. Baldwin then propounded the curious, but he clearly thought irrefutable, theory that 'in the choice of a Queen, the voice of the people must be heard'. Unless by 'the people' he meant their political representatives, who had other irons in the fire, this appears inconsistent when he had previously maintained that an election on the marriage issue would be disastrous. The King, however, was past arguing.

'I have made up my mind and nothing will alter it – I have looked at it from all sides – and I mean to abdicate to marry Mrs Simpson.'

'Sir,' said Baldwin, 'this is a very grave decision and I am deeply grieved.'[8]

As almost all the accounts are at variance with each other, it is not surprising that the Yorks were in a state of confusion and panic. Alec Hardinge, their only direct contact with the King, had been dismissed from the affair. Bertie, the Heir Presumptive, had so far been told nothing by his brother, and everything else was speculation. They heard that Mrs Simpson had told Lady Colefax that the King had never mentioned marriage to her at all.[9] Could that be possible? There was a rumour that Lady Colefax had contacted Neville Chamberlain, but Mr Chamberlain was stricken with gout and *incommunicado*. On the other hand they heard that Lord Willingdon had told his niece that if the King insisted on marrying Mrs Simpson the Privy Council would assemble and insist that he either abdicated or they resigned. What could that mean, if the King had never asked Mrs Simpson to marry him? 'I believe quite sincerely,' wrote Harold Nicolson in his diary, 'that the King has proposed to Mr Baldwin and has not proposed to Wallis.' In the middle of all this Queen Mary towered like the rock of ages. 'Thank God we have all got you as a central point,' Elizabeth wrote to her mother-in-law, 'because without that point it [the Family] might easily disintegrate.'

On the night of Monday, 16 November the King finally made his intentions clear to his mother. He had invited himself to dinner at Marlborough House (he 'suddenly appeared after dinner,' writes the Duchess of Gloucester in her memoirs). Wearing white tie and tails, he went into his mother's boudoir and was glad to find his sister Mary there as well ('having asked that his sister Mary should be present,' says Lady Donaldson, whose account is probably the more reliable of the two). The King was 'somewhat nonplussed', however, to find his sister-in-law Alice there – she had only been married to Harry for a year, almost a stranger to the family. Queen Mary put both of them at their ease by announcing with a reassuring smile that Alice was tired and would go to bed directly after dinner. ('He was in a great state of agitation,' wrote Alice, 'and asked his mother if I could leave the room ... Queen Mary was discernibly angered by this request, but with many apologies she asked me to go, which of course I did.') The meal seemed endless. They discussed the London Needlework Guild, the painting of the outside of Buckingham Palace, the Newmarket Sales. The King felt especially sorry for Alice (if she was there): 'Never loquacious, this evening she uttered not a word. And when at last we got up to leave the table ... she almost fled from the room.'[10] The King then told his mother and sister that he was in love with Wallis, determined to marry her, and aware of the fact that he would probably have to abdicate. There was no mention of the Yorks', or indeed Mrs Simpson's, possible reluctance to go along with this plan.

It was to be two years before Queen Mary would be able to put her feelings that night into coherent words. At the time, shock as a believer in the infallibility of the Monarchy, shock as a supporter of the highest moral standards and shock as a proud and loving mother almost paralysed her. The next day she stepped briskly into the room to greet Mr Baldwin with the words, 'Well, Prime Minister – *here's* a pretty kettle of fish!' What more was there to say?

The King was due to go on a tour of South Wales on Wednesday, therefore only had Tuesday to inform his brothers of his decision. Harry 'appeared little moved', just disgruntled at the idea that if he had to become Regent Designate he would have to give up the Army.[11] George, according to the King's own account, 'was reconciled to my decision'; Channon, the Kents' neighbour in Belgrave Square, said he was desolate.

And the Duke of York? His brother wrote that 'Bertie was so taken aback by my news that in his shy way he could not bring himself to express his innermost feelings at the time.'[12] He would have been deeply embarrassed if Bertie had tried; stiff upper lips had paralysed their ability to express inner feelings.

The Duchess of York had missed her opportunity of establishing, or at least making an effort to establish, a diplomatic entente with Wallis Simpson. Her overt hostility had added to the brothers' lack of mutual understanding and would destroy what remained of brotherly affection. She was left with the prospect of being married to an unwilling and possibly incompetent King and of wearing the crown she had considered too sacrosanct for David's mistress. '. . . the agony of it all has been beyond words,' she wrote to her friend Victor Cazalet a few weeks later, 'and the melancholy fact remains still at the present moment that he for whom we agonised is the one person it did not touch. Poor soul, a fearful awakening is awaiting his completely blinded reason before very long.'[13] Dorothy Laird, at one time Elizabeth's most loyal biographer, states that 'Once [Elizabeth] realises that . . . trust has been misplaced, the wound goes deep; she can forgive any act but treachery, but then she is implacable as any Scot.'[14]

The Yorks were due to leave for Edinburgh on 29 November in order that the Duke could take over his brother's position as Grand Master Mason of Scotland. During the intervening week Bertie was by no means idle. He went to see Queen Mary on Wednesday, the Prime Minister and Queen Mary again on Thursday, down to the Royal Lodge for the weekend, Queen Mary on Monday, the King on Tuesday evening. The following day he wrote to Sir Godfrey Thomas, the King's Assistant Private Secretary. 'If the worst happens & I have to take over, you can be assured that I will do my best to clear up the inevitable mess, if the whole fabric does not crumble under the shock and strain of it all.'[15]

Meanwhile there was a new complication: the proposal that the King should contract a morganatic marriage. Perhaps it was this suggestion that made Queen Mary herself very sensitive to being the descendant of such a marriage, expostulate 'Really! This might be Romania!' The whole thing had gone too far. 'I hate going to Scotland to do what I have to do as I am so worried over this whole matter,' the Duke of York wrote. 'I feel like the proverbial "sheep being led to the slaughter", which is not a comfortable feeling.' Channon commented gleefully, 'The Royal entourage must indeed be in a stew and turmoil today.'[16]

Returning from Edinburgh on the morning of Thursday 3 December the Yorks stepped out of their sleeping car to be confronted by newspaper posters proclaiming in letters a foot high 'THE KING'S MARRIAGE'. The news was out. Now, perhaps, it could be left to the people.

*

The days that followed were the most dreadful of Bertie's entire life. He spent the rest of that Thursday hurrying between his mother at Marlborough House and the King and Walter Monckton at the Palace, ending up with nothing more concrete than an arrangement to see his brother at Fort Belvedere the following day. In the morning, before leaving 145 Piccadilly, he telephoned the Fort to be told that His Majesty could not see him until Saturday. On Saturday the Yorks drove to the Royal Lodge. The Duke immediately phoned the King, but all he got was 'I will see you and tell you my decision when I have made up my mind.' He phoned on Sunday to be told that the King was in conference, but would call him back later. Prince Paul went to tea at the Royal Lodge that afternoon and found the Yorks completely in the dark about what might happen. 'The Duke of York is miserable, does not want the throne, and is imploring his brother to stay.'[17] The King did not 'phone back that day. The Duke waited until lunchtime on Monday, then rang again. The King said he might be able to see him that evening. With more than a touch of brusqueness Bertie snapped that he had to go to London, but immediately regretted it and called back to leave a message that he was still at the Royal Lodge. At 6.50 pm the King phoned and asked him to go over to the Fort after dinner. 'No,' said Bertie, 'I will come and see you at once.' He was at the Fort by seven.

The Duke of Kent had been with the King that weekend, 'never leaving him for a second and trying by every means in his power to persuade him to stay.'[18] Kent was probably under consideration as an alternative to the Duke of York, therefore however reluctant Bertie was to take over, his presence would have been awkward. The Kents possessed obvious advantages, not least of which was a son; Marina was royal by birth and George had none of Bertie's handicaps. On the other hand there was his past to consider and the last thing the Establishment wanted was another flighty King on the throne.* All things considered, there was no alternative. Bertie was told of his brother's decision that evening; there is no record of his reply. He returned to the Royal Lodge for dinner, then back to the Fort. Late that night he and Elizabeth drove to London. The following day Elizabeth took to her bed with 'flu and would remain there until things were sorted out.

The Duke visited his mother, then went to see Walter Monckton, who explained all the facts of the situation; he returned to explain them to his mother, then drove to the Royal Lodge to meet Harry, who accompanied him to the Fort to see David and Stanley Baldwin. George was already there and the four brothers, Baldwin, Monckton and other advisers all had dinner together: 'A dinner I am never likely to forget,' Bertie wrote. 'While the rest of us were very sad . . . my brother was the life & soul of the party, telling the PM things I am sure he had never heard before about unemployment centres etc . . . I whispered to WM "& this is the man we are going to lose." One couldn't, nobody could, believe it.'[19]

The next day, after seeing Baldwin and two different sets of lawyers, he took Queen Mary to the Royal Lodge for a meeting with David – she refused to meet him in his own home – and then to the Fort to see more lawyers. After driving back to London he called in at Marlborough House and 'broke down and sobbed like a child'.[20] While he was there Downing Street informed him that he was needed to witness his brother's instrument of abdication at ten o'clock the following morning at Fort Belvedere. On Thursday he was at the Fort all morning and afternoon. The tension was unbearable and he went over to the Royal Lodge for a rest but it was impossible to rest without Elizabeth and he was back at the Fort by a quarter to six. On his return to London he was amazed to find a large crowd outside 145 Piccadilly, 'cheering madly'.[21]

---

*Sir Harold Macmillan's view was that if Wallis Simpson had taken over or the succeeding royals had been frivolous, 'Brideshead', immoral, it would have been the end of the monarchy. 'Not one of them would have died for it,' he said fiercely. *Interview with PM November 1983.*

The next day he was busy arranging details of his Accession Council and seeing Sir Claud Schuster, the Lord Chancellor's representative, and Lord Wigram about David's future title. Sir John Reith, Director of the BBC, wanted to announce the former monarch before his farewell broadcast as 'Mr Edward Windsor'. Bertie soon put a stop to that:

> I replied: – That is quite wrong. Before going any further I would ask what has he given up on his abdication? S[chuster] said I am not sure. I said, it would be quite a good thing to find out before coming to see me. Now as to his name. I suggest HRH D of W[indsor]. He cannot be Mr E W as he was born the son of a Duke. That makes him Ld. E W anyhow. If he ever comes back to this country, he can stand and be elected to the H of C. Would you like that? S replied No. As D of W he can sit & vote in the H of L. Would you like that? S replied No. Well if he becomes a Royal Duke he cannot speak or vote in the H of L & he is not being deprived of his rank in the Navy, Army or R. Air Force. This gave Schuster a new lease of life & he went off quite happy.[22]

By the time Bertie arrived at the Fort with Harry that evening he was King of England. The family – himself, his mother, David, Mary, Harry, George, Aunt Alice and Uncle Algy – all had dinner together. Only Elizabeth was missing.* When they said goodbye David bowed to Bertie as his King; then they kissed and parted as freemasons.

At 2am on the morning of Saturday 12 December His Royal Highness Prince Edward sailed for Boulogne on the destroyer *Fury*. At 11 o'clock King George VI, looking haggard and desperate, attended his Accession Council. 'With my wife and helpmeet at my side,' he said slowly, 'I take up the heavy task which lies before me . . .' The Accession was proclaimed that afternoon:

> Whereas by an Instrument of Abdication dated the tenth day of December instant His former Majesty King Edward the Eighth did declare His irrevocable Determination to renounce the throne for Himself and His Descendants, and the said Instrument of Abdication has now taken effect whereby the Imperial Crown of Great Britain, Ireland and all other His former Majesty's dominions is now solely and rightfully come to the High and Mighty Prince Albert Frederick Arthur George: We, therefore, the Lords Spiritual

---

*The Queen Mother could never forget the horror of Abdication week. 'That last family dinner party was too awful,' she said to a friend years later, shuddering at the memory of her husband's agonies. 'Thank goodness I had flu and couldn't go.' Elizabeth Longford, *Elizabeth R*.

and Temporal of this Realm . . . with the Principal Gentlemen of Quality . . . do now hereby with one voice and Consent of Tongue and Heart publish and proclaim . . . God Save the King!

The King, the two Princesses and Queen Mary watched the ceremony from a room overlooking Friary Court. There was a little indecisive cheering, the band played the National Anthem, guns boomed out from Hyde Park and the Tower. During the few hours it took to read the Proclamation over the length and breadth of Britain the general feeling was one of cautious loyalty. For the country, the drama was over. For King George VI and Queen Elizabeth the long, laborious sequel was about to begin.

Later that day the new King and Queen received a telegram through the Admiralty:

> Have had a good crossing. Glad to hear this morning's ceremony went off so well. Hope Elizabeth better. Best love and best luck to you both. David.[23]

# PART THREE
## QUEEN ELIZABETH

# Chapter Nineteen

After attending an official dinner at Buckingham Palace Harold Nicolson wrote in his diary on 17 March 1937: 'The Queen ... wears upon her face a faint smile indicative of how much she would have liked her dinner party were it not for the fact that she was Queen of England. Nothing could exceed the charm or dignity which she displays, and I cannot help feeling what a mess poor Mrs Simpson would have made of such an occasion. It demonstrates to us more than anything else how wholly impossible that marriage would have been.' The idea of Wallis on the throne was preposterous, even to those who thought of it as an unnecessary piece of furniture. Whatever her other accomplishments she was a dreadful actress, incapable of appearing as anything but her unfortunate self and quite wrong for the part. It only needed a dinner party to prove the Abdication had been inevitable.

Queen Elizabeth started off with an enormous advantage. But what about the King? Not only did he have less experience and less theoretical knowledge of the job than his brother – 'I never wanted this to happen; I'm quite unprepared for it. David has been trained for this all his life. I've never even seen a State Paper'[1] – but he had no hope of competing with David's charisma. Nobody was really going to be inspired by his enthusiasm for Boys' Camps, his proficiency with a tennis racquet or the fact that he was still 'a nice honest, clean-minded and excellent mannered boy'; and that, when it came down to it, was all anyone could find to say in his favour. When he drove out to take his first levée at St James's there was only a handful of spectators – 'Not many of them, are there, my Lady?' one of the maids remarked with gloomy relish to a lady-in-waiting.[2] Warren Bradley Wells of the *New York Herald Tribune* noted that when the family left for Sandringham at Christmas:

King George VI, hat in hand, bowed right and left automatically as he drove up. Scarcely a hat was raised in reply ... [The King] and his family walked bowing across the platform. Perhaps half the men in the little throng raised their hats. There was a subdued murmur which might have been a suppressed cheer – or might not. In short, on his first public appearance after his succession to his brother, King George VI was given an extremely cold shoulder.[3]

Even the *Times* was not much of an improvement. The Queen and the Princesses had sentimental appeal, but the King was an anti-climax.

The Archbishop of Canterbury did his best: 'When his people listen to him, they will note an occasional and momentary hesitation in his speech. But he has brought it into full control, and to those who hear it need cause no sort of embarrassment.'[4]

As usual, this made everything worse. The newspapers, under the guise of staunchly denying rumours of the King's incapacity, publicised all his weaknesses: 'King George, according to those who know him best, has not so great a capacity for endurance as his brother ... and it is felt that any undue strain might have unfortunate consequences,' said the *News Chronicle*, after pointing out that the Coronation programme would be, 'in the words of a High Court official ... "almost too much to expect of any man" '. The *Sunday Referee* came out with an indignant banner headline: 'WHISPERING AGAINST THE KING.' After attributing such whispers to 'Communists and Mayfairites', the loyal editorial continued:

> The reason why the King has not appeared in public much since his Accession is that he is fully occupied learning the complicated job of kingship. His brother, as Prince of Wales, spent forty years of his life being groomed for stardom ... The fact that he [the King] did not broadcast a Christmas message; that he has paid only one visit to the British Industries Fair; that the Durbar in India has been postponed; all have been worked up by those who 'love a bit of gossip' into alarming stories of the King's health ... Once the Coronation is over, the King will appear more frequently in public; not so much as did King Edward, for he is naturally of a more reserved and conservative disposition ...

*Time* magazine for March 1937 quoted King George as saying, 'according to the papers, I am supposed to be unable to speak without stammering, to have fits, and to die in two years. All in all, I seem to be a crock.'[5] With such supporters, the unfortunate monarch did not need enemies.

Since the Heir Apparent was a minor it was necessary to appoint a new Regency Council. This led to a lengthy and stormy debate in the House of Commons about who should decide whether a reigning monarch was capable of performing his duties. The troublesome Mr Gallacher from West Fife declared: 'As a matter of fact, this is a bill directed against the present Monarch. Before the Coronation takes place, we are already discussing how we can substitute him . . . It is the present occupant of the throne who is suspect and for whom all this preparation has got to be made, and it is not in any way intended to apply to any future reign.'

The cries of 'No, No!' were not heard outside the House. Elizabeth had almost certainly read Bagehot's *English Constitution* by now and learned that the real strength of the Crown lay in 'the labourers of Somersetshire', the 'credulous obedience of enormous masses'. It was on that huge, faceless substructure of society she had to smile, while at the same time keeping her husband safely on a pedestal far above their reach.

The new Queen's history, reaching far back into the Scottish mists, was full of peril – feuds, vendettas, Jacobite plots, violent ends. Her in-laws' collective unconscious was crammed with treachery, skulduggery, battle and murder. Now, as well as the hideous spectre of Bolshevism, the exiled King was a major threat. He could be setting up pinnacled camp on the coast of France, gathering his ships for invasion. Who were the spies at Court? Nobody could be trusted. The Queen knew that her greatest support would not come from the fashionable fly-by-nights who had decorated David's court, but from the old hands, those whose conservatism and reliable absence of originality had sustained her father-in-law's regime. The few who were of any use – Churchill, the Duff Coopers – must be won over. The rest must go.

The first sign of a purge was the overnight dismissal of Lord Brownlow from his position as Lord-in-Waiting. Perry Brownlow's crime was that he had been detailed by David to accompany Wallis to France, where he had done his best to persuade her to take a fast boat to China, even booking her a state room and drafting her farewell message to the King. Brownlow foolishly considered that he had done his best for his country and expected a hero's welcome on his return. He was due to go into Waiting on 21 December, but was told that he needn't bother as King George was only receiving the Archbishop of Canterbury that afternoon for an informal meeting at 145 Piccadilly. The next morning Brownlow read in the Court Circular that Lord

Dufferin and Ava had succeeded him as Lord-in-Waiting. 'He rang up the Palace, and was told that his name could never appear in the Court Circular again and that "his resignation had been accepted". "Am I to be turned away," he asked, "like a dishonest servant with no notice, no warning, no thanks, when all I did was to obey my Master, the late King?" '6 'Yes,' was Lord Cromer's answer.

Later both Lord Cromer and Lord Wigram – Private Secretary to George V and now Permanent Lord-in-Waiting – telephoned him to say that his dismissal had not been at the King's request. Nevertheless Channon wrote uneasily in his diary, 'I feel this means there is to be a "Black List" and the Court will try to damage everyone who was a friend of the late King . . . A foolish, small-minded policy, as it will only create enemies to the new regime and make their difficult roles still more so. Are we all on the "Black List"? . . . I cannot believe that it is Queen Elizabeth's doing. She is not so foolish.'

Elizabeth was seldom foolish. It had been at the Brownlows' that Wallis had made her unforgivable wisecrack about the black stockings.

There were occasions, particularly within the family, when Bertie had to be seen to step down and voice an opinion. This was considered necessary over Emerald Cunard, a leading society hostess and one of David's most eloquent sympathisers, who had been on Queen Mary's black list for years. The Queen Dowager wrote to Prince Paul:

> The other day in my presence, Bertie told George he wished him and Marina never to see Lady Cunard again and George said he would not do so. I fear she has done David *a great deal of harm* as there is no doubt she was great friends with Mrs S at one time . . . Under the circumstances I feel none of us, in fact people in society, should meet her . . . and I am hoping that George and Marina will no longer see certain people who alas were friends of Mrs S and Lady Cunard's and also David's.7

It would be hard to believe that this was any great deprivation to Lady Cunard if we did not have Harold Nicolson's evidence that on meeting Maggie Greville soon after the Abdication Emerald, without batting a bird-like eyelid, said 'Maggie, darling, *do* tell me about this Mrs Simpson – I've only just met her.' Mrs Greville herself, that 'galumphing, greedy, snobbish old toad who watered at the chops at the sight of royalty and the Prince of Wales's set,'8 would soon tell Harold Nicolson that David 'was the only one of the family with whom she was never intimate.'9 If a cock had crowed with every treachery, the Accession of good, simple, devout King George VI would have sounded like a barnyard at dawn.

Regardless of the subversive guests round Lady Cunard's dinner table the threat was not entirely imaginary. A King's Party had existed since the previous November. It consisted of a few excitable politicians eating a prodigious number of meals – Esmond Harmsworth lunched with Mrs Simpson and Lord Lothian; Sir Samuel Hoare lunched with Lord Beaverbrook; David Margesson lunched with Winston Churchill; Tom Jones, declaring wildly that 'the country is split in two', breakfasted with Baldwin. A few days later Margesson reported 'a thickening of the Churchill-Beaverbrook brew' and a small group of MPs wrote to the former King offering their support. On 4 December Sir Henry Channon, an American convert to what he considered the British way of life, reported 'London is now properly divided and the King's faction grows; people process the streets singing "God Save the King" and assemble outside Buckingham Palace, they parade all night . . . I personally lost my temper with any Roundhead I could see, and hurled abuse at them in my Royalist fury.'

A Middlesex MP, Sir Reginald Blaker, said that a group of Conservative MPs had formed to keep the King on the throne. Such talk was dangerous.[10] By the weekend of 5 December there were 'the alarming makings of a King's Party of substantial size'. The Duke of Windsor would sum all this up with the wry remark that 'an Irish baronet of ancient lineage and antique gallantry offered to place his sword at my service in this menacing hour.'

Thanks to the deep lassitude that descends over all professional men except clergymen over the English weekend, the King's Party was dead by Monday. It would haunt King George and Queen Elizabeth for the next sixteen years, undimmed by World War II and the huge increase in their own popularity. British royalty and the Nazi Government were perhaps the only people ever to think of the Duke of Windsor as a potential revolutionary.

A further threat revived over the Abdication – that of abolishing the Monarchy altogether – could never have been taken seriously in those days by anyone except the Monarchy itself. Many relatively sane people were in favour of a change within the system – the Leader of the Labour Party, an ex-pupil of Haileybury and a gentleman, said, 'I hope we shall see a new start being made. I believe this is necessary if constitutional monarchy is to survive in the present age.' That kind of comment could be overlooked. But what about the Honourable Member for West Fife?

No one can go out before the people of the country and give any justification for clinging to the Monarchy. You all know it. You will not be able, no matter what you do, to repair the damage that has been done to the Monarchical institution. If you allow things to go on as they are going, you will encourage factions to grow, and factions will grow, of a dangerous and desperate character . . .

Then there was the Honourable Member for Bridgeton:

We are doing a wrong and foolish thing if, as a House, we do not seize the opportunity with which circumstances have presented us of establishing in our land a completely democratic form of government which does away with all the Monarchical institutions and the hereditary principle . . .

And worst of all the Honourable Member for the Gorbals:

. . . instead of having the ordinary frailties that all of us have, they will have this additional one, of being surrounded with a set of flunkeys who refuse to let them know the truth as others do. Tomorrow I will willingly take the step of going out and saying it is time the people ceased to trust these folk, but only trust their own power and their own elected authority.

One expected this sort of thing from Bolsheviks and bohemians, but these were representatives of the people – most hurtful of all, Scottish people. Never mind: the Queen would smile at them and they would come to heel eventually. Just over forty years later William Hamilton MP, Britain's last official republican, wrote an eightieth birthday greeting to the Queen Mother in the *Sunday Mirror*: '. . . my hatchet is buried. My venom dissipated. I am glad to salute a remarkable old lady. Long may she live to be the pride of her family. And may God understand and forgive me if I have been ensnared and corrupted, if only briefly, by this superb Royal trouper.'

Clearly that particular conquest took a little time. The few politically important figures in the Duke of Windsor's circle were easier to win over. Duff Cooper, Secretary of State for War, and his wife Diana had actually accompanied David and Wallis on the *Nahlin* and Duff was known to have told the Duke that if only he would wait a year, perhaps they could make Wallis Queen;[11] Diana had only recently curtsied to the woman. Surely they, if anyone, were for the block? On the contrary. In the April of Coronation year the Coopers were invited to Windsor. Duff, it turned out, had idolised Elizabeth all his life. After he had been closeted with the Queen in her boudoir for over an hour, 'the Coopers left Windsor with the impression that things would do a lot better under the new regime.'[12]

The same approach could hardly be used with Churchill. He had been shouted down in the Commons for his apparently unwavering support of the former King and he was at the nadir of his career. Even so he was a significant figure and might well come in useful. This was Bertie's department. On 18 May, six days after his Coronation, he wrote:

> My dear Mr Churchill,
> I am writing to thank you for your very nice letter to me. I know how devoted you have been, and still are, to my dear brother, and I feel touched beyond words by your sympathy and understanding in the very difficult problems that have arisen since he left us in December. I fully realise the great responsibilities and cares that I have taken on as King, and I feel most encouraged to receive your good wishes, as one of our great statesmen, and from one who has served his country so faithfully. I can only hope and trust that the good feeling and hope that exists in the Country and Empire now will prove a good example to other Nations in the world.
> Believe me,
> Yours very sincerely,
> George R.I.[13]

Churchill soon saw the error of his ways. Four years later, as one of the most powerful Prime Ministers the country has ever known, he wrote to Their Majesties that they were 'more beloved by all classes and conditions than any of the princes of the past.'[14]

# Chapter Twenty

Coronations, like royal weddings, are all much the same. The only thing that was unique about the crowning of George VI and Queen Elizabeth was that their predecessor listened to it on the radio. To provide this facility the BBC moved twelve tons of equipment and 472 miles of wire into Westminster Abbey and at the end of the ceremony inadvertently broadcast to the world an agitated official crying, 'What are we to do? The Barons are on the hoof, and we haven't got the Earls away yet!'[1], a question that remained forever unanswered. The Archbishop of Canterbury, 'ever vigilant of public interest and good taste', bustled down to British Movietone News during the evening to see the films and cut out anything he considered unsuitable for the public at large to see. The result was they saw very little but horses.

Since then, television has enabled us to see the royal family in close-up, warts and all, and it has had a profound effect on their lives. In 1937 relatively few people had ever seen them except on black and white newsreels of official occasions, when everyone seemed to be in an enormous hurry. Fleets of charabancs, special buses and private cars poured into London. Statistics, as usual, were employed to strike amazement in the minds of the public: 1,000 special trains were laid on, the Office of Works provided seating for 90,000 people made from three million feet of tubing and 850 tons of Columbian pine (the exact nature and source of the wood kept the House of Commons happy for days). The Procession would be 3,500 yards long and would take forty minutes to pass any given point; 800 Peers wearing their coronets and ceremonial robes would pay 3d a head to travel in a special Underground train from Kensington High Street to Westminster since London bus drivers had taken the opportunity to go on strike. The lead hand-horse in the Procession, ridden by the head Royal Postilion, was a Windsor grey named Silver

Fox (known as Dawey) which would be paired by a mare named Angela; there would be seventy Royal Cleveland bays and the ones with nonconformist white legs would be painted with lampblack. It would take two hours to prepare each animal. Twenty-two yards of red or blue satin ribbon would be plaited into their manes and each set of state harness weighed 128lbs. The cost of the whole thing was, for the time being, left to the imagination.

None of this meant very much to the chief performers. Elizabeth had to organise the move to Buckingham Palace, get a new crown, decide on her robes, sort out the Crown jewels, appoint a new household staff, take instruction from the Archbishop, entertain wives, learn her part, try to find time for the children. Her mother-in-law was a great help, giving her the Koh-i-Noor from her own crown, taking her granddaughters on expeditions and always ready with advice. Crawfie and Clara, on the other hand, were not very supportive. 'The little girls' lives were all upset,' Crawfie complained. 'They were always being taken from lessons to try on clothes or to have a look at something their parents felt they ought not to miss.'[2]

There was no mention of an absent son or brother at the family lunch on 10 May. They all gave Elizabeth presents – a tortoiseshell and diamond fan, a gold tea-set that had belonged to the Duke of Cumberland, miniatures and ribbons and Orders. Walter Monckton had at last persuaded the Duke of Windsor to stop telephoning the King with advice on questions of the day and he and his brother were no longer communicating. Queen Mary wrote David occasional little notes, stiffly chatty: 'I went to 2 premieres last week in aid of charities & have also been to 2 plays . . . I was interested in reading you drove through Gmunden, where in 1884 my parents, Alge & I spent 2 months with the Cumberlands . . . as far as I remember & I did go to Ischl once.'[3] A few souvenir shops outside the Palace gates displayed plaster busts of Edward VIII marked '⅙d to Clear' but very few people bought them.

Of all the descriptions of this Coronation the King's is the only one to show the slightest humour. After being kept awake since 3am by the testing of loudspeakers and the jubilant din of military bands he 'could eat no breakfast & had a sinking feeling inside'. At the Abbey he was kept waiting for what seemed hours because one of the Presbyterian chaplains in Elizabeth's procession had fainted. Finally he entered the Abbey and negotiated the flight of steps going up to the Sacrarium. He bowed to his mother and family in the gallery and after the introduction moved to the Coronation Chair, where he was eventually managed to get into the white *Colobium Sindonis*, 'a surplice which the Dean of Westminster insisted I should put on inside out, had not my Groom of the Robes come to the rescue.' When it came to taking the Coronation Oath the Bishop of Durham stood on one side of him, the Bishop of Bath and Wells on the other to support him and hold the form of Service for him to follow. Unfortunately neither Bishop could find the right place in the missal. The Arch-bishop's Higher Power prompted him to hold out his own book for the King, but 'horror of horrors his thumb covered the words of the Oath'.

After that things went from bad to worse:

> My Lord Great Chamberlain was supposed to dress me but I found his hands fumbled & shook so I had to fix the belt of the sword myself. As it was he nearly put the hilt of the sword under my chin trying to attach it to the belt . . . The supreme moment came when the Archbishop placed the St Edward's Crown on my head. I had taken every precaution as I thought to see that the Crown was put on the right way round, but the Dean & the Archbishop had been juggling with it so much that I never did know whether it was right or not . . . As I turned after leaving the Coronation Chair I was brought up all standing, owing to one of the Bishops treading on my robe. I had to tell him to get off it pretty sharply as I nearly fell down.[4]

Too many dam' parsons, as his father had said. There may even have been moments when his son would have seconded Mr G Hardie's sug-gestion in Parliament: 'If people want to see the Coronation, why can't they wait for a dry day and have it in a big field where everybody could have a chance of seeing it?' His great-grandmother's uncle, William IV, had much the same idea. If Bertie had such an eccentric thought he kept it to himself.

According to one biographer, Elizabeth 'broke down and cried: "I can't go through with it. I can't be crowned." '[5] If this is true it would seem sufficiently interesting to warrant some source or corroboration, but the author gives neither. Perhaps it came from that ubiquitous 'member of the household' on unusually intimate terms with the Queen. Perhaps it is common knowledge among the *cognoscenti* of whom there are so very many. Perhaps it should have happened. From all other accounts she sailed through the whole thing with professional, smiling dignity – 'much more bosomy' noted Chips Channon. Her own family, so unexpectedly and perilously elevated, watched her with pride. Her daughters, in lightweight coronets and purple velvet robes trimmed with ermine, behaved impeccably, apart from Margaret playing rather too noisily with her prayer-book and getting a disciplinary nudge from Lilibet.

Lord Dawson of Penn was sitting in the congregation with a primed hypodermic concealed in his robes in case divine sustenance failed.[6] To the Archbishop of Canterbury, who felt he was 'sustained by some Higher Power', the whole thing was 'a mystical experience'.[7] The Bishop of St Albans swore the King and Queen emanated some sort of 'religious radiation' and even Ramsay Macdonald felt that the couple were in states of religious trance at certain points in the ceremony.[8] The Hardinges were away, recovering from nervous prostration in India, but many of those present at the Abbey must have thought of the Coronation originally intended for this day – a solitary man, childless, standing in the King's place, no wifely throne, no peeresses, no one to go home to; or, if that scene was too heartrending, Wallis Simpson smirking under the Koh-i-Noor:

> O Lord, the giver of all perfection: Grant unto this thy servant Wallis our Queen, that by the powerful and mild influence of her piety and virtue, she may adorn the high dignity which she hath obtained through Jesus Christ our Lord . . .'

Even those who had entertained doubts now realised that 'hush-hush and rally round the new King' was the best policy.

The next day the King and Queen drove in an open carriage through the streets of London, their progress unanimously described as 'triumphal'. On the following Tuesday night they made modest history by attending 'a private dance', as the Duchess of Sutherland's Coronation ball at Hampden House was modestly described. 'The Queen was in white,' noted the industrious Channon, 'with an ugly spiked tiara . . . The King followed her, showing his teeth.' Everyone was there: Queen Mary in ice blue, Princess Olga of Yugoslavia wearing her mother's ruby *parure*, the Queen of Egypt, Prince Ernst August of Hanover, Prince Fritz of Prussia, Mrs Maggie Greville. Only one habitual guest was conspicuous by her absence. It had been suggested by Buckingham Palace that perhaps Lady Cunard might be invited after supper, by which time the King and Queen would have gone home, so Emerald waited by the telephone to be told when she could safely leave Grosvenor Square for Green Street. Such ugly little discords in the National Anthem went almost unnoticed.

King George VI sat in his study at Buckingham Palace with his crown on, practising indefatigably for his Opening Address to Parliament. King Leopold of the Belgians came to stay, and at dinner the Queen wore 'a *robe de style* of gleaming silver tissue over hooped carcase of stiffened silver gauze, with a deep *berthe* collar of silver lace encrusted with glittering diamonds[9]. A few weeks later Their Majesties toured Cornwall to receive the feudal dues from the tenants of the Duchy. They were presented with a pound of pepper, a hundred shillings, a grey cloak, a brace of greyhounds, a pair of gilt spurs, a salmon spear, a load of wood, a *bow d'arbus* and a pound of cumin. During the summer they stayed for a quiet weekend with Mrs Greville at Polesden Lacey and had dinner with three dukes, four duchesses, an unspecified number of marquesses, and Osbert Sitwell.[10] On Saturday, 13 November there was a discreet paragraph in the *Times*:

> The King and Queen will attend morning service tomorrow at the parish church of St Paul's Walden, near Hitchin, where the Queen will unveil a stone tablet to commemorate the fact that she was born in the parish and baptized in the church. Their Majesties wish the service to be a very quiet one and the congregation will be limited to the usual worshippers resident in the village. Admission to the service will be by ticket only.

Lady Strathmore was not present at this ceremony and Lord Strathmore is not mentioned. As Queen Elizabeth unveiled the tablet she was probably the only person present to know that one line of its tribute – 'BORN IN THIS PARISH' – was untrue. The *Sunday Times* revealed the discrepancy over forty years later.[11] The tablet, with God's blessing, remains.

The rest of the world's royalty did nothing of any particular interest. King Alfonso of Spain, exiled in Vienna, was reported to be lunching off boiled beef and apple tart in the Hotel Bristol; the Duc de Guise, Pretender to the French crown, issued a manifesto declaring that he had decided to claim the throne of his fathers, after which he relapsed into a profound silence; at Serowe, in Bechuanaland, ex-Queen Bagakgametsi pleaded guilty to trying to harm the Queen Mother with 'mystic potions and incantations'.

Meanwhile, regardless of who occupied the British throne, Europe marched at a brisk pace towards World War II; or Germany, packed and ready, marched briskly, while Great Britain mislaid its bits and pieces and flurried about, nagged by Churchill and delayed by Chamberlain. Guernica was destroyed by Fascist bombers and four thousand Basque Catholic child refugees arrived at Southampton, only to reveal that they were mostly neither Basque nor Catholic, but Asturian, Galician and Castilian infidels.[12] This caused a brief moral quandary to the Catholic Church and Salvation Army. Germany and Italy left and returned to the Non-Intervention Committee so often that nobody could keep track; as the Committee itself was unable to agree about anything, it didn't seem to matter. Hundreds of Trotsky sympathisers and hardline Communists were executed in the Soviet Union. There were pogroms in Poland, strikes and riots in Trinidad, riots in Barbados, a ninety-day 'state of war' in Brazil, violence in Palestine and the Sino-Japanese war in China. On 21 August HMS *Leander* annexed three uninhabited islands in the Pacific Ocean for Great Britain.

Compared with 1911 there was less glamour about this Coronation year and far less amazement at the achievements of man. Acts of God were unoriginal: 671,000 homeless and 400 drowned in floods in the Ohio Valley, floods in the Fen country, floods in Syria, forty deaths caused by storms in the Oriente Province of Cuba. Nobody discovered much apart from the only known mummy of a noble of the 1st Dynasty and a new comet of the 7th magnitude. The longest solar eclipse of modern times was visible in the South Pacific, the Moon occultated Mars and the near approach of Jupiter to the earth was noticed in July. Even the air was relatively dull: Flight Lieutenant Adam reached an altitude of 53,937 feet and two Japanese airmen in their aircraft *Divine Wind* flew from Tokyo to Croydon in 94 hours 18 minutes; the German airship *Hindenburg* was destroyed by fire at Lakehurst, New Jersey, the majority of French aviators seemed to survive. There were a couple of attempted assassinations but the only one to succeed was of BagirSidqi, Chief of the Iranian General Staff. William Morris, after giving away millions of pounds to deserving causes, was made a Viscount and Mr Neville Chamberlain opened a campaign for a Fitter Britain, perhaps as a substitute for the Archbishop of Canterbury's Back to God campaign, which had achieved no noticeable support. In Berlin on 5 July the American journalist William Shirer wrote in his diary, 'The Austrian Minister tells me that the new British Ambassador here, Sir Neville Henderson, has told Goering, with whom he is on very chummy terms, that Hitler can have his Austria so far as he, Henderson, is concerned.[13]

The King and Queen invited the rest of the family to spend Christmas at Sandringham. Last year, when their reign was not yet two weeks old, Queen Mary's staff had run everything, the old lady herself had been unwell. This year Elizabeth took charge. The vast tree glistened, soft cries of delight welcomed the unwrapping of Fabergé ornaments and diamond trinkets, the King wore a paper crown and Queen Mary thoroughly enjoyed herself. On the last day of Coronation Year she wrote in her diary, '. . . a very wonderful and interesting year. We saw the interesting film *Marie Walewska* after dinner & at midnight sang Auld Lang Syne & had a snap dragon. Very nice being altogether.'[14]

# Chapter Twenty-One

Most people did not see or, if they did, fully understand the statement in the *London Gazette* of 28 May:

> The King has been pleased by Letters Patent under the Great Seal of the Realm bearing the date the 27th day of May 1937 to declare that the Duke of Windsor shall, notwithstanding his Instrument of Abdication executed on the 10th day of December 1936, and His Majesty's Declaration of Abdication Act 1936, whereby effect was given to the said Instrument, be entitled to hold and enjoy for himself only the title style or attribute of Royal Highness so however that his wife and descendants if any shall not hold the said title style or attribute.

The Duke of Windsor had wanted a morganatic marriage – let him have one. Short of giving up his own royal title, David was to live for the rest of his life with a superior social status to Wallis and she, as the *Times* put it when objecting to the proposal, 'must carry in solitary prominence the brand of unfitness to be a member of the Royal Family.' The ostensible reason for this insult was that if Wallis divorced her third husband, as she had done the previous two, the family did not want an ex-wife wandering about as HRH. Slightly less cynically, they did not want the same thing to happen if David should predecease her, as in fact he did.

The result was disagreement among the rest of the family. The King's nephew George – later Lord Harewood – was in his first year at Eton: 'It was hard,' he remembered, 'for the younger amongst us not to stand in amazement at the moral contradiction between the elevation of code of duty on the one hand, and on the other the denial of central Christian virtues forgiveness, understanding, family tenderness.'[1] His mother and father had been among the exiled Duke's first visitors in Austria; so had Louis Mountbatten, but cousin Louis could be counted on to keep an even keel whichever way the wind blew. The Duke of Kent was a frequent guest, though Sir Walter Monckton reported that his Duchess stubbornly refused to go with him.[2] Marina had been instructed by Queen Mary that 'being a foreigner' she must not also be 'the first female member of the family to call on [Wallis]',[3] who was in the south of France anyway, waiting for her divorce absolute. The upshot was that Marina earned the approval of both Queens and 'a coolness grew up between the Duke of Windsor and the brother who had been so close to him.'[4] In the thick of this family squabbling Queen Mary could be counted on to support the throne regardless; otherwise it must be assumed that Coronation Year was an uneasy time for the royal conscience.

For some obscure reason the King was responsible for deciding where the Windsors' wedding should take place. He and Queen Elizabeth chose the Château de Candé, which they had never seen, owned by a naturalised American called Charles Bedaux who nobody had ever met. However, of the various suggestions put forward, the Château seemed furthest removed from the Riviera and its implications of flightiness. The command went out that nobody should attend the ceremony. David Low drew a cartoon for the *Evening Standard* entitled 'Guests to the Duke's Wedding' – the ghosts of Romeo and Juliet, Tristan and Isolde, Abelard and Heloise, Paris and Helen, Antony and Cleopatra, filing into church being filmed by Great Love Stories Inc.

When Elizabeth married the Duke of York their presents had been stacked in crates; three thousand invitations were sent out and five Lords Spiritual, headed by the Archbishop of Canterbury, joined the innocent pair in holy matrimony. Two days before the former King of England married Wallis Simpson, Lady Alexandra Metcalfe noticed that George and Harry were the only members of the family to have sent presents. There were twelve guests at the wedding: the bride's Aunt Bessie, the Duke's assistant private secretary Hugh Thomas, his legal adviser Walter Monckton, his solicitor George Allen, Lady Selby, wife of the British Minister in Vienna, the Metcalfes, Wallis' friends the Herman Rogers, Charles Bedaux and his wife, who the wedding couple had only just met and, saving the day for England, Randolph Churchill. Cecil Beaton was taking wedding pictures until the previous day and longed to remain, but realised that 'I could scarcely be permitted . . . when so many intimates had been excluded.'[5]

Walter Monckton brought congratulations from King George and

Queen Elizabeth in the form of a letter containing the news published in the *London Gazette* five days before: 'as an exception to "the settled general rule that a wife takes the status of her husband", his bride would not. They hoped that this painful action they had been forced to take [by whom and why was not explained] would not be regarded as an insult.'6 The letter appeared to have been timed to send them to the altar in a state of humiliation and, perhaps, remorse.

But what altar? The Windsors were simple, conventional souls and they wanted God's blessing. This could only be transmitted through a minister of the Church of England to which, more or less, they belonged. The Church refused to have anything to do with it. A Reverend R A Jardine from Darlington wrote and offered his services and the former Defender of the Faith was naïvely delighted to accept this improbable representative of the Almighty. 'A gallant little fellow,' wrote Lady Alexandra Metcalfe. 'HRH is so pleased to be having a religious ceremony. We found a chest suitable for an altar, put a lamé and horn tablecloth of Wallis's round it & with the aid of Mrs Spry's flowers it looks quite pretty.'7

Informed of Jardine's project, the Bishop of Durham lost no time in announcing 'Mr Jardine has no authority whatever to officiate in any other diocese than Durham ... If the marriage of the Duke of Windsor were taking place in the Diocese of Durham, the Bishop of Durham would consider himself in duty bound to inhibit him or any other clergyman within his jurisdiction from officiating at the marriage.' Under the circumstances he turned the profligate over to the Bishop of Fulham, who was in charge of the diocese of Northern and Central Europe. Fulham, London and Canterbury conferred on the telephone with Durham and York. 'I have been very worried about the whole thing,' said Prebendary F A Cardew, Church of England Rural Dean in France. 'Mr Jardine is down there on his own initiative. He represents nobody but himself.'8

This is no place for philosophical or ecumenical debate: simpler to say that it all worked out in the end. 'I, Edward Albert Christian George Andrew Patrick David, take thee Bessie Wallis to my wedded wife, to have and to hold from this day forward, for better or worse, for richer or poorer, in sickness and in health, to love and cherish till death do us part . . .'; Wallis faltering slightly, promised to love, cherish and obey, the Duke endowed her with all his worldly goods and the Revd Jardine blessed them.

In spite of being wholehearted supporters of Chamberlain's appeasement policy Their Majesties were outraged by the Duke of Windsor's efforts to achieve the same end and quite ready to believe Wallis had been plotting with Ambassador Joachim von Ribbentrop, a member of the social set now being ostracised by the two Queens, to get Hitler's support for an Edward VIII *coup*. In September 1937 they were told that the Windsors were planning to visit Germany 'for the purpose of studying housing and working conditions'. This could only be a cover-up for a more sinister purpose. Directives were sent flying and when the Duke and Duchess arrived in Berlin they found the British Ambassador had been unexpectedly called away and the Chargés d'Affaires told to ignore their presence. A month later Lord Halifax, in his capacity of Master of the Middleton Foxhounds, attended an international hunting expedition organised by Goering and visited Hitler at Berchtesgaden. Chamberlain viewed this visit as 'a great success'. There was the right sort of friendliness and the wrong sort of friendliness. The plight of German Jews, the offensiveness of Nazi beliefs and the unappealing nature of the Reich Chancellor had little to do with it.

Six months later Hitler accepted Sir Nevile Henderson's offer and took over Austria. 'A pleasant state of affairs!' was the caustic comment from Marlborough House.

# Chapter Twenty-Two

'I *will* not have another war,' King George V bellowed at his Prime Minister in May 1935, '*I will not!* The last war was none of my doing, and if there is another one and we are threatened with being brought into it, I will go to Trafalgar Square and wave a red flag myself sooner than allow this country to be brought in!'[1] For King George VI, unable to see things in red, white and blue as his father had done, the problem was far more complex. He tried to keep track, working at his boxes until all hours of the night, constantly anxious.

Apart from such duties as going to an exhibition of hand-quilting by unemployed miners and inspecting Air Raid Precaution Centres, it sounds as though the Queen was taking it fairly easy at this time. Kenneth Clark, Surveyor of the King's Pictures, stayed at Windsor Castle in the Spring of 1938 and was 'shocked to see how little she, and the King as well, did with their day: she never rose before 11.'[2] It was quite out of character for the King to be idle; Clark must have been trying to protect Elizabeth. Perhaps she was still *distrait* from her Coronation; in any case there is more than a hint of boredom and discontent in Clark's account of this visit. There were hardly any guests and the place was as dreary at night as it had been under King George V and Queen Mary. Clark and the Queen went for long walks and 'spent one evening tasting country wines in one of the lodgekeeper's rooms.'[3] Clark, whose impression on first meeting her had been 'that she was not much better than the kind of person one met at a country house', found that the Queen had a hitherto dormant passion for contemporary art. In fact she was most delightful and congenial, apart from her poor taste in clothes. In fact 'he might have been a little in love with her'.[4] Remembering their 'romantic friendship', he said 'they saw as much of each other as they dared', adding that 'the King became unreasonably jealous and twice made scenes, once

157

at Windsor Castle and again at Buckingham Palace.'[5] This might be more convincing if it had not involved Lord Clark, whose ego was phenomenally inflated even without a flirtatious Queen's assistance.

Whatever 'romance' there actually was, the Queen's sudden interest in art was certainly due to his influence. Clark arranged for her to be painted by Augustus John, but the old man felt unable of capturing the essence of the Queen of England. 'She has been absolutely angelic in posing so often and with such cheerfulness,' he wrote to Mrs Cazalet on 13 June 1940. 'But he could make no contact with her – she was not real. He wanted to make her real . . . Good God! It was an impossible situation!'[6] In 1961 the unfinished portrait was discovered in one of the cellars under John's studio and presented to the sitter. Elizabeth, whose taste was somewhat different from Augustus John's, told him, 'it looks so lovely in my drawing room, and has cheered it up no end! The sequins glitter and the roses and the red chair give it a fine glow, and I am so happy to have it . . .'[7] Augustus had hoped to sell it to Hollywood.

Queen Elizabeth had something more melancholy to occupy her mind in the spring of 1938. Her mother had been gravely ill for some time and died in London on 23 June in the presence of her family and her royal son-in-law. Lady Strathmore was a formidable personality. She had brought up nine children and, as she would have said had her circumstances been different, buried four. In her youth she was handsome, with large patrician features inherited by the elder children but dwindling into winsomeness in her youngest daughter. Photographs of her in old age look slightly grotesque, like a distinguished General playing Widow Twankey. The old lady was taken from London to Glamis where, in the pouring rain, they buried her in a grave lined with rhododendrons. Cosmo Lang conducted a Memorial Service at St Martin-in-the-Fields. 'She raised a Queen in her own home,' he said, as though this were a unique accomplishment, 'simply by trust and love.' Among the many mourners were the Honourable James Stuart, by now Deputy Chief Whip in Chamberlain's government, and Mrs Arthur James.

After a short period of mourning at Birkhall Their Majesties returned to London to prepare for the State Visit to France postponed because of Lady Strathmore's death. Norman Hartnell, taking as his precedent the wedding of Princess Alice and Prince Louis of Hesse seven months after the Prince Consort's demise in 1862, re-made Elizabeth's entire wardrobe in bridal white which, without irony, is considered acceptable mourning. Their Majesties crossed the Channel on the First Lord of the Admiralty's yacht *Enchantress*. His wife, Lady Diana Cooper, told her husband in a letter that the King, suddenly realising he had forgotten his hot-water bottle, ordered a frenzied message to be sent to the ship and 'a child was dispatched to Boots' Cash Chemists on a bicycle before it was realised that he would never edge his way back through the crowds and the guards, but the clever Puck got back in forty seconds.'[8] That crisis over, they had a pleasant crossing: 'The Queen nobbled everyone, naturally, from the Commander-in-Chief to the marine who always occupies on all fours the bathroom. The First Lieutenant, Mr Costabadie, is like the ailing Knight at Arms. I doubt his being able to cast it off.'[9]

Paris was *en fête*:

> ... roofs, windows and pavements roaring exultantly, the Queen, a radiant Winterhalter, [is] guarded by too many security measures. The Minister responsible for their safety told me that their fears and safeguards were such as to put plain-clothes policemen in every window on the route and to have hefty citizens lean in a ring against the suspect trees lest they should fall on the procession. ... At the Opera we leant over the balustrade to see the Royal couple, shining with stars and diadem and the Legion d'Honneur proudly worn ... The Elysée and the Quai d'Orsay outshone each other in splendour and *divertissement* ... At Versailles we lunched in the Galerie des Glaces, with thirteen glasses apiece for thirteen precious wines, all bottled on the birthdays of presidents and kings ...'[10]

'A Royal Family sweetens politics by the seasonable addition of nice and pretty events,' said Walter Bagehot. Fighter planes, demonstrating the solidarity between France and Britain, roared in formation over nymphs dancing round the stone horses of the Sun and shepherdesses tending their lambs under trees garlanded with roses.

Hitler was demanding 'the return' of Sudetenland. On Elizabeth's thirty-eighth birthday, while the Royal Family was sailing peacefully up the east coast in the *Victoria and Albert* en route for Balmoral, the King was much relieved to be told that Lord Runciman had arrived in Prague to mediate between the Czech government and the Sudeten party. He must have thought it over when they arrived, because his letter to the Prime Minister shows a certain bewilderment: 'The German attitude to what you are trying to do to help the Czechoslovakian situation, certainly gives cause for anxiety, &

their partial mobilisation on the Czech frontier under the guise of large-scale manoeuvres, might mean all sorts of things.'[11] Meanwhile William Shirer, in Prague, was writing in his diary 'Lord Runciman arrived today to gum up the works and sell the Czechs short if he can . . . [the] whole mission smells . . .'[12]

On 4 September President Beněs ceded the Sudetenland outright to Germany in order that, in the words of the *Times*, Czechoslovakia might become a more 'homogeneous state'. On 12 September Bertie's cousin Prince Arthur of Connaught died, necessitating another plunge into mourning, and Hitler made a violently aggressive speech at Nuremberg. On 13 September Chamberlain wrote a long letter to the King:

> It has been obvious . . . that we must be prepared for a sudden change for the worse and, if then we have any time at all for action, we must know beforehand what action we are going to take. In these circumstances I have been considering the possibility of a sudden and dramatic step which might change the whole situation. The plan is that I inform Herr Hitler that I propose at once to go over to Germany to see him . . .

After putting the pros and cons of this suggestion at some length the Prime Minister added a hasty postscript saying that he had already contacted Hitler and was ready to leave. 'I trust that my action will have Your Majesty's approval.'[13] Since the King had to travel to London to attend Prince Arthur's funeral he went to the lengths of telephoning his blessing. By the time he arrived at Buckingham Palace on the morning of 15 September his Prime Minister was off and away.

The King noted a bag of 450 grouse and four hares in his Game Book that week; the weather was fine and they were joined by the ladies for a picnic in the heather. He was not idle at Balmoral, however. With great thought and care, he had prepared a draft of a personal letter to Hitler appealing to him 'as one ex-serviceman to another' to spare the youth of Britain and Germany from the horrors of another world war.'[14] He knew that his father, though a far more militant pacifist, would never have done such a thing; nevertheless, in his diffident way, he thought it would be worth a try. It was disappointing that Lord Halifax was not more enthusiastic.

Chamberlain achieved nothing at Berchtesgaden but the promise of a week's grace before the invasion of the Sudetenland. When the week was up he flew to Godesburg, only to be told that Hitler now demanded immediate occupation. Chamberlain again appealed for time and was granted until 1 October. He returned home very gloomy and was not greatly encouraged by the King's longing to try a personal appeal himself – if not as an ex-serviceman, then how about as King to Führer? No, said Chamberlain, and the draft was again put back in the drawer.

On 25 September the Air Raid Precautions system was put on a war footing and cellars and basements were commandeered as shelters. The following day thousands of children were evacuated from the cities, each labelled, some snivelling, most larky. It is unlikely that the Queen saw much of them on her way up to Glasgow that night to deputise for her husband at the launching of the *Queen Elizabeth*. Her own children, then safely tucked up at Balmoral, joined her at Glasgow station next morning and they all crossed over to Clydebank where the huge, inanimate hulk lay in John Brown's shipyard waiting for the breath of life.

Launching a ship is not something most of us are accustomed to. Cynthia Asquith, attended by 'a delightful sailor' holding a bouquet and umbrella, says she had a confused feeling she was being married. 'At the magic moment I pulled the lever and the ship shivered into life . . . and away she slithered like a lovely, lithe animal, very fast and with wonderful grace . . . When she reaches the sea she curtseys deep and settles down in her element . . .'[15] This is how one imagines it, but perhaps the *Champion* was more skittish than the *Queen Elizabeth*. There was a long, awkward pause while the last props were being removed. The Queen studied a book of photographs and the Princesses examined models of the completed liner. Suddenly there was a cry of 'She's off!' Startled, the Queen rushed forward, seized the bottle of champagne, just had time to say 'I-name-this-ship-Queen-Elizabeth-and wish-success-to-her-and all-who-sail-in-her' and swing the bottle before the great thing lumbered away. The bell meant to announce the moment of launching rang as the ship's stern touched the water; steam-whistles shrieked, drag-chains screamed and the whole thing was enveloped in a rising cloud of red iron dust. Elizabeth made the usual speech about being of good cheer in spite of the dark clouds and placing entire confidence in the leaders who, under God's providence, were striving their utmost. Queen Mary, who had just been fitted for her gas mask, listened on her wireless set. 'She made her speech admirably. Bertie's really.'[16] When Elizabeth returned to London she found Bertie extremely upset because Chamberlain, at the end of his tether, had told him in no uncertain terms finally to abandon the idea of sending a personal message to Hitler.

On 28 September Queen Mary and Princess Marina went to the House of Commons to hear Mr Chamberlain's further statement on the crisis. They sat in the Ladies' Gallery and the old Queen listened impassively but intently as the Prime Minister recounted the whole shoddy tale. Suddenly, at twelve minutes past four (Harold Nicolson had just glanced at the clock), there was a flurry on the Government bench and Sir John Simon, a piece of Foreign Office notepaper in his hand, tugged at the Prime Minister's coat. Chamberlain 'adjusted his *pince-nez* and read the document that had been handed to him. His whole face, his whole body, seemed to change . . . he appeared ten years younger and triumphant. "Herr Hitler," he said, "has just agreed to postpone his mobilisation for twenty-four hours and to meet me in conference with Signor Mussolini and Signor Daladier at Munich." '[17] There was silence for a second. Nobody thought of asking why M. Daladier had suddenly become Italian. Queen Mary was 'so much moved I could not speak to any of the ladies in the Gallery, several of them, even those unknown to me, seized my hand, it was very touching. Let us pray now that a lasting Peace may follow – I went to see Bertie – A most wonderful day – God be praised.'[18]

Two days later the King and Queen appeared on the balcony of Buckingham Palace with the Chamberlains. Everybody smiled and waved, the crowd cheered, the world had once more been saved for democracy. It was too late for most people to make up for their ruined summer holiday, but they went back to work with renewed vigour. The Royal Family returned to Balmoral. Before leaving, Bertie 'issued to his peoples a message of sober thanksgiving and gratitude' and wrote to the Archbishop of Canterbury: 'I am sure that some day the Czechs will see that what we did was to save them for a happier future.'[19]

# Chapter Twenty-Three

On 10 March 1939 the Prime Minister announced that 'the outlook in international affairs is tranquil'. He had recently been to see Mussolini in Rome – a more enjoyable visit than those to Godesburg and Munich – and was satisfied that all our troubles were over. Five days later Hitler and his armies entered Prague. Speaking from the Hradschin Castle, the palace of the Kings of Bohemia, the Führer proclaimed that Czechoslovakia had ceased to exist. Queen Elizabeth, perhaps hoping to see some last-minute drama as her mother-in-law had done, went to hear for herself what they were saying in the House of Commons. According to Hansard she listened to a debate on a Government bill to provide fifty large camps to be used by school children if peace continued and by evacuees in the event of war. According to another account 'the business before the House was not unamusing, for the witty A P Herbert was asking leave to bring in a Bill to restore public passenger steamers to the Thames.'[1] On Good Friday, just as Their Majesties and family were settling down for a peaceful Easter weekend at Windsor, Queen Mary was horrified to hear 'that the Italians had kicked out Zog, King of Albania . . . The poor Queen had to leave with her baby son of two days old.'[2] This, unlike Czechoslovakia, was a personal matter. She could sympathise with family dramas Upstairs; what went on Downstairs, among the Hitlers and Mussolinis and Stalins and their like filled her with incredulous rage.

Joseph Kennedy, the American Ambassador, was a guest at Windsor at Easter and was taken to see the Air Ministry's new secret weapons – Balloon Squadrons manned by aviators with telescopes and binoculars. Mr Kennedy was impressed. On 20 April (according to gossip, anyway) King George sent congratulations to Hitler on his fiftieth birthday.[3] The next day Lilibet received a ciné camera and projector from her Uncle David on the occasion of her thirteenth.[4]

The previous September Joseph Kennedy had delivered a personal letter to the King from President Roosevelt. After saying that he had learned in confidence from Mackenzie King that there was a possibility of Their Majesties visiting Canada in the summer of 1939, the President invited them to stay 'for three or four days of very simple country life at Hyde Park . . . if you bring either or both of the children with you they will also be very welcome, and I shall try to have one or two Roosevelts of approximately the same age to play with them.'

After the anxiety of the Czechoslovakian business this was something to look forward to, though Bertie had his usual qualms of conscience about going away. 'I feel we must start for Canada on Saturday unless there is any really good reason as to why we should not,' he wrote gloomily to his mother.[5] Keeping Bertie's spirits up was no easy task; he never seemed convinced that everything was such fun, so long as one kept smiling, or that he would enjoy it when he got there. Queen Mary and the children came to see them off at Portsmouth; Margaret said 'I have my handkerchief,' and Lilibet said sternly, 'To wave, not to cry.'[6] As the *Empress of Australia* ploughed steadily across the Atlantic towards the New World even the King cheered up a little.

Eight days later they were stuck in dense fog in the middle of an ice field. 'We nearly hit a berg the day before yesterday,' Elizabeth wrote chattily, 'and the poor Captain was nearly demented because some kind cheerful people kept on reminding him that it was about here the *Titanic* was struck, & just about the same date!'[7] In the end the crossing from Portsmouth to Quebec took twelve days, but even though Bertie felt revived, it was not without a touch of complaint: '. . . I should not have chosen an ice field surrounded by dense fog in which to have a holiday, but it does seem to be the only place for me to rest in nowadays.'[8]

In their specially-built train – the private coaches contained a drawing room and dining room, two bedrooms and an office – Their Majesties travelled 4,281 miles. Some Canadians felt this was not enough. The royal couple visited no universities, schools, charitable organisations or factories. Local officials who had been practising their welcoming addresses for months were not allowed to present them in order 'to save the strain upon the King and Queen'. Those who remembered how the Prince of Wales would clamber down from his observation platform and talk to the people standing beside the track, how he went off into the wilds with Indian guides and bust a bronco at Saskatoon and bought a ranch in Alberta found his younger brother a decided disappointment.

Elizabeth consequently shone all the brighter. 'The Queen,' said Lord Tweedsmuir, 'has a perfect genius for the right kind of publicity. The unrehearsed episodes here [in Ottawa] were marvellous.' In fact she spent ten minutes talking to some Scottish masons 'in full view of 70,000 people' and did a short walkabout among 10,000 veterans after unveiling the War Memorial. Still, it was better than nothing and the official verdict was that the whole tour had been a triumphant success.

Roosevelt's invitation may have sounded casual but Mrs Roosevelt found that although the King and Queen were going to stay only two nights at the White House formidable preparations were necessary. William Bullitt, the US Ambassador in Paris, sent her a secret memorandum based on the State Visit the previous year. This confidential document contained every detail of the royal requirements, down to 'a linen blanket for the Queen's couch'. Although Mrs Roosevelt puzzled a good deal, she was unable to understand what a linen blanket might be.[9] The British Ambassador's wife told her the head butler should be provided with a stopwatch, because the King must be served at meals precisely thirty seconds before the Queen. But what about the White House rule that the President was always served first? FDR solved the problem by saying that he and the King would be served simultaneously by two butlers; then, after the requisite thirty seconds, the Queen and Mrs Roosevelt in the same manner.

But how should they be placed at table? Should the President sit with the King on his right and the Queen on his left and his wife on the King's right? It was at last decided that the King should sit on Mrs Roosevelt's right and the Queen on the President's right. This meant that instead of having Mrs Roosevelt, King, President, Queen, you had Queen, President, King, Mrs Roosevelt – much more satisfactory.

But what should they sit on? The Roosevelts used two special high-backed chairs in their dining room, one for the President, one for his First Lady. It might show disrespect to the Queen if the King sat in one of these, so two more identical chairs were purchased. Still more chairs were needed for messengers to sit on outside the royal bedrooms. 'This last demand seemed foolish to me,' the exhausted Mrs Roosevelt complained, 'since the rooms were just across the hall from each other'; anyway there were plenty of telephones. Chairs were nevertheless provided and presumably the messengers sat on them.

While the Roosevelts hurried off to Hyde Park to make further preparations for Their Majesties' promised 'rest and relaxation', the King and Queen sailed for New York on board the President's yacht, escorted for some of the way by their friend J P Morgan in his Corsair. After a fiercely hot, humid, noisy, ticker-tape New York day they arrived at Hyde Park hours late for dinner and in a state of collapse. Franklin said to Bertie, 'My mother does not approve of cocktails and thinks you should have a cup of tea.' Bertie answered, 'Neither does my mother,' and took a cocktail.[10] This was the start of a friendship that was to play no mean part in winning the future war.

Seven weeks after their parents' departure Lilibet and Margaret, in the charge of Crawfie and Clara, sailed out into the Solent on board the destroyer *Kempenfelt* to meet the returning *Empress of Britain*. After the kissing and hugging and how they've grown and don't they look well there was a hilarious lunch in the ship's dining room; the King threw balloons out of portholes, Lord Airlie popped some with his cigarette 'and everyone was very youthful and gay.'[11] There was another wild welcome from the crowds packed along the dock at Southampton; in London the masses, and Harold Nicolson, were hysterical with joy – 'Such fun . . . the bells of St Margaret's began to swing into welcome and the procession started creeping round the corner. They went very slowly, and there were the King and Queen and the two Princesses. We lost all our dignity and yelled and yelled. The King wore a happy schoolboy grin. The Queen was superb . . . in truth one of the most amazing Queens since Cleopatra. We returned to the House with lumps in our throats.'[12] In the evening a vast crowd roared like hungry children for a sight of the scrumptious family on the Palace balcony. They had been starved without them, nothing but bread and Scrape. Business had been bad; for those who cared about such things the Season had been a flop; nobody had bothered to come to London and Belgravia tradesmen were in despair. Now they were back, the darlings, all pink and white and delectable, even the King in his Admiral's uniform looking good enough to eat. When they disappeared for a while 10,000 voices were raised in 'The Lambeth Walk' and 'Under the Spreading Chestnut Tree'; it was midnight before the last surfeited revellers straggled down the Mall.

What had happened? Reading the enthusiastic reports of Their Majesties' visit to Canada and the United States people had suddenly become aware that this amazing couple belonged to *them*. Anything

Ottawa and New York could do they could do better. This explanation seems likely, but there were other reasons. Strong sentiments had been stirred up during the Abdication, then frustrated. Sex had been connected with the throne for the first time in living memory. Institutional religion was withering away and people had learned from the cinema, even from the radio, that not all extra-terrestrial beings were dead saints and inaccessible angels. King George V had been God the Father, rumbling away behind the clouds and occasionally coming out to shine; King Edward VIII, made flesh, was a kind of precursor of James Dean, a meteoric upset; Bertie and Elizabeth, after flickering uncertainly for a time, exactly fitted the rôles left empty by Douglas Fairbanks and Mary Pickford – fallible yet perfect, exalted in themselves but nearly always seen dealing with danger, fluttering in tight corners, winning through. It was not simply that they had been away and were suddenly seen with new eyes; if they had stayed at home inspecting air-raid shelters, the same thing would have happened. 'George the Good' and his Cleopatra were, at that moment, an historical necessity.

Stardom suited the Queen perfectly. She must have some new pictures – what about that nice young man Cecil Beaton, who had done the Kents and Princess Olga? Beaton appeared, properly nervous. They discussed what she should wear: 'You know, perhaps the embroidered one I wore . . . in Canada? And I thought perhaps another evening dress of . . . tulle? And a . . . tiara?' All this, Beaton recalled, 'wistfully said, with a smile and raised eyebrows', as though it was rather daring of her tentatively to suggest what she had already decided and he must be the final judge. Beaton was captivated. Snap-snap he went, photographing her 'with monkey-like frenzy'. 'It is so hard to know when *not* to smile,' Elizabeth murmured, tidying her shoulder-straps meticulously and placing her fan just so. She disappeared for a quick costume change. 'I changed the tiara. And these diamonds – are they all right?' She was insatiable. 'Do you mean to say she's gone off to change once more?' asked the superintendent in despair. 'Why, she hasn't had her tea yet, has she? Well, it means the poor King will have to have his tea alone.' Finally, stricken as Lord David Cecil, Beaton bowed himself away. 'But in my pocket was hidden, scented with tuberoses and gardenias, a handkerchief that the Queen had tucked behind a cushion . . . I had stolen it. It was my particular prize, one which would have more romance and reality than any of the photographs.'[13]

The King, in his own way, was also rising to the occasion. He had made a fluent, powerful speech in the Guildhall, about the ideals of the Commonwealth; it had been hailed as a declaration of beliefs, an indication that Britain was prepared to defend her democratic institutions, a clarion call to mankind. 'A change from the old days,'[14] he commented dryly. He wondered anxiously how Hitler could be made to take Britain seriously – Hitler was now demanding Danzig and Britain had changed its official policy from appeasement to threats but he didn't take a blind bit of notice when 20,000 Civil Defence troops paraded in the Park. The King had another of his ideas. Georgie had recently been in Italy and talked with their Nazi cousin, Prince Philip of Hesse, who was also the King of Italy's son-in-law. Philip had served as personal liaison officer between Hitler and Mussolini and was believed to be on friendly terms with the Führer. 'Do you think it would be possible to get him over here,' Bertie wrote eagerly to the Prime Minister, '& use him as a messenger to convey to Hitler that we really are in earnest?'[15] Unfortunately neither the Prime Minister nor the Foreign Secretary appreciated the importance of family in such matters.

Since there seemed little he could do to resolve the international situation the King decided to take a few days off and show the family his old school. They sailed to Portsmouth on the Royal yacht, dropped anchor in the Dart at the bottom of the Royal Navy College steps. A very pleasant two days were spent recalling old times and playing croquet with the cadets, among whom was Lilibet's cousin, Cadet Captain Prince Philip of Greece. Then the King visited his Boys' Camp, which was held this year at Abergeldie, conveniently near Balmoral. Elizabeth and the girls went over to supper, but Lilibet did not appear particularly taken with any of the two hundred selected boys nervously downing their baked beans. After abandoning them for the day to inspect the Reserve Fleet Bertie wrote to his mother, 'It is wonderful the way in which all the men have come back for duty at this time, & I feel sure it will be a deterrent factor in Hitler's mind to start a war.'[16] Thus reassured, he returned to Balmoral to prepare for the shooting season.

This was the happiest time of the King's year:

> Punctual to the minute he would come from his room where he had already conferred with Gillan as to the day's plan, his face displaying his pleasure at what lay before him. In one hand would be a long walking-stick, in the other, very often, some special article

of apparel of his own planning for combating any possible trick of the weather: a cap, a scarf, or some ingenious kind of coat, for he was always a great contriver. We would all clamber into the bus, which at once became full of chatter, and about once a week whoever was nearest the door would lower the window a little, in order to inspire the storm of imprecation which instantly followed an act of such suicidal folly, for the King always unshakeably maintained that the exhaust and the window were fatally conjoined, and always had been.[17]

On driving days most of the house party joined the guns for lunch, which was always in the open. Hampers were taken to some favourite spot, plaid rugs spread on the heather and bogmyrtle, and since 'by one of the most hallowed of shooting conventions' the ladies usually arrived before the guns had returned from the hillside, they had often already unpacked 'the delicious contents which nobody who had enjoyed them could ever forget.' On Sunday afternoons there might be an expedition to the far end of Loch Muick for tea in the Glassalt and some light-hearted trout fishing, or perhaps they would all go to 'the Queen's charming little cottage. There a more serious and less reputable form of fishing often produced some salmon, bearing mysterious marks almost suggestive of foul hooking.'[18] As the days went by and the sun shone and the grouse fell in their hundreds it began to seem that Hitler had taken the lesson of Weymouth to heart.

News of the Soviet-German Non-Aggression pact burst into this idyll on 22 August. The King returned to London, leaving Elizabeth in Scotland. 'I feel deeply for you,' Queen Mary wrote, knowing what it was like to be left sitting on a mountain. The King was determined to take action. Make friends with Japan – that was the answer. Alec Hardinge (restored to health and now the King's Private Secretary) wrote to the Permanent Under-Secretary of State for Foreign Affairs: 'His Majesty wonders . . . if it would help in any way if, at an opportune moment, he were to send a friendly message direct to the Emperor . . . he feels that, when dealing with orientals, direct communication between Heads of States may be helpful.'[19] The Foreign Office politely declined the offer. Then *what* about a personal appeal to Hitler? King Leopold had sent one, so had President Roosevelt and Prime Minister Mackenzie King and the Pope . . . Chamberlain promised that he would keep it in mind. Elizabeth came down from Balmoral, though Bertie hardly had time to see her what with meetings of the Privy Council, audiences to Ministers, visits to the War Office, the Admiralty, the Air Ministry and the Central War Room, keeping track of Ambassador Henderson's comings and goings, the promises, the threats, the rumours (Goering is going to get rid of Hitler and restore the Hohenzollerns – if only that were true).

It was almost a relief when Germany invaded Poland on Friday. Elizabeth felt she must return to Balmoral and explain it all to the children, so the King went to bed alone the first night of the blackout. The British Government's ultimatum received no reply. On Sunday morning Queen Mary went to the church of St Mary Magdalene at Sandringham, where the rector had installed his wireless in the nave. She and tens of millions of her people heard Neville Chamberlain declare war somewhere between the Absolution or Remission of Sins and the Benedicite. Anthony Eden, Harold Nicolson, Bob Boothby and Duncan Sandys listened to the housemaid's wireless in Ronnie Tree's house, since the Trees didn't have one themselves. This was the first time that radio had been used for such a purpose, but Nicolson was unimpressed. 'The PM,' he commented laconically, 'was quite good and tells us that war has begun.' Barely a quarter of an hour later, when the air-raid sirens sounded over most of Britain, everyone, except the insensible and the indifferent, knew why.

Winston Churchill, on whom the King, Queen and half the world would rely for the next five years, went up to the flat roof of his house to see what was going on:

> Around us on every side, in the clear, cool September light, rose the roofs and spires of London. Above them were already slowly rising thirty or forty cylindrical balloons . . . [Then] as the quarter of an hour's notice which we had been led to expect we should receive was now running out we made our way to the shelter assigned to us, armed with a bottle of brandy and other appropriate medical comforts.[20]

# Chapter Twenty-Four

It is appropriate at this point to mention the astonishing fact that the Royal Family remained in Great Britain for the duration of World War II. 'We Stay With Our People! We Are Not Afraid!' ran the headlines, implying that any other Royal Family would have scuttled off, pale with terror, clutching the Crown Jewels. It is true that the Cabinet formally advised the King that the children should be sent to Canada out of harm's way and that their mother said, 'the Princesses would never leave without me, and I couldn't leave without the King, and the King will never leave,' but that they remained has never ceased to strike the British public – most of whom had no alternative – with incredulous awe.

Queen Elizabeth's most significant contribution to history, apart from her rôle in the Abdication, was during the war years. Owing to her rôle as the King's confidante, adviser and supporter, Bertie managed to do his job well. What was his job, exactly? All he had actually sworn to do in the Coronation service was to be merciful and just and support the clergy. In practice he had to endorse the routine machinery of government, bestow his warrant on its decisions, personally to meet senior public servants, ambassadors, administrators and the recipients of all titles bestowed in investitures, appear as a figurehead on national occasions and in times of crisis, visit all aspects of the nation at work and at war, represent the country, Commonwealth and Empire to the rest of the world and fulfil his commitments as Head of the Armed Forces.[1] The only things he could do on his own initiative were to advise, encourage and warn the government in the event of there being any controversy, this inalienable right being known as the Royal Prerogative and a great bore to many politicians.

Apart from all that he had to embody the indefinable mystery of monarchy and so on. It was a fairly demanding job in peace-time for those who took it seriously. In war it was non-stop. With his wife and helpmeet by his side the King tackled it in his own conscientious way. He brought his diary up-to-date every Sunday: 'After 3 weeks of war, many strange things have taken place. It is an amazing puzzle.' He then summarised Russia's invasion of Poland, its possible effect on Italy, the unacceptability of Hitler's peace terms and the puzzling fact that 'Germany has not interfered with our mobilisations in any way, & has not raided us from the air. Why? We must wait and see.'2 Waiting, as he said in his Christmas broadcast, was a trial of nerve and discipline. He occupied himself by inspecting the Maginot Line and placating the Turkish military mission, which had been about to go home in disgust at the British government's parsimony. His Christmas broadcast, in which he quoted a poem by Miss Marie Louise Haskins, was received extremely well. It also turned Miss Haskins into a bestseller which since she had lived in total obscurity since 1908, when her one and only collection of verse was privately printed, pleased her a great deal.

During the first weeks of the war Elizabeth was distracted by domestic problems: Buckingham Palace had to be packed up and the staff reorganised; Crawfie recalled from holiday to arrange sewing parties at Birkhall and take the children to the dentist. When nothing happened it seemed safe to bring them down to Sandringham for Christmas. In the New Year, when they moved to the Royal Lodge, the Queen found time to send a copy of *Mein Kampf* to the Foreign Secretary, Lord Halifax, in case he was unclear what the country was fighting for. 'I . . . do not advise you to read it through, or you might go mad, and that would be a great pity . . . Even a skip through gives one a good idea of his mentality, ignorance and obvious sincerity.'3

'We have been at War for 6 months today,' the King wrote on Sunday, 3 March. 'There have been several "peace" moves, & "scares" that Germany would invade Holland & Belgium . . .'4 Chamberlain, dismissing the 'scares', declared triumphantly on 4 April, 'Hitler has missed the bus!' On 9 April Germany invaded Denmark and Norway and the war began.

Everyone leaped into action, particularly the critics of the Prime Minister. The King felt left out: 'I have spent a bad day,' he wrote that evening. 'Everyone working at fever heat except me.'5 British troops landed at Namsos and Andalsnes but they had no support against German air power and had to be withdrawn. The King chafed while Parliament debated the disaster and finally turned Chamberlain out; then, with some apprehension, he sent for Winston Churchill. 'He looked at me searchingly and quizzically for some moments, and then said, "I suppose you don't know why I have sent for you?" ' Adopting his mood, Churchill replied, 'Sir, I simply couldn't imagine why.'[6]

The wartime triumvirate was now complete. Winston supplied the fiery personality, Bertie the reliable image, Elizabeth the perfumed oil to throw on troubled waters. She got on with the Prime Minister very well, though sometimes he punctured her effusiveness with mild irony and he couldn't tolerate her passion for charades and wordgames. Perhaps as a sly rebuke for these awful pastimes he gave her *Fowler's Dictionary of Modern Usage* for Christmas. (The King, who received one of Winston's specially designed siren suits, was not above doing a little teasing himself: 'At last the Army has come into its own,' he wrote in Churchillian tones to his Prime Minister in 1942, '. . . ably helped by the forces of the air & of those that work under the surface of the sea.'[7]) Everything was made even more fun by the fact that Churchill had appointed James Stuart as his Chief Whip. Now very much a family man, Stuart still had his dry humour and his lackadaisical charm. There were quite a few laughs along with the blood, toil, tears and sweat.

The things for which Elizabeth are best remembered were her secondary occupations – visiting bombed cities, re-laying foundation stones, doing her duty as Commander-in-Chief of the WRENS and the WRAFS and the WAACS, inspecting munition factories, entertaining royal refugees and having 300 land-girls to tea. 'She enjoyed a threepenny lunch with other people's children [sic] evacuated from London. She ate jam tarts and drank water from a bakelite mug. "This is all very good," she told one of the children around her in the calm of the countryside.'[8] Tripping across bomb-sites in her high heels, always modestly decked in three rows of pearls and the unobtrusive diamond, she was constantly sympathetic and encouraging.

Or almost constantly. Very occasionally – so seldom that the onlookers felt they must have been mistaken – the smile froze and the voice slapped out hard and cold. 'Visiting a factory [she] was shown the spot where nineteen workmen had been killed by a bomb. "Poor things," she said, and walked on.'[9] Presented with an enormous civic lunch in Lancashire, which had probably used up all their catering rations for a month, she snapped acidly at the Mayor, 'We don't have any more food on the table at Buckingham Palace than is allowed to the ordinary householder according to the rations for the week.' 'Ah well then,' the Mayor replied amiably, 'thou'll be glad of a bit of a do like this.'[10] A newsreel camera inadvertently caught for posterity 'the expression of distaste as she picked her way through a group of dejected and no doubt smelly citizens huddled in some public building the day after their homes had been destroyed in an air-raid.'[11] The writer was quick to add that the Queen's expression no more indicated contempt or dislike than the grimace of a mother mopping up her baby's vomit.

At five in the morning on 13 May 1940 Bertie was woken up by a police sergeant informing him that Queen Wilhelmina of the Netherlands was on the phone. 'It's not often one is rung up at that hour,' he commented mildly, 'and especially by a Queen. But in these days anything may happen, & far worse things too.'[12] Queen Wilhelmina, who had recently confronted Hitler by threatening *'Touchez à mes pays bas et je vous inonde!'*[13] wanted the King to send some aircraft to defend Holland. He passed this message on to the appropriate department and went back to bed.

Later in the morning Queen Wilhelmina telephoned again, this time from Harwich. The sixty-year-old royal lady, realising that her earlier request might not have been treated with proper urgency, had left The Hague and embarked in the British destroyer *Hereward* at Rotterdam. 'I suppose this is bomb-proof?' she enquired, sitting herself down in the deckhouse. The commander did not disabuse her, but asked her to wear a helmet, which she put on top of her hat. Then she told him to take her to Zeeland in order to join her remaining army. The commander obediently set course, but on the way received a message that the place was in flames and overrun with Germans. Wilhelmina told him to sail further south; on being informed that the Germans were there too she replied, 'Then take me to England.'[14] Her intention was to have a few words with King George and the British Government and return to Holland in the evening.

King George dissuaded her from this plan with difficulty and told her to catch the next train for London. He met her at Liverpool Street – though he had never seen her before she was instantly recognisable – and took her to Buckingham Palace. Her mind being on other things, she had not packed so much as a toothbrush and only possessed the clothes she so firmly sat down in.

The Queen took the problem in hand and arranged for her own dressmakers to come in, but none of their regal confections appealed to Wilhelmina. Once the prettiest and most sought-after Queen in Europe, all she wanted now were a few aeroplanes and a couple of sensible tweed suits. Boxes of hats were unpacked but she scorned them all. At last, noticing the plain black felt worn by one of the cringing underlings, she declared, 'There you are. That is the hat for me!'[15] Thus garbed she marched off to conduct the Dutch resistance from her rooms in the Palace. 'She has little S.A.' said Field Marshal Wavell sadly.[16]

Just over a fortnight later the Belgian army capitulated and the evacuation of Allied troops from Dunkirk began. The King was in a ferment. Every day he wrote down the number of soldiers evacuated, until finally he could record that the last of the British Expeditionary Force had been brought safely back. By 5 June the operation was complete – 335,000 troops rescued, including 111,000 French. On 10 June Italy declared war on Britain and France: 'Mussolini gave no reason,' the baffled King wrote in his diary.[17] On 16 June France surrendered.

Queen Wilhelmina had been joined at the Palace by Prince Bernhard, Princess Juliana, King Haakon and Prince Olav of Norway. The foreign royals were, not unnaturally, sensitive to the possibility of German invasion and felt that perhaps more than the Queen's target practice with her .303 rifle and .38 revolver was necessary.[18] Haakon, as spokesman for the exiles, asked what precautions the Palace had taken against a parachute attack. The King explained the method of alerting the guard, but since his Norwegian uncle was clearly sceptical he pressed the alarm signal and they all went out into the garden to observe the magnificent result. There was no result. It seemed the police-sergeant on duty had told the officers of the guard that no attack was impending 'as he had heard nothing of it', so the guards had gone back to filling in their racing forms. Shortly afterwards a number of guardsmen entered the gardens at the double and, to the horror of King Haakon, 'proceeded to thrash the undergrowth in the manner of beaters at a shoot rather than men engaged in the pursuit of a dangerous enemy.'[19]

The precautions were soon looked into, and just as well. On 16 July 1940 Hitler issued 'War Directive No. 16', known as Operation Sealion: 'As England in spite of her hopeless military position has so far shown herself unwilling to come to any compromise, I have decided to begin preparations for and, if necessary, to carry out the invasion of England . . .'[20] The date decided on was 15 September, when according to the German Naval Staff's estimate, 1,722 barges, 471 tugs, 1,161 motor-boats and 155 transports would be needed to ferry the 16th and 9th Armies across the Channel; meanwhile

German bombers were to obliterate Channel shipping and demolish south coast ports and airfields. By mid-August the barges were assembling in the estuaries of the Maas and the Scheldt while Spitfires and the Luftwaffe fought the Battle of Britain over deserted holiday beaches and towns.

It is difficult not to romanticise this sky-high battlefield. 'Many a young Englishman,' wrote John Wheeler-Bennett (who was safely in Political Warfare), 'made the discovery in sacrifice that "Death opens unknown doors. It is most grand to die".' 'Just ordinary young men,' the King wrote more sanely, 'who come from all trades & professions [and] are now flying & using the most intricate & modern inventions.'[21] Unfortunately there weren't enough of them. By 6 September, although they had made enough trouble to cause Hitler to postpone the invasion for a further week, the resources of Fighter Command were stretched to the limit and things looked bad.

His Royal Prerogative meant the King had to be told everything that was going on and a great deal of this information must have been discussed with Elizabeth. After the first fierce daylight raid on London there was anxious speculation about the imminent invasion, news of which had been issued by GHQ Home Forces under the curious code-name CROMWELL, enough to give any monarch a sleepless night. But the Luftwaffe, surprised and unnerved by the fighter opposition, kept away and the following day was ominously peaceful. On Monday London was attacked again, nearly half the bomber formations were turned back, the rest scattered and the invasion postponed for another three days. British bombers and guns pounded the embarkation ports in northern France: the invasion was postponed until 27 September. 'Even though victory in the air should not be achieved before another ten or twelve days,' Hitler declared hopefully, 'Britain might yet be seized by mass hysteria.'[22]

On 15 September a German bomber flew straight down the Mall and dropped two bombs in the forecourt of Buckingham Palace, two in the quadrangle, one on the Chapel and one, carelessly, in the garden. The King and Queen lunched in the air-raid shelter, which Elizabeth had furnished with gilt chairs, a regency settee, a large Victorian mahogany table and a supply of glossy magazines.[23] 'A magnificent piece of bombing, Ma'am, if you'll pardon my saying so,' one of the police constables remarked.[24] It was shortly after this that the Queen made the famous and outrageous claim that she was glad the Palace had been bombed, claiming that 'it makes me feel I can look the East End in the face.' Huddled in their flimsy Andersons, crammed into

Underground stations, searching for Mum and the kids through last night's rubble, the people of the East End were genuinely impressed. Mass Observation tracked down a few sceptics, but that organisation was known to have a left-wing bias and must be unreliable. If there really was a housewife who complained 'it's all very well for them traipsing around saying how their hearts bleed for us and they share all our sufferings, and then going home to a roaring fire in one of their six houses'[25] she deserved all she got.

The following Sunday Goering attacked London with everything he had – five fighters for every bomber, flying thick as hornets. The battle raged for an hour before the German formations were scattered and hunted home. That night and the following night Bomber Command destroyed or damaged twelve per cent of the invasion barges and transports due to cross the Channel. The rest would soon follow. On the afternoon of 17 September the War Diary of the German Naval Staff reported Hitler's decision: 'The enemy air force is still by no means defeated; on the contrary, it shows increasing activity. The weather situation as a whole does not permit us to expect a period of calm. The Führer has therefore decided to postpone Operation Sealion indefinitely.' On 19 September the remainder of the invasion force skulked ignominiously away, without even attempting so much as a raid on the coast of Britain.[26]

The possible invasion of Hawkhurst and Petersfield became material for *Dad's Army* as war erupted over the entire world. The King went through long periods of depression and bewilderment. The whole situation in North Africa was an enigma. Ploughing through his daily reading of Cabinet papers and Foreign Office telegrams, he found it 'almost impossible to keep a clear mind on all that is going on.'[27] I do wish people would get on with the job and not criticise all the time, but in a free country this has to be put up with.'[28] It had never been easy for Bertie to put up with things. In the early days, when he knew most of the people involved – Boris of Bulgaria, Leopold of Belgium, George of Greece, and of course the Yugoslavs – he felt he was doing something useful by writing letters ('I send you my best wishes for the happiness and prosperity of your Majesty and of Bulgaria during these troublous times.'). One thing that comforted him was his friendship with Roosevelt. They went out of their way to be personally amiable to each other's Ambassadors and never wrote to each other without recalling those happy days at Hyde Park. Even so, the whole business had got out of hand since Pearl Harbor. 'Anything can happen,' he wrote, feeling helpless, '& it will be wonderful if we are lucky anywhere.'[29] Even Elizabeth found his pessimism hard to deal with. 'He feels so much not being in the fighting line,' she wrote to Queen Mary.[30] Gloomy and frustrated, for two nights a week at 6pm on the dot the King put on his overalls and worked at a bench making parts for RAF guns.[31]

By the spring of 1943 it seemed safe to take a trip to North Africa – the first time he had set foot out of England since he inspected the Maginot Line in 1939. The King was unable to view even this exciting prospect without the usual doubt and conjecture: 'As the time draws nearer for my departure on my journey, I wonder if I should go, but I know I shall be doing good.'[32] Travelling incognito as 'General Lyon', he set off in Churchill's luxurious transport plane on the evening of 11 June. Elizabeth said goodbye to him at Northolt and went home to wait for news. 'I have had an anxious few hours,' she wrote next day to Queen Mary, 'because at 8.15 I heard that the plane had been heard near Gibraltar and that it would soon be landing. Then after an hour & a half I heard that there was thick fog at Gib. & that they were going on to Africa. Then complete silence until a few minutes ago, when a message came that they had landed in Africa & taken off again. Of course I imagined every sort of horror & walked up & down my room staring at the telephone.'[33]

Harold Macmillan, Minister Resident at Allied Headquarters, was one of the party welcoming 'General Lyon' at Algiers. His job of going through the programme of the tour with the King was not easy:

> Unfortunately, he was very tired from the journey and had not slept at all. So I had a good deal of difficulty in getting him to agree to the various items . . . The real trouble is that the courtiers are deplorable. Joey Legh does his best, and, although looking quite halfwitted, is not so. But Alec Hardinge seems to me beyond the pale. He is idle, supercilious, without a spark of imagination or vitality. And his whole attitude to the visit makes one wonder why he advised the King to undertake it at all. However, after a lot of cajoling and so forth, we got the first two and a half days agreed.[34]

After a bath and a sleep at the Villa Emma the King recovered his spirits and his temper. The tour was a success and he enjoyed every minute of it, particularly the stately entry into Valletta harbour on the cruiser *Aurora*, when he stood alone in his white naval uniform on the bridge acknowledging the thunderous welcome of troops, sailors, airmen and civilians lining the cliffs, packed into the narrow streets, perilously perched on rocks, lamp-posts, bollards and rowboats while choirs sang and bands played. He was piped ashore like a conquering hero and that night, sailing over a calm sea to Tripoli, he felt like one. 'Mussolini called the Mediterranean *Mare Nostrum*. The King, in a cruiser with four destroyers, has crossed it twice in thirty-six hours.'[35] Alec Hardinge, who according to Macmillan 'would have been out of date in the 1900s', resigned a month later, ostensibly because of another bout of exhaustion and ill-health.

A King could not be expected to lead his invading troops from an office desk. A year later, as D-Day approached, Bertie passionately wanted to repeat this experience. He found to his consternation that Churchill had the same idea. Not content with flying to Tehran by way of Cairo to meet Stalin, Chiang Kai-shek and Roosevelt, the Prime Minister glibly informed his monarch that 'he hoped to see the initial attack from one of the bombarding ships'. The King was reduced to suggesting that he should go with him, though it wouldn't be quite the same thing. He had noted with some asperity that Churchill 'likes getting his own way with no interference from anybody and nobody will stand for that sort of treatment in this country'[36] and now the old man was going to steal what should be the Sovereign's thunder. It was a bit much, but since he wanted so badly to be involved in the invasion he would have to put up with it. 'I told Elizabeth about the idea & she was wonderful as always & encouraged me to do it.'[37]

Alan Lascelles, his new Private Secretary, was appalled at the suggestion. Who would Lilibet choose for her Prime Minister if both her father and Churchill were killed? No Commander could fight a major battle and look after his King and Prime Minister at the same time. The King reluctantly agreed to sleep on it and in the morning he wrote to Churchill asking him to reconsider; 'the right thing to do', he advised through gritted teeth, 'is what normally falls to those at the top on such occasions, namely, to remain at home and wait.'[38] Next day he and Lascelles went to see Admiral Ramsay, the Allied Naval Commander-in-Chief, at the Downing Street Annexe. Churchill was already there, looking ominously smug. Admiral Ramsay, who had no idea that the King might be involved in this absurd enterprise, told Churchill that apart from risking mines, torpedoes, air attack and shells from shore batteries, the Prime Minister wouldn't be able to see a thing anyway. The Admiral was asked to withdraw for a few minutes and there was a quick conference. When he was called back it was to be told that the King, actually, rather wanted to go too.

The Admiral's reaction was, to say the least, violent. Churchill said blandly that of course he would have to seek Cabinet approval for the King joining the expedition; unfortunately he would be unable to recommend them to give it. 'Fair enough,' said the King, until it rapidly became clear that the Prime Minister had no intention of applying this wise decision to himself.

Lascelles and Ramsay tried everything. Churchill sat plumply smiling.

'Your face is getting longer and longer,' the King said to his Secretary.

'I was thinking, Sir, that it's not going to make things easier for you if you have to find a new Prime Minister in the middle of "Overlord".'

'Oh, that's all arranged for,' said Churchill, 'and anyhow I don't think the risk is a hundred-to-one.'

Lascelles argued that he had always understood no Minister of the Crown could leave the country without the Sovereign's consent. He would be on a British man-of-war, said Churchill, and therefore on British territory. The King and his Private Secretary, defeated, left in dudgeon.

Bertie was very angry but controlled himself to write Churchill a long, reasonable letter:

> Please consider my own position. I am a sailor, & as King I am head of all three services. There is nothing I would like better than to go to sea but I have agreed to stop at home; is it fair that you should then do exactly what I would like to do myself? You said yesterday afternoon that it would be a fine thing for the King to lead his troops into battle, as in the old days; if the King cannot do this, it does not seem to me right that his Prime Minister should take his place ... I have been very worried & anxious over the whole of this business & it is my duty to warn the P.M. on such occasions. No one else can & should anything dreadful happen I should be asked if I had tried to deter him.[39]

After reading this Churchill nipped into his special train and sped to General Eisenhower's headquarters near Portsmouth. The King telephoned Lascelles and threatened to drive to Portsmouth himself to prevent Churchill embarking. Lascelles telephoned Churchill's train. The Prime Minister, knowing when he was beaten, gave in with a bad grace. If only the train had left half an hour earlier, he would have got away with it.

Churchill's account of the drama differs slightly. He sat down in the early hours and dashed off a letter to the King, which he sent by dispatch rider to Windsor:

> Sir, I cannot really feel that the first paragraph of your letter takes sufficient account of the fact that there is absolutely no comparison in the British Constitution between a Sovereign and a subject . . . as Prime Minister and Minister of Defence I ought to be allowed to go where I consider it necessary to the discharge of my duty, and I do not admit that the Cabinet have any right to put restrictions on my freedom of movement. I rely on my own judgement . . . I must earnestly ask Your Majesty that no principle shall be laid down which inhibits my freedom of movement when I judge it necessary to acquaint myself with conditions in the various theatres of war. Since Your Majesty does me the honour to be so much concerned about my personal safety on this occasion, I must defer to Your Majesty's wishes, and indeed commands.[40]

Thinking it over in later years Churchill, perhaps unwittingly, expressed the King's own feelings about the war: 'A man who has to play an effective part in taking, with the highest responsibility, grave and terrible decisions may need the refreshment of adventure. He may also need the comfort that when sending so many others to their death he may share in a small way their risks . . .' The King was just as frustrated as his Prime Minister, but he put up with it, for once, with more grace.

Three days later Allied forces landed in Normandy. The business of the House of Commons concerned a question as to why a disabled soldier had been refused a permit to open a shop in Wimbledon and a request from Lady Apsley, Conservative Member for Central Bristol, for an issue of berets to the ATS. Sir James Greig, the War Minister, replied that this was no time for new hats for the ATS and Sir Archibald Southby, Conservative member for Epsom, made a short and moving appeal for the right of women to new headgear in springtime. That night the King broadcast to his people: 'If from every place of worship, from home and factory, from men and women of all ages and many races and occupations, our intercessions rise,' God would see that we won the war. Bertie had a simple, filial belief in the Almighty; the probability the Germans were interceding just as unanimously did not trouble him. 'I am glad you liked my broadcast,' he wrote to his mother. 'The Bishop of Lichfield helped me with it.'[41]

# Chapter Twenty-Five

On 12 May 1940, after Churchill had taken over the government and war had begun, Elizabeth telephoned Crawfie at the Royal Lodge: 'I think you'd better go to Windsor Castle, anyway for the rest of the week.' Clara, still unable to understand any crisis that wasn't to do with dill-water, packed enough socks and knickers for a weekend and the two young Princesses were taken to the Castle for five years.

Windsor Castle covers something like thirteen acres. Lilibet, aged fourteen, slept with Bobo the nursery maid, Margaret with Clara. All the paintings had been taken down and the valuable furniture removed. Every room was lit by one bare light bulb; there was no heating and electric fires were seldom used, partly out of patriotism, partly because of power cuts. The air-raid shelter was a hastily converted dungeon and Crawfie's bathroom was out on the roof.

A company of Grenadier Guards, whose war-work was to defend the Princesses from possible kidnap or worse, soon arrived to liven things up. Daddy and Mummy came at weekends. Lilibet wore her Mickey Mouse gas mask for precisely the recommended period each day and carefully cleaned the eyepieces every evening with the ointment provided. She was a conscientious, worried girl. Crawfie and Margaret were distressingly frivolous. There was hide-and-seek and 'sardines' with the young Guardsmen and treasure hunts and the Madrigal Society and the Girl Guides; and, of course, the pantomimes.

*Cinderella*, the first of these, featured Lilibet as Prince Charming and Margaret as poor, deprived little Cinders. It all ended with a chorus of Guardsmen unfurling a Union Jack and everyone, the King and Queen included, singing their heads off. For this production Lilibet wore white satin knee-breeches but the following year, for *Sleeping Beauty*, she persuaded them to order a classic Principal Boy costume of jerkin and tights. Because or in spite of the fact that his daughter had reasonably attractive legs, her father snapped, 'Lilibet can't possibly wear that. The tunic is too short!' By 1943 and *Aladdin* Lilibet was seventeen, Philip of Greece in the audience and the costumes decorous if not particularly becoming. This was compensated for by what Lady Longford terms 'the Princesses' aptitude for rollicking satire':

*Widow Twankey*: There are three acres and one rood.
*Princess M.*: We don't want anything improper.
*Widow Twankey*: There's a large copper in the kitchen.
*Princess E.*: We'll soon get rid of him.[1]

After the finale the Queen might sing 'A Sailor's Wife a Sailor's Star Must Be' in duet with Philip's Aunt Edwina, accompanied at the piano by the skilful young Margaret. The Queen was also very fond of the songs of Vera Lynn and gave some poignant renderings of 'We'll Meet Again' and 'The White Cliffs of Dover'.

The girls' education obviously suffered from their confinement at Windsor. Elizabeth, not particularly concerned, agreed to Crawfie taking on a Mrs Montaudon-Smith to help out with French while Lilibet studied constitutional history with Henry Marten, the Vice-Provost of Eton, who addressed her, when necessary, as 'Gentlemen'.[2] Old Archbishop Lang's last act before his resignation was to prepare the heir to the throne for Confirmation: 'The night before I spent at the Castle and had a full talk with the little lady alone ... though naturally not very communicative, she showed real intelligence and understanding. I thought much, but rightly said little, of the responsibilities which may be awaiting her in the future.'[3]

Four months before the end of the war Lilibet joined the ATS as No. 230873 Second Subaltern Elizabeth Alexandra Mary Windsor, but slept every night at Windsor, possibly still with Bobo. On VE night both girls were set free for half an hour in the Mall. Chaperoned by Crawfie, Mrs Montaudon-Smith and a Major Phillips they weren't allowed to go to Piccadilly Circus but ran down St James's Street and shouted outside the Palace, 'We want the King! We want the Queen!' Then they went back by the garden gate and were given sandwiches by their mother. 'Poor darlings,' was Bertie's perplexing entry in his diary that night, 'they have never had any fun yet.'[4]

The rest of the family spent the war usefully, according to their lights, though none of them actually fought in it. Prince Henry Duke of Gloucester was gazetted as Chief Liaison Officer with the British Expeditionary Forces. 'My role as I see it,' he said, 'is to keep my wicket up for a time and just take the edge off the bowling until the star-turns on the side are ready to go in.'[5] Unfortunately the star-turn in France turned out to be his brother David, Duke of Windsor. Junior in rank to Harry, he took all the salutes and left Harry plodding along behind. The Duke of Gloucester, 'without knowing quite what he could have done, did feel that perhaps he ought to have done something.'[6]

His Duchess was pregnant again after suffering several miscarriages. Her X-rays were duly forwarded to Harry at the front, who desperately wanted the opinion of his commanding officer, Brigadier Fanshawe. 'The latter, not unnaturally, did not feel competent to give an opinion, and . . . was so anxious to avoid doing so that he slipped off to bed. Before he had undressed, however, he heard the Duke's foot on the stair and presently his knock at the door. Fanshawe, still in uniform, jumped smartly into bed. Prince Henry entered; Fanshawe feigned sleep; Prince Henry shook him . . .' The Duke was so taken up with the X-rays that he failed to enquire why his commanding officer had gone to bed in full uniform.[7] They sat for hours puzzling over the Duchess's pelvis.

Harry's next job was a diplomatic mission to the Near and Middle East and India, which ended with much hilarity bicycling along the passages of the Viceregal Residence in Delhi squirting Billy Ednam and Andrew Elphinstone with a fire hose. The Duchess of Gloucester gave birth to two sons during the war and at the end of 1944 the Duke, accompanied by his family, went off to be Governor General of Australia.

This post had been intended for George Duke of Kent but on the outbreak of war it was decided to keep him at home, presumably 'in case', a phrase constantly uppermost in royal minds. He was attached to the naval intelligence division of the Admiralty and spent the first year visiting naval establishments in Britain, finding plenty of time to rearrange his 'rich treasures . . . gold boxes, *étuis* and pretty, expensive objects' at Coppins, idly strumming Debussy while Marina occupied herself with backgammon.[8] The Kents might not have enjoyed Australia but the decision to keep him at home had tragic consequences.

In 1940 Georgie was appointed Staff Officer in the training command of the RAF and a year later toured Canada and the United States, where he hoped to meet his brother David, by then Governor of the Bahamas. This was not permitted. His brother-in-law, Prince Paul of Yugoslavia, was also in disgrace, having given in to the Axis and escaped with his wife to Greece, leaving the eighteen-year-old Peter (he who nearly drowned in the font) in charge. The Kents hurried off to Chequers to try and persuade Churchill to be merciful to Paul and Olga. Perhaps he was – they were sent to Kenya as 'privileged prisoners', which was certainly better than being captured by the Germans, but distressing and embarrassing to the Kents. Their elegant, brittle world was falling apart: David and Wallis, Paul and Olga, all banished; their friends cold-shouldered by the family, Elizabeth – who long ago had been one of them – unapproachable.

The Kents' younger son, Michael, was born in July 1942. On 25 August George started out from Invergordon in a Sunderland Flying Boat en route for Iceland. Half an hour later the 'plane crashed into a mountain-side and he and his entire crew, bar one, were killed outright. 'He was killed on Active Service,' the King wrote in his diary. It was the only consolation. After the misery of the funeral at Windsor he returned to Balmoral and went to the site of the crash: 'I met Dr Kennedy, who found him, the farmer Morrison & his son who led search parties . . . the ground for 200 yds long & 100 yds wide had been scored and scored by its trail & by flame. It hit one side of the slope, turned over in the air & slid down the other side on its back. The impact must have been terrific as the aircraft . . . was unrecognisable when found. I felt I had to do this pilgrimage.'9

Queen Mary, desolate, went to Coppins to comfort Marina. King George sent a cable to Princess Olga in Kenya asking her to return immediately. Olga used almost every known form of transport and, on the King's instructions, was given priority all the way; her journey, via Uganda, the Cameroons, Nigeria, Portugal and Ireland, took only a week.10 Nevertheless a month after her arrival a furious attack was launched against her in the Commons by Captain Alec Cunningham Reid, Conservative MP for Marylebone: 'We have deliberately brought this sinister woman over to the British Isles and have allowed her, to all intents and purposes, complete freedom . . . If you are a quisling and you happen to be royalty, it appears that you are automatically trusted and forgiven.'11 Again and again during the autumn of 1942 Captain Cunningham Reid tried to get Princess Olga incarcerated or sent back to her 'dangerous tiger . . . traitorous rat' of a husband. Nor was he entirely without supporters in this curious obsession.

There were some curious accidents during the war. In July 1943 one of the Queen's closest friends, Colonel Victor Cazalet MP, was killed in an unexplained aircrash over Gibraltar, together with General Sikorski, C-in-C of the exiled Free Polish forces. Around that time Marie Belloc Lowndes, an indefatigable diarist and know-all, dined with 'an airman friend': 'He told me a most curious secret, that an accident exactly similar to the Duke of Kent's had befallen a whole Air Mission going back to Russia. Every man was killed and apparently Russia thought it had been done on purpose. [He] seemed worried about the Duke of Kent's accident and said it should not have occurred, that the pilot should have been much higher in the sky.' But who could have had a sinister grudge against the inoffensive Georgie? Either Marie's airman friend was trying to impress, or knew more than was good for him.

Elizabeth and David Bowes-Lyon were 'alike as two pins'; their intimacy had survived both their marriages and he was a constant visitor at Sandringham and Balmoral. After he was sent to New York to take over the political warfare and propaganda work of British Security Co-ordination his sister must have been able to keep track of many devious schemes unknown to the public, including those that affected the Duke and Duchess of Windsor.

Bowes-Lyon's appointment was not popular, though many Americans were impressed by his royal connections and his charm. 'Both are wasting assets,' Sir Robert Bruce Lockhart wrote, 'because David has a poor mind and no knowledge of Europe. Moreover, he is full of suspicions and is quite incapable of "playing straight". In Jack's opinion [John Wheeler-Bennett, King George VI's official biographer] he is a bad man.'[12] Although Sir David quickly established a powerful social position in Washington it was soon reported that he was exceeding his powers and trading on his special status to assume functions far beyond the limited range of his ability. Brendan Bracken thought him 'an intriguer' and wanted to get rid of him, but Lord Halifax, now British Ambassador in Washington, supported him, so nothing could be done.

By the end of 1944 he was in serious trouble. 'Jack Wheeler-Bennett, who has an intimate knowledge of David Bowes-Lyon, has a low opinion of David's character and thinks that his capacity for intrigue and untruthfulness has almost no limit ... Young Miall [R Leonard Miall, a BBC executive], a former protégé of David's, told Jack today that David, whom Halifax allows to see the most secret telegrams, including those of the Prime Minister and the President, has a photographic apparatus in his Washington office and takes

photostats of important secret documents which he is permitted to
see but not to keep . . . These photostats he used to send to Miall in
New York, although they had no bearing whatever on his work. If this
were known in London, David would be sacked, King's brother-in-law
notwithstanding.'*

Princess Mary must have spent her war much like tens of millions
of other women, worrying about her sons, both of whom were active
soldiers, and trying to make ends meet. She and Lord Harewood frequently stayed with the Beauforts at Badminton, where her mother,
under the guise of being a guest, conducted what amounted to a court
in exile.

Apart from George's death, the bombing of Marlborough House
and her constant anxiety about the royal relations, Queen Mary had
a wonderful war. The day after it was declared she set out with most
of her staff, sixty-three persons and their dependents, and drove via
Peterborough, Oundle and Northampton to Althorp, where she had
a pleasant lunch with Lord and Lady Spencer. On through Oxford,
Chippenham and Swindon – 'a lovely drive' – to be greeted at Badminton by her niece, the Duchess of Beaufort, with a certain degree of
apprehension – the convoy sweeping up to the house seemed endless.
The Queen Dowager lost no time in organising herself and the entire
household. She selected a bedroom on the first floor with an adjacent
sitting room and bathroom and splendid outlook across the park; she
also chose a dining room and decided that the Beauforts' dining room
– which they never used, after all – would do very nicely for receiving
guests she did not invite upstairs. 'Pandemonium was the least it could
be called!' the Duchess wrote to Osbert Sitwell. 'The servants revolted,
and scorned our humble home. They refused to use the excellent
rooms assigned to them. Fearful rows and battle royals fought over
my body – but I won in the end and reduced them to tears and pulp.
I can laugh now, but I have never been so angry! . . . The Queen,
quite unconscious of the stir, has settled in well, and is busy cutting
down trees and tearing down ivy. Tremendous activity.'[13]

Queen Mary was not a countrywoman. She had never learned

*When Sir David Bowes-Lyon KCVO died on 13 September 1961 his obituary in
the *Times* went no further in explaining Sir David's work as head of the Political
Warfare Mission than to say 'some of [this] work has remained secret. Certainly
Bowes-Lyon's range went much further than his ostensible brief and beyond the
terms of reference that have been made public.'

to ride, seldom owned a dog, her gardening consisted of tours of inspection. But she passionately hated ivy. On 25 September: 'Lovely morning which we spent clearing ivy off the trees while Jack Coke [Major the Hon. Sir John Coke KCVO] hacked off branches of 2 chestnut trees & an elm & the gardeners began to clear a wall of ivy near Mary B's bedroom.' Next day: 'Lovely morning which we spent clearing ivy off trees – we watched a whole wall of ivy of 50 years standing at the back of Mary B's bedroom being removed – most of it came down like a blanket.'[14] When most of the ivy had been demolished (she learned to destroy the roots after realising that nature niftily replaced the rest), she turned her attention to Wooding, setting off in her old green Daimler every afternoon with hacksaws and other lethal implements tied to the back. The Queen Dowager conducted the operations, poking at recalcitrant branches with her walking stick, and the casualty list was formidable: two chauffeurs knocked out, quite apart from splinters, wounds, sprains and fractures.[15] The Duke narrowly escaped having his ancient and historic cedar tree felled to the ground. Luckily the Queen's attention was diverted to Scrap.

Scrap may have helped to satisfy her craving for collecting – a piece of bone left by a fox, fragments of old iron, bottles galore, tins and wire and shards of china, she pounced on it all. One day she returned from a walk in triumph, dragging behind her a large piece of rusty old iron to add to the royal dump. It turned out to be a plough belonging to a neighbouring farmer – 'and will Your Majesty graciously give it back to him, please, at once, as he can't get on without it.' The alternative, perhaps more likely version of this story is that the plough was quietly returned to its owner without the Queen's knowledge.

Owing to the proximity of Bristol and Bath there were constant air-raid warnings. Until she learned to disregard the tiresome things Queen Mary was always first in the shelter, composed, perfectly dressed and sitting bolt upright doing the crossword while everyone else shuffled in half asleep.[16] She followed the news with passionate personal interest that gives the impression she would have set about Hitler with a rolling pin had she been able: 'What a vile enemy, I feel very bitter – Poor Christian of Denmark and poor Charles of Norway!'[17] One of her greatest pleasures was giving lifts to pedestrian soldiers, sailors and airmen, particularly Americans. There was no condescension in her interest, no need to exert her charm. In her stately way she was humble, eager to learn about the people from whom she had been segregated so long. On VE Day she listened to Bertie's speech and dear Mr Churchill's, then went to the local pub where the village was celebrating: 'We sang songs, a friendly affair and amusing.'[18]

When at last she had to go home, back to her pedestal, Queen Mary wept in public for the first time in her life. 'Oh, I *have* been happy here! Here I've been anybody to everybody, and back in London I shall have to begin being Queen Mary all over again!'[19] She was seventy-five, too old to abdicate. Perhaps the delights of Wooding and Scrap and waging war against ivy would have palled in peace-time. Even so it is sad to see her disappearing once more into her calm, doomed world of privilege.

# Chapter Twenty-Six

There have been countless books and much controversy about the treatment of the Duke and Duchess of Windsor, but there is still no satisfactory explanation. What evidence there is gets exploited in the interests of those who sympathise with it. The majority, despising him for giving up the throne and frittering his life away, refuses to believe any argument in his favour, however well substantiated; the few elderly Cavaliers still in love with the image of the Prince of Wales ('in love' may seem a curious term, but it most accurately describes their feelings), can have it proved to them chapter and verse that he was a petulant ne'er-do-well, but they won't believe it. Until the present heir to the throne made the mistake of not getting on with his wife, David Windsor and Hamlet were the two princes in history to provide topics of inexhaustible speculation.

Almost no one doubted Queen Elizabeth's sweet and charitable nature until historian Michael Bloch suggested a different version.[1] After that various writers began implying that far from being the darling little creature she appeared, she had conducted a single-handed vendetta against the Windsors and ruthlessly, without a tremor of pity, destroyed them. Even if this could have been proved it would not have convinced her adorers. Nor would it have made the slightest difference to Wallis, or to others on the receiving end of British policy towards the Windsors at that time, if they had been given irrefutable evidence of the Queen's generosity of heart. What people believe is very seldom based on fact; opinions are formed by personal taste, the result of God knows what individual experience.

Begging the question as to why David was in exile at all, let alone why he had to be humiliated over his wife's title and so thoroughly ostracised, there is no doubt that he made the first wrong move. On 1 September Walter Monckton telephoned the Duke to say the King would send a plane of the King's Flight the next day to fly him and the

Duchess back to England. This could not have been an easy decision for Bertie and Elizabeth. War was about to be declared, they were up to their eyes in problems. David himself might be kept busy in some fairly remote corner of the British Isles, but what about Wallis? Nevertheless the tiresome couple couldn't just be abandoned.

The Duke, apparently unable to grasp the situation, refused to go without a personal invitation from Their Majesties to stay at Windsor. Monckton foolishly repeated this to Bertie and Elizabeth. The plane was cancelled. A week later Monckton arrived at Antibes in a small, dilapidated Leopard Moth, clearly impractical for transporting the Duke and Duchess, let alone their luggage and dogs. He brought the news that the former King would only be allowed to return if he agreed to become either Deputy Regional Commissioner in Wales or Liaison Officer with the Howard-Vyse Mission in France.[2] The Duke agreed to these conditions and on the night of 12 September, in the pitch blackout, he and Wallis arrived at Portsmouth from Cherbourg. Churchill had organised a guard of honour and a Royal Marine band to play God Save the King but otherwise they were met by two people – Walter Monckton and Lady Alexandra Metcalfe. There was no representative of the family, no message, no car, and nowhere to stay. 'Officially, the Royal Family had decided to treat the ex-King, as much as possible, as though he were a dead person.'[3]

Since he had been its Prince and rashly promised that something would be done about it, the Duke felt vaguely responsible for Wales and decided to take the job of Deputy Regional Commissioner. On 14 September he went to see his brother at the Palace, a meeting Monckton had been able to arrange only by 'the exclusion of women'. The brothers were together for an hour. 'He seems very well,' the King wrote to Chamberlain, '& not a bit worried as to the effects he left on people's minds as to his behaviour in 1936. He has forgotten all about it.'[4] Something must have been said, however, or implied that worried him. After discussing it with his closest adviser, he wrote to the Minister for War, Leslie Hore-Belisha, that his brother would be most suitably employed in France rather than Wales. Next day Hore-Belisha told the Duke of this decision. The Duke asked whether he could first be attached to various Commands in England, in order to get to know soldiers again; and, he added, he would like to take Wallis with him.

The reply was inevitable. The following morning Hore-Belisha was summoned to the Palace. The King 'thought that if the Duchess went to the Commands she might have a hostile reception, particularly in Scotland. He did not want the Duke to go to the Commands in England. He seemed very distressed and walked up and down the room. He said the Duke had never had any discipline in his life . . . HM remarked that all his ancestors had succeeded to the throne after their predecessors had died. 'Mine is not only alive, but very much so.' The King thought it better for the Duke to proceed to Paris at once.'[5] On 27 September Major-General HRH The Duke of Windsor sailed for France.

General Sir Alan Brooke, Chief of the Imperial General Staff, noted that Major-General Howard-Vyse 'has instructions to guard against his endeavouring to stage any kind of "come-back" with the troops out here.'[6] The instructions were in vain; British and French troops gave the Duke an uproarious welcome. He was back at work (something which his younger brother should have understood), 'full of go and interest'.[7] 'We passed into Br. Sector & went to our GHQ and there met Gort and his chief-of-staff also the Duke of Gloucester.' 'Fruity' Metcalfe wrote to his wife: 'Everyone here was delighted to see HRH & the visit could not have gone better. It was very important to HRH as you can well imagine.'[8] Shortly after, the Duke of Windsor automatically returned the salute of a company guard intended for his senior-ranking brother Harry. The two men may have found this quite a joke, but some days later the former King was severely reprimanded for violating military etiquette. 'David shrugged the incident off,' wrote Wallis, 'but . . . we had two wars to deal with, the big and still leisurely war, in which everybody was caught up, and the little cold war with the Palace, in which no quarter was given.'[9]

Secret instructions went out from the Court to ensure that in future the Duke acquired no personal publicity or prestige. He was to be 'punished' by a period of inactivity.[10] 'My brother-in-law [the King] arrives in France tomorrow,' Wallis told her Aunt Bessie, 'but competition still exists in the English mind – so one must hide so there is no rivalry. All very childish except that the biggest men take it seriously. Anyway the Duke can leave the front and spend those days with me so that the cheers are guaranteed.'[11] Once Bertie was safely back in England David set off to visit the Second French Army and sent a prescient report. It was disregarded.

On 9 April Germany invaded Denmark and Norway. Harry was winched out of Boulogne and flown back to England in advance of the retreating British Army, but the Duke of Windsor received no instructions or information. A month later he went to the British

Embassy and asked Sir Ronald Campbell if he could be temporarily seconded to the Armée des Alpes, where he could inspect the French forces drawn up along the Italian frontier and pack up his possessions at La Croe. For once his suggestion was accepted. The Windsors arrived in Antibes on the day the British Army began the evacuation of Dunkirk.

Ten days later the French government fled from Paris to Tours and Italy declared war on France and England. The Riviera emptied but there was still no word from England as to what the Windsors were expected to do. France surrendered on 16 June. The German armies were at Dijon, heading for the Rhone Valley. David 'phoned the British Embassy to ask if he and Wallis could be evacuated by the Royal Navy. He was told it was out of the question.

On 19 June, with the Germans only 200 miles to the north, they joined a convoy of consular-refugees heading for the Spanish frontier. '*Je suis le Prince de Galles. Laissez-moi passer, s'il vous plaît,*' the Duke shouted at every barrier, and they did. Then he was refused visas at the border on the grounds that he might become a charge on the neutral Spanish government. A 'phone call to the Spanish Ambassador in France put matters right and on 20 June they finally arrived in Barcelona. The Duke cabled Churchill: 'Having received no instructions have arrived Spain to avoid capture. Proceeding to Madrid. Edward.'

With a decisive slamming of the stable door, Churchill cabled: 'We should like Your Royal Highness to come home as soon as possible,' and told him that two flying-boats had been ordered to proceed to Lisbon to pick them up. At the same time Alec Hardinge wrote a furious letter to the Foreign Office saying 'the King has noted with extreme displeasure that the Duke and Duchess had been referred to as "Their Royal Highnesses". His Majesty's express wish is that steps be taken to ensure that such an official error should never occur again.'

At the risk of falling into the usual trap I cannot believe this ceaseless persecution was instigated by the King. Bertie was fussy, intensely correct and could be childish but there is no indication that he was actually vindictive, except towards Lady Sybil Graham's dog. It is unlikely that Alec Hardinge and his colleagues acted without consulting him. Basically it was a family situation and David, after all, was his brother. Who had sufficient influence to make him behave in this uncharacteristic way?

In July 1940 the German Ambassador in Madrid reported to

the German Foreign Ministry that Miguel Primo de Rivera, leader of the Madrid Falangists, had just returned from Lisbon: 'He had two long conversations with the Duke of Windsor; at the last one the Duchess was present also . . . The Duke and Duchess have less fear of the King, who was quite foolish, (*"reichlich töricht"*), than of the shrewd Queen, who was intriguing skilfully against the Duke and particularly the Duchess.' This could be the Windsors' paranoia or Teutonic make-believe.

On the same day the Windsors reached Lisbon Churchill was summoned to the Palace. The Duke received a telegram the following morning: 'I am authorised by the King and Cabinet to offer you the appointment of Governor and Commander-in-Chief of the Bahamas . . . Personally I feel sure that it is the best option in the grievous situation in which we all stand. At any rate I have done my best.' Lord Beaverbrook remarked that the Duke would be very relieved. 'Not half as much as his brother will,' Churchill replied.[12]

The Duke had already made arrangements to return to England on the flying-boat of RAF Coastal Command waiting, as promised, in Lisbon harbour. He dropped every condition for his return except one: that he and Wallis should be received just once by his brother and sister-in-law, if only for a few minutes, and that notice of the fact should appear in the Court Circular. The result was a rap over the knuckles: 'Your Highness has taken active military rank, and refusal to obey direct orders of competent military authority would create a serious situation. I hope it will not be necessary for such orders to be sent.'[13] Any kind of life the Duke and Duchess might lead in England would clearly be intolerable. The ex-Liege Lord, by the Grace of God, of Great Britain, Ireland and the British Dominions beyond the Seas, Defender of the Faith and Emperor of India accepted the job. Churchill explained to the Dominions: 'The position of the Duke of Windsor on the Continent in recent months has been causing His Majesty and His Majesty's government embarrassment . . . There are personal and family difficulties about his return to this country . . .'

David, perhaps trying to keep some shreds of dignity and self-respect, made a foolish fuss about getting two servants released from the Army. Vitriolic cables shot back and forth. The German invasion was expected any day, but that did not prevent a long wrangle about how the Windsors were to get to Nassau. The obvious route via America was not allowed. Finally, on 1 August the Duke of Windsor sailed from Lisbon on the SS *Excalibur* (re-routed and insured at a cost of $17,500) as a representative of the Crown that refused to grant his wife a five-minute audience.

Although the Battle of Britain was said to be taking up all Their Majesties' energies, even in the Bahamas, the uttermost end of the earth, the Windsors were not let off the hook. Senior Government House officials in Nassau had already received a message from the Lord Chamberlain: 'You are no doubt aware that a lady when presented to HRH the Duke of Windsor should make a half-curtsey. The Duchess of Windsor is not entitled to this. The Duke should be addressed as "Your Royal Highness", and the Duchess as "Your Grace".'14

Nassau was hot, uncomfortable and deadly dull; there was plenty of time to brood on it all. The Duke wrote long letters protesting bitterly about 'the mean and petty humiliations in which a now semi-Royal Family' – a direct and snobbish dig at Elizabeth – 'with the co-operation of the government has indulged itself for the last four years.'15 Possibly they were never sent, but they helped to relieve his misery and anger. He did his job competently, even well, but it was not what he had been trained for. His long experience enabled him to put a royal face on it, but as a man he was crumbling.

David heard the news of Georgie's death on the Empire Service of the BBC. Telegrams from Queen Mary and Lord Halifax followed, but nothing from Balmoral. It was a knockout blow. The brothers had understood each other's deviations from the royal norm; he had supported George through all the early scandals; even if there were some tricky moments when his younger brother's loyalty had seemed questionable, their devotion to each other withstood David's abdication and marriage. That they had not been allowed to meet either in Portugal or America added bitterness to his misery. There was no substitute for his relationship with George, any more than there could be a substitute for Wallis.

He wanted to share his grief with his family, but he had no family. Like his brothers, he had never been what is known as a 'strong' character and had even less grasp of reality. David's best qualities were a naïve, almost childish goodwill, enormous energy and a talent for being loved. After his brother's death these qualities began to disintegrate until finally, as an old man, the Duke of Windsor seemed little more than an empty husk.

Wallis too, in spite of her efficient work with the Red Cross, her Infant Welfare Clinics and successful efforts to keep up appearances, began to suffer a long, painful deterioration that would continue for the next thirty years. Approaching fifty and in constant pain from various abdominal troubles, her letters to Aunt Bessie became increasingly agitated and indecipherable – some RAF officers were leaving, 'one hopes there will be more adonises and Don Juans in the new lot'. By the end of the war the brisk, witty, odd-looking Wallis Simpson, who had coped so admirably with her unlooked-for rôle in the Abdication, was unrecognisable to anyone but her love-blinded husband.

The Duke resigned his Governorship in March 1945. On VE Day he and Wallis were in Palm Beach and the following month they left for Europe on the US troopship *Argentina*. The ship called at Plymouth en route for Le Havre but the Windsors did not disembark. They appeared on deck, waved at the crowds in the best balcony tradition and the Duke told reporters yes, he would very much like a job. On 5 October he flew from Paris to London and stayed with his mother at Marlborough House: 'At 4 David arrived by plane from Paris on a visit to me – I had not seen him for nearly 9 years! It was a great joy meeting him again, he looked very well – Bertie came to dinner to meet him.'[16]

The following Sunday David went to see Bertie alone – a meeting that seems to have given him much encouragement, for he wrote shortly afterwards from Paris:

> Dear Bertie,
>    I was very glad to see you in London after so long an interval and to find you looking so well and vigorous after the strain of the last six years of total war . . . don't forget that I have suffered many unnecessary embarrassments from official sources uncomplainingly in the last nine years, but I have reason to believe from the spirit of your recent two long talks with me that it is now your desire that these should cease.
>    The truth of the whole matter is that you and I happen to be two prominent personages placed in one of the most unique situations in history, the dignified handling of which is entirely yours and my responsibility, and ours alone. It is a situation from which we cannot escape and one that will always be watched with interest by the whole world. I can see no reason why we should not be able to handle it in the best interests of both of us, and I can only assure you that I will continue to play my part to this end . . .[17]

The King did not reply for a month. When he did so it was to the effect that there was no question of official work for his brother in peace-time, but that everything would be done to facilitate any plans he might have to leave Europe for good and spend the rest of his life in America.

# Chapter Twenty-Seven

On 2 August 1945, three months after the end of the European war, the King met President Truman on board the battlecruiser *Renown* in Plymouth Sound. Most of the conversation over lunch was concerned with the atom bomb.

'It sounds like a professor's dream to me,' growled Admiral Leahy.

'Would you like to lay a little bet on that, Admiral?'

Four days later Hiroshima and 200,000 of its citizens disappeared in a mushroom cloud. Three days after that 150,000 people were wiped out in Nagasaki. Japan surrendered. Services of National Thanksgiving had already been held in St Paul's and St Giles' Cathedrals for the defeat of Germany and God received no extra thanks for this latest miracle.

The new method of waging war brought with it a new method of conducting peace. The keynote from now on would not be prosperity, equality, the advancement of civilisation or simply having a nice time, but survival. From the word go it was extremely dreary. Anyone who was conscious in the late Forties and Fifties will remember that everything seemed sludge-coloured. People moved about with weary caution in clothes that looked as though they had been made out of something else, and frequently were: skirts made out of curtains, trousers out of overcoats, nameless garments out of dishcloths and old ribbon. Bread was rationed for the first time; taxation went up. The Labour Government was in again, showing the country's gross ingratitude to Churchill. By September 1947 the King was writing to his mother, 'I do wish one could see a glimmer of a bright spot anywhere in world affairs. Never in the whole history of mankind have things looked gloomier than they do now.'[1]

On the other hand, the Queen, who bore the family off to Balmoral that summer, determined they should enjoy themselves, appeared to be 'a happy little woman who might easily break into

"Lily of Laguna" at breakfast time or while away a motor drive with "Daisy, Daisy" . . . Eating what she liked, regardless of her figure. A lover of sweets. A woman who . . . referred to her Hartnell creations as "my props" . . . A non-photogenic woman . . . A woman whose courage and love had helped to cure the King's impediment. A woman with a dog. Not smart, not sporty . . . A woman who knew that change was coming, and went with the tide. The woman who knew, when she married Bertie, that a wife could make or mar him. The woman who had made Bertie.'[2] Even given the fact that it was taken in brilliant sunshine, not a cloud in the sky, the picture is endearing.

It was an indifferent year for grouse so the King and Lilibet set off with their party on a lethal treasure hunt to see how many kinds of wildlife they could shoot or trap. They ended up bagging nineteen varieties, including one mountain hare, two capercailzie, a heron, a sparrow hawk, three rabbits, one roedeer and six ptarmigan, while Lilibet felled a stag. Lord Eldon, whose friendship with Elizabeth went back to the old Glamis days, was detailed to collect fish. He caught two salmon and after being rowed up and down the loch for two hours by 'one of the ladies', a few small brown trout. In spite of the bewildering lack of any spoils of war the King recorded in his game book that it had been 'a lovely day'.

That autumn Lady Airlie went to Sandringham for the first time in six years. She found many changes:

> In the entrance hall there now stood a baize-covered table on which jigsaw puzzles were set out. The younger members of the party – the Princesses and several young Guardsmen – congregated round them from morning till night. The radio, worked by Princess Elizabeth, blared incessantly . . . One sensed far more the setting of ordinary family life . . . It was in the way in which the King said, 'You must ask Mummy' when his daughters wanted to do something . . . In Princess Margaret's pout when the Queen sent her back to the house to put on a thicker coat . . . In the way both sisters teased, and were teased by, the young Guardsmen to whom Queen Mary referred when we were alone together as 'The Body Guard'.[3]

After six years of being cloistered at Windsor the Princesses were making the most of their freedom, even if the most they could make of it was to do jigsaw puzzles, flirt with a carefully selected group of officers and shoot the odd stag. Lilibet, however, was better off than her sister; she now had a regular *beau*. 'They have been in love for the last eighteen months,' Queen Mary told Lady Airlie in strictest confidence. 'In fact longer, I think. I believe she fell in love with him the first time he went down to Windsor, but the King and Queen feel that she is too young to be engaged yet. They want her to see more of the world before committing herself, and to meet more men. After all she's only nineteen, and one is very impressionable at that age.'[4]

Prince Philip of Greece was dazzlingly handsome at that time, whatever his other merits. Unfortunately he was not only a Greek national, but sixth in succession to the Greek throne, the whereabouts of which, at the time, were far from clear. The Prince, who spent much of his early life in England, was sent to Cheam preparatory school when he was nine years old. Two years later he had a short period at Kurt Hahn's Salem school on Lake Constance. Hahn was arrested by the Nazis, released after a direct appeal from Ramsay Macdonald to President Hindenburg and came over to start Gordonstoun in Scotland on the same spartan and highminded principles as Salem. Philip was there for four years before he joined the British Navy.

In 1940, when Italy invaded Greece, he became an ally and was transferred from convoy duty to active service, but if he wished to have a permanent commission in the Navy, let alone marry the Heir Apparent, he would have to become a British subject. His cousin, King George II, had given his permission; but his cousin was in Cairo and no one knew whether he would ever return to the Greek throne. If Philip were given British citizenship it might be thought that Britain was supporting the Royalist cause; on the other hand it might look as though the prospects for the Greek monarchy were so bad that members of the Greek Royal Family House were leaving a sinking ship. Therefore the King was advised that it would be wiser to postpone the question of Philip's naturalisation until March 1946, when they would know the result of the Greek plebiscite on the monarchy.

The plebiscite resulted in a declaration calling on George II to return to Athens – good news. But now there was a further complication. If Philip, as a Greek royal in direct succession to the throne, were to renounce his nationality immediately after the restoration, it would be very unhelpful to the Greek King's cause. Again the best course was to wait.

When a suitable time had passed, the problem was tackled once more. What would the young man be called? He decided on 'Lieutenant Philip – R.N.' Excellent, but Lieutenant Philip what? The Royal House of Greece and Denmark did not have a family name

– it had never been considered necessary – so something must be invented. What about 'Oldcastle'? It was an anglicisation of 'Oldenburg', the original name of the House of Schleswig-Holstein-Sonderburg-Glucksburg. Perhaps not. What about 'Battenburg' then, already translated into 'Mountbatten'? Splendid. The announcement that Lt Philip Mountbatten R.N. had taken British citizenship was made at last in the *London Gazette* of 18 March 1947, at which time his intended fiancée was in South Africa with her family.

The South African tour of February 1947 was primarily intended for the opening of the Union Parliament in Cape Town, but it also provided a change after the rigours of war and a breathing space for Lilibet who might, even now, change her mind. It was an unfortunate coincidence that conditions in Britain were at their worst. Sixteen degrees of frost were recorded in London. Iceburgs were observed off the Norfolk Coast. Trains stopped running and froze to their sidings, power stations ran out of coal, there was no electric power for many industries, the export rate was nil. Unemployment rose to 2½ million, cattle and sheep died in their thousands, old people and children in their hundreds. As the entire Royal Family, with an accompanying entourage of ten courtiers, slipped away from Portsmouth in the *Vanguard*, claims of 'We Stay With Our People, We Are Not Afraid' had a distinctly hollow ring. It was all very well to share their sufferings in spirit, but the people felt that their King and Queen should be at home, tripping through fourteen-foot snowdrifts, looking the power cuts in the face.

So, of course, did the King. On their arrival at Cape Town one of the first things he did was cable Prime Minister Attlee expressing Their Majesties' 'sympathy with the people of Britain and their earnest hope for an early alleviation of their present hardships.'[5] In spite of this reassurance reports of criticism continued to arrive. Attlee felt that it would be bad for morale to curtail the tour, as the King had anxiously suggested, especially in the eyes of foreign observers. There was nothing for it, then, but to face the sunshine with courage.

There were one or two mishaps at the opening of Parliament: the King and Queen were nearly swept off their feet when the red carpet caught on the royal car while it was reversing and the King lost his temper with the guard of honour because they failed to present arms at the right time. It was something of a relief to set off on their two-month tour in the proudly named 'White Train'.

The royal party was accompanied by the Press, among whom was a rather bemused James Cameron:

> The King kept saying he should be at home and not lolling about in the summer sun; never was a man so jumpy . . . One evening he called some of us Press people along to his dining car, ostensibly because he had a communication to make, but more probably to relieve the deadly boredom . . . We found him behind a table covered with bottles of all sorts of things, with which it would seem he had been experimenting with some dedication. 'We must not f-forget the purpose of this t-tour,' he said . . . 'trade and so on. Empire cooperation. For example. South African b-brandy. I have been trying it. It is of course m-magnificent, except that it is not very nice. But,' he said triumphantly, 'there is this South African liqueur called V-Van der Humm. Perhaps a little sweet for most. But now, if you mix half of brandy with half of Van der Humm . . . Please try.

The Pressmen tried. A hundred or so miles of South Africa passed very pleasantly. When the train stopped at some wayside halt (the organisers had learned the lesson of Canada), Elizabeth would entreat her agonised husband, 'Oh, Bertie, do you see? This is Hicksdorp! You know we've always wanted to see Hicksdorp! Those people there with the bouquets – they must be the local councillors. How kind! And those people at the far end of the platform, behind that little fence – I expect they are the Bantu choir. How kind! *Wave*, Bertie!' And with a little nudge, the King found himself on terra firma, clearly wishing he were anywhere else on earth, with his wife just as clearly having waited all her life to see Hicksdorp.[6]

Sometimes the King commanded the train to stop so that he could have a swim. One evening it drew to a halt on the verge of a broad beach near Port Elizabeth. Police appeared on the sands and roped off the vast crowd of onlookers into two halves.

> Down the path from the Royal Train walked a solitary figure in a blue bathrobe, carrying a towel. The sea was a long way off, but he went. And all alone, on the great empty beach, between the surging banks of the people who might not approach, the King of England stepped into the edge of the Indian Ocean and jumped up and down – the loneliest man, at that moment, in the world.[7]

Everyone else reported the usual triumphant success. 'Laughing boys and girls, cool and clean and sunburnt, their fair hair blown by the wind, cheered them through the streets . . . (In the Rand) hundreds of thousands of sweating, screaming, frenzied blacks lined the route and hollered their ecstatic joy at this sight of this little family of four, so fresh and white.'[8] The King's equerry, Peter Townsend, gave a moving description of Africans who had waited all day at wayside halts on the veldt bursting into song as the train steamed in, 'haunting, melodious airs, drifting on the limpid night air, under a starry sky.' He and the Royal Family nearly split their sides when they heard a police officer explaining to a group of piccaninies: 'That is Mr King and next to him Mrs King; then just behind, Princess Elizabeth King and Princess Margaret King.'[9] How charming they were, these simple people.

But although the King and Queen believed implicitly in their black subjects' loyalty, Nelson Mandela had already formed the African National Congress Party and there were times when they felt a little uneasy. The King was definitely edgy the day they left the train to drive to Benoni. His back-seat driving became intolerable to everyone but his wife, and even she was unable to calm him down. As they drove into Benoni 'a black and wiry' man, clutching something in his hand, sprinted purposefully after the car and grabbed the handle of the passenger door. The Queen, with great presence of mind, attacked him with her parasol, breaking it in two. It was later revealed that the assailant had been trying to give Lilibet a ten shilling note for her birthday. 'I hope he was not badly hurt,' the King said kindly.[10]

By 21 April they were back in Cape Town for Lilibet's coming-of-age broadcast to the Dominions. 'I declare before you all,' she piped in her schoolgirl voice, 'that my whole life, whether it be long or short, shall be devoted to your service and the service of the great Imperial Commonwealth to which we all belong. But I shall not have strength to carry out this resolution unless you join in it with me, as I now invite you to do; I know that your support will be unfailingly given. God bless all of you who are willing to share in it.' In the same city nearly half a century later Nelson Mandela, President of the South African Republic, gave a banquet in her honour. Tactfully replacing her request for God's blessing by hope for good weather the Queen said, 'Next year I look forward to welcoming you, Mr President, on the first ever visit to Britain by a South African head of State. It will happen as we approach the end of the twentieth century and peer into the next. The view may sometimes be a little obscure, but the events in South Africa of the last few years have helped to bring rays of sunshine to pierce the mist. May the sun shine ever brighter.'

Meanwhile the Princesses galloped along the sands and across the veldt, Lilibet 'competent and classic', Margaret 'pretty and dashing', until Peter Townsend beat them by a neck back to the train. Bertie and Elizabeth knew their youngest daughter had 'a terrific crush' on Townsend but they didn't take it seriously. It was rather sweet that their sixteen-year-old baby worshipped him – just like a big brother. They returned to England to face the more significant and complex problem of Lilibet's marriage.

Philip had been invited to Balmoral for a month the previous summer so that they could assess his character, behaviour, habits and prospects. Bertie may secretly have hoped to find him lacking. Although Philip passed the test, it was certainly not for his ease of expression: 'I suppose one thing led to another. I suppose I began to think about it seriously, oh, let me think now, when I got back in 'forty-six and went to Balmoral. It was probably then that we, that it became, you know, that we began to think about it seriously and even talk about it. And then there was their excursion to South Africa, and it was sort of fixed up when they came back. That's what really happened.'[11]

On 10 July 1947 Buckingham Palace announced that Their Majesties' daughter, the Princess Elizabeth, was betrothed to Lieutenant Philip Mountbatten R.N., son of the late Prince Andrew of Greece and Princess Andrew. At the beginning of October Philip was received into the Church of England by Geoffrey Fisher, Archbishop of Canterbury, who had 'talked to my beloved old Archbishop Germanos, the representative of the Ecumenical Patriarch in England, a grand man. He saw the point.'[12] On 20 November the couple were married in Westminster Abbey. The bride, it was announced, had been allotted a hundred extra clothing coupons for her trousseau and her bridesmaids twenty-three each. Her mother, playing this rôle for the first time, was barely mentioned. Chips Channon, who had not been 'commanded', was rather off-hand about the whole thing. He did, however, go to the reception at St James's Palace to view the wedding presents, which apart from his own, Queen Mary's and the Nizam of Hyderabad's, he thought 'ghastly'.[13] *Plus ça change . . .*

'We keep wondering whether Philip realises what he's in for,' the King was heard to say at a cocktail party that autumn.[14] Whatever his private opinion of his son-in-law, he was as miserable about his daughter's marriage as his father had been about Princess Mary's. Perhaps it says something about royal marriages in general; or, more likely, the relationship of sovereigns to their daughters.

Queen Victoria had much preferred her daughters to her sons; their weddings had all the sprightliness of funerals. King Edward VII didn't seem to suffer from this intense possessiveness, but his wife did. 'Alix found them such companions, that she would not encourage their marrying, and ... they themselves had no inclination for it.'[15] Perhaps this is a common phenomenon, but the isolation royalty imposes on itself is not common. Bertie had found a friend in his twenty-one-year-old daughter. They were very alike – practical, conscientious and pessimistic. Margaret and her mother were what Queen Mary called 'espiègle' – mischievous, roguish, arch, perpetually playing games. He was going to miss Lilibet dreadfully. 'I was so proud of you & thrilled at having you so close to me on our long walk in Westminster Abbey, but when I handed your hand to the Archbishop I felt that I had lost something very precious,' he wrote in one of those customary, blighting honeymoon letters. '. . . Your leaving has left a great blank in our lives but do remember that your old home is still yours & do come back to it as much & as often as possible. I can see that you are sublimely happy with Philip which is right but don't forget us is the wish of Your ever loving & devoted Papa.'[16]

If it was necessary for Elizabeth to think of her husband as her King, which according to her mother-in-law it was, then presumably it was equally necessary to think of Lilibet as the Heir Apparent. From that point of view Philip seemed as suitable, in his way, as Albert had seemed to Victoria, Duchess of Kent (not that the Duchess had much say in the matter). Lilibet and Philip were third cousins through the lineage of Queen Victoria, second cousins once removed through Christian IX of Denmark, and fourth cousins once removed through collateral descendants of George III. Therefore as Prince and Princess they were clearly made for each other.

As a man he was possibly a little Philistine for Elizabeth's taste. Like young Margaret, she preferred a lean and hungry look, a hint of sensitivity, a touch of rumpled charm. Philip's family, too, presented difficulties. She did not altogether trust the Mountbattens and Philip's mother, née Princess Alice of Battenberg, was definitely odd. A wonderful woman, of course; but odd. Elizabeth in her baby-blue, with her lilting voice and winsome ways and rippling giggle, was indeed a remarkable contrast to the gaunt, sombre Greek princess in her nun's habit. Twenty years later, when Lilibet was Queen, Alice would make her home in Buckingham Palace where, according to Lord Louis Mountbatten, she had more influence on the Queen than anyone. 'The Queen adored her . . . she is fond of her mother, but got on infinitely better with my sister.'[17] As Elizabeth waved goodbye to her daughter and son-in-law on their way to honeymoon at Uncle Dickie's country estate she knew that having Mountbattens in the family was not going to be easy.

# Chapter Twenty-Eight

Apparently forgetting the disaster of White Lodge, the King and Queen had chosen Clarence House as a suitable residence for their daughter and son-in-law, who thought it dilapidated and uninhabitable. The government voted £250,000 for its repair since 'even a nation in economic difficulties was not willing to see its heiress presumptive [sic] and her husband housed indefinitely in three rooms in the Palace.'[1] This wasn't strictly the case, as the King had also given them Sunninghill Park, near Ascot, for a country retreat. For some curious reason, never disclosed, this burned down while they were on honeymoon. 'Oh, Crawfie,' Lilibet wrote to her ex-governess, 'how could it have happened? Do you really think someone did it on purpose? I can't believe it. People are always so kind to us. I don't for one moment believe it was the squatters.'[2] Her father gave them Windlesham Moor in Berkshire to make up for it.

In any case Lilibet was going to join Philip in Malta very shortly, where Uncle Dickie would lend them his own luxurious villa. In the meanwhile it was no doubt unsettling not to have a permanent London roof over their heads. On the evening of Their Majesties' Silver Wedding Queen Elizabeth broadcast to her people: 'At this time my heart goes out to all those who are living in uncongenial surroundings and who are longing for a time when they will have a home of their own. I am sure that patience, tolerance and love will help them to keep their faith undimmed and their courage undaunted when things seem difficult.'[3]

But patience, tolerance and love were not, as Elizabeth herself knew, inexhaustible. The occasional grumble became more frequent, making itself heard in the strangest places. Many of the old aristocracy disapproved of Mountbatten for 'giving away' India; they had never thought very highly of the 'new' royal family anyway. Even the labourers of Somersetshire, on whose uncritical loyalty the throne depended, were feeling disgruntled. The loss of India diminished the romance and dignity of the Crown. Where, after all, had their support got them? They were worse off than before – rationed, cold, frequently homeless and without even an Empire to boast about. The independence of India and Pakistan was declared on 15 August 1947 and that same day Lord Listowel, Secretary of State for India, delivered up his seal of office to the Emperor at Balmoral. Bertie asked if he could have the flag from the Lucknow Residency as a souvenir of the Empire he had never seen.[4] Queen Mary wrote on the back of the envelope containing her son's latest letter, 'The first time Bertie wrote me a letter with the I for Emperor of India left out, very sad,'[5] and filed it away with the others.

At the beginning of 1948 the King complained of an odd sort of cramp in his legs. Too much sitting at his desk no doubt. Lilibet and Philip were still living at the Palace during the week, so his fears of losing her were calmed for the moment, and Margaret had a crowd of new friends who brightened the place up, even if they did make an awful row. Lilibet was pregnant, the Queen responding charmingly to the inevitable cries of 'I can't believe you're going to be a grandmother!' Bertie could well believe he was going to be a grandfather. At the age of fifty-two he felt old and tired.

Still, there were compensations. Elizabeth felt they could relax their vigilance a little now the war was over and although they still had nothing to do with the old 'smart set' (Lady Cunard died that summer) they were seen out and about more often, enjoying the invasion of American entertainers such as Danny Kaye and Frank Sinatra. Mae West was also in England and the King rather wanted to meet her. Unfortunately she was snapped up by Mrs Sacheverell Sitwell, who invited Lady Cunard (before her demise) to her party, so Miss West was sadly beyond the pale. Princess Marina was there, in spite of Queen Mary's instructions twelve years before.

Her parents were delighted to see Margaret taking her responsibilities seriously, as well as having a lot of healthy fun. In the autumn of 1947 she had flown to Belfast to launch a new liner. When a young sailor presented her with a bouquet of roses she immediately plucked one out and gave it to him – just like her mother. A year later, accompanied to Amsterdam by the Duke of Beaufort, Princess Alice and dear Peter Townsend, she did very well at the Investiture of Crown Princess Juliana as Queen of the Netherlands. Her chief *beau* seemed to be 'Sunny', Marquess of Blandford – or was it Johnny, Earl of Dalkeith? Anyway, there was safety in numbers. Young Porchester, Peter Ward, Colin Tennant, Angus Ogilvy, Simon Phipps, Dominic Elliot, Billy Wallace – it was hard to keep track.

Mrs Roosevelt had been over to England in 1942 to see for herself what rôle British women were playing in the war. The three British women with whom she came in closest contact were Queen Elizabeth, Queen Mary and Mrs Churchill. She got on very well with the latter, but her visits to the first two were quite a strain. At Buckingham Palace she had been given Elizabeth's bedroom, the windows patched up with wooden frames and isinglass. The almost inedible wartime food had been served on gold and silver plates and after dinner they all sat, wrapped in every available fur and woolly, and watched Noël Coward's *In Which We Serve*. At Badminton she almost froze to death and conducted a difficult conversation with Queen Mary, who had retired to bed as the only place where she could keep warm. Impressed though Mrs Roosevelt was with their fortitude, she had caught a terrible cold and earned a scolding from her aunt for 'using those nasty little tissues and wadding them in your hand while the King used such lovely sheer linen handkerchiefs.'[6] It had been a relief to get back to Washington.

In the spring of 1948, now a widow, Mrs Roosevelt ventured to England again. This time she stayed at Windsor and found the conditions, though far more comfortable, almost equally strange. She had been reassured earlier in the day by the normal family atmosphere – Margaret and her friends playing the gramophone too loud and being yelled at by Bertie to turn it down, Elizabeth's 'skill . . . in keeping their family life on a warm friendly level' – but at dinner a kilted Highlander marched round the table playing the bagpipes and 'there was, of course, much formality'. After dinner they were all commanded to play 'The Game – a form of charades. Queen Elizabeth acted as a kind of master of ceremonies . . . She puzzled for some time over various words and occasionally turned to Mr Churchill for assistance, but without success. The former Prime Minister, with a decoration on the bosom of his stiff white shirt and a cigar in his hand, sat glumly aside and would have nothing to do with The Game.'[7] Chips Channon, ear to the ground, reported that 'the house party . . . became quite childish with the Queen wearing a beard etc. A wonderful scene it must have been. Mrs Roosevelt was exhausted.'

Perhaps it was reaction from the war, perhaps it was 'her age' or the company of her youngest daughter's friends or the prospect of becoming a grandmother, but Elizabeth certainly seemed to be becoming sillier – or, as Channon phrased it, more 'slack'.[8] Of course she still presented the public image, making the right speeches in the right places and appearing eagerly interested in the poor and the deprived, but there was more than a hint that after all those years of effort she was out to have a good time. Unfortunately it all went sadly wrong.

In July they went into their customary residence at Holyrood House in Edinburgh, where Margaret took ghoulish pleasure in showing Townsend the very spot where Rizzio, Mary Queen of Scots' rather too intimate secretary, had been stabbed to death. One evening the King and Townsend walked up to Arthur's Seat. The younger man normally had a job keeping up with the King's long, dogged stride, but that evening he was clearly in difficulties and kept muttering 'What's the matter with my blasted legs? They won't work properly.'[9] During August Elizabeth knew that her husband was in discomfort most of the time. By October, when they got back to London, his left foot was numb all day and the pain keeping him awake at night. The trouble moved to his right foot. Elizabeth insisted on calling in Sir Morton Smart, Manipulative Surgeon to the King. Smart was gravely alarmed and requested the second opinion of Sir Maurice Cassidy, the King's general medical adviser. Ten days later both these gentlemen examined him and also took the opinion of Sir Thomas Dunhill, Sergeant-Surgeon to the King. Their unanimous opinion was that Professor James Learmonth, Regius Professor of Clinical Surgery at Edinburgh, should be consulted. On 12 November Learmonth's examination disclosed early arteriosclerosis, with a danger of developing gangrene. He feared the King's right leg might have to be amputated.

Lilibet was told none of this, on the grounds that it might distress her during her pregnancy. Possibly she thought her mother's unnaturally glum face was due to her own condition, or to some tactless remark of Philip's, or worry about 'Sunny' Blandford. On the evening of 14 November she was moved into 'the delivery room', once her nursery. Philip changed into flannels and went off with Michael Parker for a game of squash. Shortly afterward, he received the message that Lilibet had given birth to a boy.[10]

The Palace was in a frenzy. Queen Mary noted the child's remarkable resemblance to the Prince Consort and twelve temporary typists were hired to acknowledge the sackfuls of letters and presents. Elizabeth hurried from husband to daughter to grandson. The doctors issued a bulletin saying the King was suffering from an obstruction in the arteries of the legs and that complete rest and treatment to improve the circulation must be maintained for an immediate and prolonged period, adding that 'there is no doubt that the strain of the last twelve years has appreciably affected his resistance to physical fatigue.'* Nobody mentioned then or later that he had been an exceptionally sickly child and a chain-smoker the whole of his adult life. Elizabeth, refusing to believe in the will of God, needed something or someone to blame. She decided on Wallis Windsor. If Wallis had not 'blown in from Baltimore', Bertie would have been perfectly healthy. Perhaps this fantasy helped her deal with her husband's impatience and her own anxiety.

The King tried to be philosophical. After a fortnight of inactivity he told his mother that he was 'getting tired & bored with bed as I am feeling so much more rested which is a good thing',[11] and a fortnight later he was present and correct at his grandson's christening. One of the official photographs of this occasion shows the King, looking ill and haggard, standing between David Bowes-Lyon and Philip; both Margaret and Queen Mary appear in a bad temper and only Lilibet wears a delighted grin. Charles Philip Arthur George, dressed like a bishop, sleeps soundly in a sort of side-saddle position on his mother's knee. Where was Elizabeth? The absence of coquettish grandma, with her talent for looking so pleased with herself and life, gives a sudden realisation of what the royal family would have been without her – dignified, honourable, and stodgy. Five days later a Dr Jacob Snowman, then in his eighties, made the long trek from Hampstead to circumcise the infant.[12]

---

*Brigadier Stanley Clark OBE whose dates in his Palace Diary are at variance with John Wheeler-Bennett's, says the King at this point was diagnosed as having Buerger's Disease: an inflammatory or toxic condition which attacks the arteries and veins in a limb, generally in young men; also known as thrombo-angitis. It is associated with heavy smoking and often leads to gangrene. Treatment takes the form of exercises to improve the circulation in the affected limb.

# Chapter Twenty-Nine

Elizabeth's grandson would play an important part in her future but in the meanwhile her major concern was Bertie's health. It was no good pretending it wasn't happening or retiring with some minor indisposition: nothing could convince her that her husband was anything but a very ill man. For the first time in her life she had to live with an uncompromising reality, while at the same time condemned to look as though she was constantly enjoying herself. Thousands of women go through this ordeal. That Bertie was King of England, and his health a matter of national concern, made it no easier.

At the beginning of March the doctors concluded that either the King must continue to lead the life of an invalid, for which he was temperamentally unsuited, or they must perform a lumbar sympathectomy. There was a right royal row: so all this treatment had been a waste of time, why the hell couldn't the bloody quacks learn their business? After he calmed down it was tentatively suggested that it might be more practical if he went into the Royal Masonic Hospital. That set him off again: 'I suppose I've a good right to go to a Masonic Hospital, but I've never heard of a King going to a hospital before!'[1] Nobody was going to tell him it was high time he did. A complete surgical unit was established in the Palace and a sombre crowd waited for news outside the Palace railings: when the bulletin was posted saying the operation had been successful newsboys scrawled 'HE'S ALL RIGHT' on their placards, the crowd cheered and hurried away.

In Professor Learmonth's opinion 'the problem was both psychological and physical.' On the Professor's final visit he was somewhat alarmed when the King, after demanding his dressing gown and slippers, whipped out a highly polished sword from the bedclothes or other place of concealment, and chuckled maliciously, 'You used a knife on me, now I'm going to use one on you.'[2] The Professor was much relieved to find himself being knighted.

The Queen, trying to keep her husband calm in the intervals between having tea with old ladies in council flats, looking at portraits of war leaders, being seen at serious theatre like *The Wild Duck* (Margaret went to *Harvey* that night, lucky girl) and smiling at photographers, was under considerable pressure. Nothing was made any easier by those tiresome Labour people making a fuss about the repairs to Clarence House. How could the House of Commons claim they had spent £250,000 on it, instead of the £50,000 they had been given? True, the Ministry of Works had said the work would exceed the estimate by ten per cent, but Philip said that always happened with estimates. Lilibet was so excited about everything he was doing there: he had studied the plans with the Ministry of Works architects and told them exactly where they had gone wrong and how to put it right. Canada had given them the white maple panelling for his study and the City of Glasgow presented them with all the white sycamore wall fitments for his bedroom. Lilibet herself had mixed the paint to get exactly the right shade for the apple-green walls of the dining room and Philip had cleverly found someone to make the carved and gilded light brackets which looked for all the world as though they were genuine George III.[3] He was simply furious with the secretary of the London District Committee of the Amalgamated Society of Woodworkers when their lazy carpenters went on strike. After all, they only had £50,000 a year between them – Philip's share of that was shockingly small – and there was a baby to consider.

By the early summer of 1949 the Edinburghs had survived their troubles and were about to move in. Margaret was in high spirits after a European Grand Tour which had left the *paparazzi* exhausted and the King's condition was much improved. Perhaps it was time to show the country that the royal family was not downhearted. In June a memorable ball was held at Windsor to which, there being no problem about Lady Cunard, almost everyone who was anyone was invited. The rooms were banked with flowers, chandeliers winked down on diamonds, every woman had a new gown and the men were swathed and studded with honours. After the guests had waited for about twenty minutes the doors were flung open to reveal the King and Queen. 'He seemed brown,' Channon noted (the King had started using heavy make-up to disguise his pallor), 'and she, though unfortunately very, very plump, looked magnificent in a white satin semi-crinoline number, with the Garter and splendid rubies . . . Mrs Greville's, I suppose.'[4] The King rested his foot on a stool but Elizabeth was indefatigable, allowing Maurice Winnick's band to go on playing until quarter to five in the morning.

The meat ration was reduced to one shilling a week and the sugar ration to eight ounces. The King plunged into renewed gloom at the prospect of having to deal with another crisis, but Balmoral restored his spirits; he improvised a harness with a long trace attached to a pony to pull him up hills and had it fitted with a quick-release mechanism in case the pony bolted. When Bertie said in his Christmas broadcast that 'None of us can be satisfied till we are again standing upright and supporting our own weight and we have a long way to go before we can do that,' only the most insensitive listener could have thought, as he undoubtedly did, that he was talking about economic aid from America.

The General Election of 23 February 1950 brought the Labour Government back with a majority of eight. The King was in a ferment of worry about what he should advise, encourage or warn Clement Attlee to do if he asked for a Dissolution but luckily, on Churchill's advice, he didn't. Lilibet was sailing around the Mediterranean on HMS *Surprise*, escorted by Philip in *Magpie*, a cruise only loosely connected with his command in the Navy. 'Princess full of beans,' *Surprise* would signal to *Magpie* and *Magpie* would signal back 'Is that the best you can give her for breakfast?'[5] Anne Elizabeth Alice Louise was born at Clarence House in August; three months later Lilibet left the children in the charge of their grandparents and joined Philip in Malta. 'Like the wife of any naval officer,' said the Press, 'she is joining her husband on his station,' adding that she had already sent out her car, forty large cases of clothes and a new polo pony for Philip.[6] Her father missed her bitterly.

The day his granddaughter was born the King was alone at Balmoral worrying about Korea and the deteriorating relationship between Britain and America. If only Roosevelt were still alive he could have telephoned and asked how things were at Hyde Park before mentioning that it might be helpful if the United States resisted blowing up the world. Nobody listened to kings any longer, but as head of the British Commonwealth he surely ought to be able to do *something*. The last straw was on Christmas Eve when the Stone of Scone – a sacred object safely stowed under the Coronation Throne for six-and-a-half centuries – was stolen from Westminster Abbey. At least this was one occasion when the King could make himself heard.

Majestic edicts were sent out and all jokes about the heinous crime cut from radio programmes and variety shows – even *Take It From Here*, Their Majesties' favourite listening, was censored.

Elizabeth had her own reasons for dissatisfaction. Her nephew Timothy, 16th Earl of Strathmore, was selling off thousands of acres of family property and opening Glamis to the public, charging 2/- entrance fee. She herself had actually been criticised. The *Sunday Pictorial* (surely nobody actually read such a paper?) had been deliberately insulting about her appearance at the Somerset-Thynne wedding:

> Her hat is too large, too heavy and too drooping . . . the pattern of the dress would be better on a furnishing fabric, the skimpy cape is both broadening and shortening, the dark edging makes the dress look like a dressing-gown with the sash undone, the gloves are too heavy-looking and add unnecessary bulk to the figure and peek-a-boo shoes have been considered inelegant for two years.

The King and Queen were not alone in their apprehension of the future. 'So ends a horrible year with worse to come,' Harold Nicolson wrote in his diary on 31 December 1950. 'It is sad to become old amid such darkness.'[7]

# Chapter Thirty

The Festival of Britain was intended to commemorate the Great Exhibition of 1851, a demonstration of British achievement in the arts, sciences and design. Queen Mary resolutely toured the Dome of Discovery, inspected the sculpture, murals and mobiles by Moore, Piper, Hepworth, Sutherland, Topolski and Epstein, peered up at the Skylon and tested the tree walk. The whole thing struck her as 'really extraordinary and very ugly'.[1] The King, the papers said, looked well.

In fact he was exhausted. Elizabeth insisted on taking him to Balmoral for a rest, accompanied only by Margaret, one lady-in-waiting and Peter Townsend, whose marriage was going through a difficult phase. It was a splendid holiday. 'The sun warmed the scent from the pines,' Townsend remembered nostalgically, 'and the crisp nights were full of stars.'[2] Neither of these delights prevented the King from going down with 'flu. The doctors found that his left lung was inflamed and put him on penicillin. Bertie was deeply interested in his own condition and wrote a detailed account of it to his mother, explaining the results of his X-rays and the cause of his cough, but as the weeks went by his interest flagged and he became despondent at 'not being able to chuck out the bug'.

Elizabeth went on trying to convince people nothing was wrong. Eighty-year-old King Haakon came to stay and since Bertie was unable to entertain him she met the old man at Westminster pier, took him to the Royal Tournament and laid on a State Banquet. At Ascot 'the Queen was in lilac and looked sublime'. Chips 'watched all the real Princesses of the Blood Royal as they kissed and curtsied to her, and really marvelled at her self possession.' In July, however, Philip was brought home on indefinite leave.

Back at Balmoral all went well at first – the weather was good and Bertie could enjoy a full day's shooting. Margaret asked Johnny Dalkeith and Billy Wallace to stay for her twenty-first birthday.

One night when they were making a particularly deafening noise downstairs the King rang for his equerry: 'I found him standing there, a lonely, forlorn figure. In his eyes was that glaring, distressed look which he always had when it seemed that the tribulations of the world had overcome him: "Won't those bloody people ever go to bed?" '³ On the birthday itself the King went out with a shooting party and bagged 300 grouse, some of them not fully grown, but there was a cold wind and he caught a chill. His doctors insisted he should return to London for X-rays, so he went alone on the overnight train, flying back to Dyce Airport the following day. The first thing he did on his return was go to the sand-table model of the moors and ask for every detail of the day's shooting. Elizabeth, anxious as she was, had to wait.

After doctors had examined the X-rays they advised a bronchoscopy to remove a portion of tissue from the lung for histological examination. The King and his party clocked up thirty-eight hares, one pigeon and a further 302 grouse, then he took the night train for London. Elizabeth learned the ominous verdict two days later.* She flew south with Lilibet and Philip, leaving Margaret and the grandchildren at Balmoral. An operation for lung resection was arranged for Sunday. Early that morning Elizabeth and the family drove to Lambeth Palace to pray with the Archbishop of Canterbury for Bertie's recovery. He, in something of the same spirit, gave instructions for three brace of grouse to be delivered to the Duke of Windsor, who was staying in London. 'I understand he is fond of grouse,' he said.†

The lung resection was performed without a hitch, but in the process it was discovered that some of the nerves of the larynx would have to be sacrificed. Peter Townsend saw him shortly after the operation: 'He smiled warmly, almost apologetically . . . when he spoke it was not in his firm, deep voice, but in a thin whisper.' It was probable that Bertie would never be able to talk in a normal voice again.

*'Those close to Queen Elizabeth – even her own family – were never allowed to know whether she fully understood the full implications of the doctors' reports upon the King's health'. (Dorothy Laird *Queen Elizabeth the Queen Mother*). The King himself never knew – or was never told – that he had cancer.

†The Duke of Windsor's autobiography, *A King's Story*, was about to be published. The royal family had certainly read it by now, and had presumably been responsible for 'a few wisely chosen omissions' in the English edition. Their reaction to the book is not known. The reviews were excellent.

Recovery was slow, but at last there was some good news: October's General Election brought the Conservatives back and Churchill, aged seventy-six, returned to Downing Street 'with no sign of doubt or anxiety as to his ability to govern on the score of age or any other.'[4] James Stuart became Secretary of State for Scotland and the Edinburghs were having a predictable success on their tour of Canada. By 9 December it was considered safe to hold a National Day of Thanksgiving for the King's recovery. The Commonwealth thanked God, and the King knighted some more doctors.

Prolonged illness had given him a curious new distinction and grace; what Cecil Beaton described as 'the raw, bony, medieval aspects of that handsome face' had blurred into a kind of haunted gentleness. He longed for the country. 'I have been through a great deal in recent times,' he wrote to the Australian Minister for External Affairs, a Mr R G Casey, 'but my main task is getting well. I am going to dedicate myself now to that task of getting well. I am a man who likes outdoor life. I love all the things England offers in such wealth outdoors, and one of the things I do not get is country life. Kingship keeps me in this room, talking affairs of state constantly, even when I am not quite up to it. I just yearn for the country.'[5]

Thank God it was soon time to go to Sandringham. The vigilant doctors allowed him to go shooting again, provided he didn't stay out too long and always moved about in his Land Rover. At Christmas Queen Mary, plagued with rheumatism in the dank Norfolk climate, supervised the arrangement of the family's presents in the ballroom.

Chips Channon, in pensive mood, consulted the oracle of his diary: 'What will this new Parliament unfold? The deaths of Winston, Queen Mary and the Monarch? A Coronation, some sort of show-down with Stalin? Shall I survive it? Shall I die, or be made a Peer, or just resign?'[6]

Dr Malan, South Africa's reactionary Prime Minister, offered the King and Queen his official residence in Natal to escape the worst of the British winter. Peter Townsend was sent out to look it over; since his report was encouraging they arranged to leave England on 5 March. Although the King was now 'esteemed to the point of tenderness' by the public,[7] this projected visit came in for much criticism both in Parliament and the Press. Elizabeth, believing that 'if the dividing lines in South Africa go deep, the reconciling appeal of royalty goes deeper still'[8] ignored it. The King left Sandringham for London very worried about the trouble in the Suez Canal and what he called 'our unhappy relations with Egypt' – something of an understatement considering that Shepheards Hotel, Barclays Bank, the BOAC offices, four cinemas and a number of petrol stations in Cairo had been set on fire the day before.

The Edinburghs were replacing Their Majesties on another tour, this time a 'Commonwealth Tour' to East Africa, Australia and New Zealand. As a farewell celebration the whole family went to *South Pacific* at Drury Lane and were deeply moved by the company's rendering of the National Anthem, followed by rousing cheers from the audience. The next day they all went to London Airport to see Lilibet and Philip off. Television cameras were there – something Bertie could never get used to – and tens of thousands of viewers watched the King, bare-headed, gaunt, his hair blown about by the January wind, 'almost madlooking',[9] staring after his daughter's 'plane until it was no more than a speck in the sky. When they got back to the Palace Queen Mary came to tea after seeing a delightful exhibition of French drawings from Fouquet to Gauguin at the Arts Council. That evening Elizabeth had to go to Finsbury Barracks to visit the City of London Squadron of the Royal Auxiliary Air Force, of which she was honorary Air Commodore; a bleak thing to do under the circumstances, but she carried it off with her usual aplomb.

They went back to Sandringham the following day, taking the grandchildren with them. The *Times* reported that Nairobi had given Philip and Lilibet a royal welcome. They were now at the Sagana Hunting Lodge taking pictures of elephants and lions – there was a waggish Leader under the title 'Leo Sapiens' – and at the nearby Treetops Hotel baboons had just eaten all the new lampshades. It took Bertie and Elizabeth back to those happy days – 1924 was it? – when they had hunted with guns, not cameras.

There was no such milksop feeling here, thank God. February 5th was 'Keepers' Day' at Sandringham, when all the tenants, estate workers, neighbouring small farmers and local worthies joined in the King's shoot to pick up the remains of game left at the end of the season. Elizabeth and Margaret took the opportunity of lunching with Edward Seago, the painter, at his home in Ludham. After they had admired his paintings and sketches and chosen those they liked best, Seago took them out on Barton Broad in a hired motor-cruiser and on to tea with some friends at Barton Hall. It was late when they got back. Elizabeth hurried straight to Bertie's room and was relieved to find him in topping spirits. Seago's pictures had been propped up in the hall. The King, though his knowledge of art could have been considerably greater, was enchanted with them. They had 'a truly gay' dinner[10] and Bertie, exhausted but happy, went to bed. A valet took him a cup of hot chocolate and he read until around midnight, when a watchman in the garden saw him fastening the latch of his bedroom window.[11] The next morning, while Elizabeth was drinking her tea, Sir Harold Campbell, the equerry-in-charge, came to tell her that Bertie was dead.

# PART FOUR
## QUEEN MOTHER

# Preface to Part Four

The death of the Prince Consort was the central turning point in the history of Queen Victoria. She herself felt that her true life had ceased with her husband's . . . Nor is it possible that her biographer should escape a similar impression. For him, too, there is darkness over the latter half of that long career. The first forty-two years of the Queen's life are illuminated by a great and varied quantity of authentic information. With Albert's death a veil descends . . . the rest is all conjecture and ambiguity . . . We must be content in our ignorance with a brief and summary relation.

*Queen Victoria*, Lytton Strachey

However profound her mourning, Queen Victoria was still an Empress; a Queen Consort ceases to exist the moment her husband dies. The title, which gives its bearer a clearly defined status in the Constitution, goes into cold storage and from then on she is known officially as 'Queen Dowager', with far fewer prerogatives (it is impossible, for instance, to be treasonable to a Queen Dowager). Elizabeth, disliking the connotations, decided on 'Queen Elizabeth the Queen Mother'. In this way she managed to be called 'Queen' twice over, but it made no difference to the fact that she now owed allegiance to Lilibet. Lilibet was a chip off the old block – 'Just like the young Queen Victoria,' the Duke of Devonshire said, 'with the old Queen's sagacity. She makes it very plain to [her mother] that whereas she . . . is a commoner, she, Princess Elizabeth, is of royal blood.'[1] The new Queen Mother felt much like the Duchess of Clarence after her daughter Victoria's accession: '*Il n'y a plus d'avenir pour moi! Je ne suis plus rien!*'

The uncertainty of her position made mourning even harder to bear. She had spent two thirds of her life creating a King out of unpromising material and in doing so had made a man on whom she could rely. Over the years their rôles had merged into

223

a more mutual dependence; Bertie had learned to apply his mind to problems and take decisions, smooth her path and surround her with comforts. She was convinced that if he had not been forced to the throne he would not have developed lung cancer and died from coronary thrombosis, ignoring the fact that a longer life as Duke of York, subservient to his eldest brother and occupied with minor duties, would never have given him the opportunity to become the man he did. Bertie was certainly more fulfilled, if not happier, with greatness thrust upon him than he would have been without any greatness at all. As widowed Duchess of York the Queen Mother would not have been able to tell the British people, 'He loved you all, every one of you, most truly,' as she told them after the King's funeral.

Elizabeth had been cruelly demoted, but there was more to it than that. She was only fifty-one, a 'man's woman' dismayed to find herself in the no-man's-land of respectable widowhood. Was she expected to become a vaguely endearing old nuisance like Alexandra, a formidable matriarch like her mother-in-law, or should she consider returning to the obscurity she was reputedly reluctant to leave thirty years ago?

'My only wish now,' she said, 'is that I may be allowed to continue the work we sought to do together.' But what work? For fifteen years, which included a major war, she had been a King's adviser and confidante: 'the great task of service' sounded more amorphous than ever. The Queen Mother would, in fact, spend the rest of her life doing the donkey-work of royalty – inspecting, opening, patronising charities, being seen so that she might be believed. Little of this gives any indication of spontaneity, none of it made history or is of interest except to those concerned in it at the time. A certain amount of conjecture and ambiguity will be necessary if the picture of the next half-century is to represent more than pages in the Queen Mother's engagement book.

# Chapter Thirty-One

'The King is regarded in law as both a body politic and body natural. The death of the body natural is termed the demise of the Sovereign; the body politic is immortal.' Lilibet inherited the body politic on the night of 5–6 February when she was sitting in a tree with Philip and her cousin Pamela Mountbatten watching elephants by artificial moonlight. From that moment she was Queen of England, and it is as 'the Queen' I shall refer to her from now on.

On Thursday 7 February the Queen and the Duke of Edinburgh arrived at London Airport to be met by the Duke of Gloucester, Winston Churchill, the Mountbattens, Anthony Eden and Clement Attlee. The Duke of Windsor sailed from New York on the *Queen Mary* the same day, leaving Wallis behind. Royal persons and dignitaries all over the world cancelled their engagements and prepared to set out for London. The weather was appalling.

The King still lay in the bed where he had died. Sixteen years ago, at the same lowest ebb of winter, he had waited downstairs with David, Harry and George while Cosmo Lang delivered his father's soul. Elizabeth had been ill then; now, with Margaret, she walked through the rain to the parish church of St Mary Magdalene and back again to the house, where Seago's paintings were still propped against the wall. The Sebastopol bell in the Round Tower at Windsor tolled once for every year of the King's life. The great bell of St Paul's tolled for two hours over the drenched City of London.

The Queen attended her Accession Council the following day: '. . . I pray that God will help me to discharge worthily this heavy task that has been laid upon me so early in my life,' she said in her high, certain voice. (David had asked for support 'in this heavy task'; Bertie had 'taken up this heavy task' – was there ever a Sovereign who took on the job with optimism?) During the few hours it took to read the Proclamation, over the length and breadth of Britain mourning for the dead King was suspended and everyone became officially jubilant.

> We, therefore, the Lords Spiritual and Temporal of this Realm . . . with the Principal Gentlemen of Quality . . . do now hereby, with one Voice and Consent of Tongue and Heart, publish and proclaim that the High and Mighty Princess Elizabeth Alexandra Mary is now, by the Death of our late Sovereign of Happy Memory . . . become Queen Elizabeth II, by the Grace of God, Queen of this Realm, and of her other Realms and Territories, Head of the Commonwealth, Defender of the Faith . . . God Save the Queen!

Bands played, guns boomed and the Queen made history by watching it all on her black and white television. People outside in the rain, craning their necks round jostling umbrellas, believed that since she was young, healthy, even pretty in an average sort of way, everything was going to change for the better. Piqued by twenty years of royal disapproval, the 'smart set' was even more optimistic: '*Mirabile dictu* . . . The young Queen has invited [Prince] Paul over for the funeral . . . I rejoice in the new reign and welcome it. We shall be the new Elizabethans . . .'[1]

Though devastated by her son's death, Queen Mary made a point of going to Clarence House to do homage to the new Sovereign: 'Her old Grannie and subject must be the first to kiss Her hand.'[2] The Queen, the Duke of Edinburgh and their children then drove to Sandringham, where her mother and sister were waiting. At five o'clock that evening Bertie was put into his coffin and taken the short distance to the church, where a series of workers on the estate – gamekeepers, foresters, carpenters in tweed knickerbocker suits and polished boots – guarded him four at a time until the following Monday.

On Sunday morning the Queen Mother and her family went to church for early service; then the doors were unlocked and employees and tenants from the late King's villages and farms filed past the coffin for the rest of the day. Bertie had been 'in a real sense, father of his family in this village and, indeed, in all the villages which make up the Sandringham estate,' said the local cleric, Revd H V Anderson. 'He cared most deeply for its people, its homes, its woods, its fields and farms . . .' Some of them remembered Prince Albert shooting his first woodcock, his first partridge and his first grouse in King George V's Coronation Year; many were the same men who had guarded his father's coffin.

Rain changed to snow. The added chill of a Royal death made

it a typical Sandringham winter. On Monday morning the cortège travelling from Sandringham to Wolferton Station was almost exactly the same as King George V's. The Queen replaced her grandmother and there was no riderless pony, but the gun carriage rumbled as slowly along the lane, there was the same muffled clopping of horses, crunch and shuffle of feet emphasising the winter silence. There is no mention of a piper and if a pheasant careened free across the sky no one noticed it.

At King's Cross the Imperial State Crown had been placed on a pedestal under a purple covering. The train pulled in at the red-carpeted platform, the doors of the funeral coach slid open to reveal purple curtains and draperies. Lieutenant-Colonel Sir Terence Nugent, Comptroller of the Lord Chamberlain's Office, lifted the crown and carried it into the funeral coach. There was a long pause, then the Queen Mother and her daughters, shrouded in black, stepped out of the train followed by the Duke of Edinburgh and the Duke of Gloucester. Another pause before eight lofty Guardsmen shouldered coffin and crown and slow-marched to the waiting gun carriage. Harry and Philip fell in behind them and the women were left alone.

Sparrows chirping in the roof, the dull roar of traffic from the Euston Road. They waited, appearing uncertain what to do. Finally the Queen and her mother whispered to the attendant Nugent. Given his signal, the royal car drew up to its proper place. The women disappeared inside it after graciously acknowledging the salute from the guards of honour. The guards marched off, the props were cleared away.

Among the many eulogies delivered that day in Parliament Viscount Samuel's was the most realistic: 'What is needed in a constitutional monarchy,' he told the House of Lords, 'is not brilliance, or mere cleverness or eloquence, but a sincere good will and a sound common sense.' As King George VI had grown more familiar with death he had seemed to be outgrowing even those sterling qualities. He had taken on the magical 'look of Weltschmerz', finally acquired the talent to be loved.

James Cameron was in Westminster Hall waiting for the cortège to arrive. He felt strongly about many things but he was not often choked with emotion. The piece he wrote for the *Illustrated London News* was choked:

> While the King lived we spoke of him as this, and as that, endowing him with all the remote virtues of an infallible man; such men do not die. But the King died; and we found somehow

a different thing: that we loved him ... the sudden shadow fell momentarily across the heart of every man; loyal men and cynics, the rich and the dispossessed, reactionaries and radicals ...[3]

Reports of King George VI's lying-in-state are almost interchangeable with those written sixteen years before. 'The public ... began to arrive in numbers so astounding that every plan was upset, every traffic arrangement entangled ... By the afternoon of the third day 80,000 people were waiting in what was almost certainly the longest queue the world has ever seen ... a vast strip of humanity over three miles long, stolidly facing a five-hour wait in the toothed wind ...' Queen Mary, erect but tottering, heavily veiled, came with her eldest son. The Kings and Queens of Norway, Sweden, the Hellenes and the Netherlands, together with various members of the British Royal Family, crept in and out pretending not to be noticed. Cameron found it 'strange – almost incredible – to see these opaque veiled figures and recognise them for the ladies whose professional uniforms – that they may fulfil their duty and be conspicuous – are light pastels. It was difficult to adjust oneself to the new titles: Queen, Queen Mother. And those who photographed them ... did a strange thing: they found for the first time perhaps in twenty years a picture of the King's widow without a smile.'[4]

Queen Mary's only surviving sons, David and Harry, did not stand guard over the coffin; neither did Elizabeth's son-in-law, peaky with anxiety. ('I never felt so sorry for anyone in all my life,' Michael Parker said after telling Philip of the King's death. 'He looked as though you'd dropped half the world on him.'[5]) At the Palace the young Queen was being whisked from engagement to engagement with barely time to speak to her husband, let alone her mother: Churchill brought a deputation from the House of Commons, she received the Prime Minister of New Zealand, gave lunch to the Swedens and the Netherlands and the Mountbattens, received the High Commissioners of Commonwealth countries, Ministers, Ambassadors and Foreign Ministers and the representatives of Ireland, the President of the French Republic, the President of the Turkish Republic and the President of the Praesidium of Yugoslavia. On Wednesday the Duke of Windsor had tea with the Queen, Prince Philip and the Queen Mother.[6]

On 15 February Elizabeth's standard flew over Buckingham Palace: at least the day of Bertie's funeral was hers. The long, melancholy cortège lumbered from Westminster Hall to Paddington.

The Duke of Windsor, in the uniform of Admiral of the Fleet, followed the coffin on foot with Harry; Philip, Edward Kent and a battalion of minor royalties marched behind. The women, shadowy in their nylon veils, swayed like sea-grass behind the windows of the funeral carriages. Queen Mary had asked Lady Airlie to keep her company at Marlborough House. 'We sat alone together at the window, looking out into the murk and gloom. As the cortège wound slowly along the Queen whispered in a broken voice, 'Here *he* is' ... I could not speak to comfort her. My tears choked me ... We held each other's hands in silence.'[7]

Queen Mary had not been present at her mother-in-law's funeral because George had German measles, but she remembered how beautiful 'beloved Grandmama' had looked after death – 'like a marble statue'. Her father-in-law's had been an agitated affair, with Alexandra insisting on a precedence not hers by right and George and herself, as the new King and Queen, 'very busy with dull things of all kinds.'[8] Then 'that terrible day of sadness' of her George's funeral when, dressed in the peaked coif and thick crêpe veils of German royal mourning, she stood alone at the foot of the coffin as her daughter-in-law did now. She watched the cortège arriving at Windsor, the procession to St George's Chapel and the final interment on her television set. It was strange, from such a distance, to see her son lowered into the vault with his father and ancestors; almost as though she were already with him on the Other Side.

# Chapter Thirty-Two

Advice from eminent ecclesiastics did not succeed in comforting the Queen Mother. She went to stay with her friends the Vyners in Scotland, where she received a recently published anthology of poetry from Edith Sitwell. In her thank-you letter she told Dame Edith that she had read it sitting by the river: 'It was a day when one felt engulfed by great black clouds of unhappiness and misery . . . and thought how small and selfish is sorrow. But it bangs one about until one is senseless.'[1]

It was Winston Churchill, successfully if not comfortably married for over forty years, who took the problem in hand. He paid her a surprise visit, and whatever was said between them, three months after Bertie's death she flew from Windsor to Fife to inspect the First Battalion of the Black Watch before it left for Korea. Though in telling them that whatever they were facing she knew honour would be won for Scotland and the Black Watch it sounded as though she were sending them off with drum and fife to attack Napoleon's army rather than snipe Communists in the Korean jungle, the cheers were just as rousing. A few weeks later her old friend 'Bobbety' Cranborne, Marquess of Salisbury, arranged a joy-ride in a brand new Comet. Margaret, Peter Townsend and two of Elizabeth's chauffeurs joined the party that flew 1,850 miles to Bordeaux and back, picnicking over the Alps. At one point the Queen Mother took over the controls of the taxpayers' priceless machine and 'the mach needle crept towards the coloured danger sector . . . Suddenly the Comet began to porpoise . . . had that gone on much longer, the wracking on the structure could well have precipitated a rupture of the skin of the kind that caused subsequent tragedies.'[2] Elizabeth was so pleased with her performance that she sent a telegram to the City of London Squadron of the RAAF to tell them about it.[3]

Peter Townsend, recently made Comptroller of the Queen Mother's Household, was supervising repairs and redecorations at Clarence House, for which Parliament had voted an inadequate £8,000 on the grounds that at a conservative estimate £100,000 had been spent on it for Lilibet and Philip three years before. Meanwhile Elizabeth was permitted to stay in her own suite on the first floor of Buckingham Palace. The Queen and her husband had taken over the Belgian Suite on the ground floor, Charles and Anne lived in the nursery suite on the second floor and Margaret, sensibly, in the suite over the Visitors' entrance. In 1937, when the Yorks first moved in, all the food had to be transported from the kitchens at Buckingham Palace Road to the dining rooms at Constitution Hill. Elizabeth had modernised the place considerably, but nothing could be done to make the royal tenement any cosier. There were telephones, messengers to spring down miles of corridor and antique lifts to crank people up and down when they went calling; even so, at the end of the day with the grandchildren asleep and Margaret entertaining her friends and Lilibet either working or preoccupied with her family, the newly widowed Queen Mother was lonely and dejected. The Sultan of Brunei brought her some silver candlesticks from Borneo (she might have preferred one of the gold sarongs he had presented to Margaret and Queen Mary), but there seemed precious little else for a woman who had been accustomed to the constant love and attention of a King.

She returned to Scotland and, as always, responded promptly to her surroundings. Perhaps dignified, if gradual, retirement was the answer; go back to her roots. So she bought Barrogill Castle, a dilapidated property overlooking the Pentland Firth on the remote coast of Caithness. Though there was no tongueless girl or hidden Monster there were said to be shoals of mermaids disporting themselves in the warmth of the Gulf Stream along the Caithness coast and sea-serpents too, surging in great stately hoops from Dunnett Head to Hoy. It was a bleak landscape, barren moors, desolate lochs, towering cliffs, whirlpools. The castle itself had the requisite bricked-up rooms and dungeons and may have seemed her spiritual home. Unfortunately it was physically inadequate, three years' work being needed to make it habitable. Having changed its name to the Castle of Mey she left it to builders and returned to London.

The Press had gone on for months about her grief and people were curious to see her in action again. Barely two months later she accompanied the Queen and Margaret to Freddie Lonsdale's

*Aren't We All?* at the Haymarket Theatre. She and the Queen both wore tiaras, the Royal Box was imaginatively decorated with bronze and yellow chrysanthemums. Cecil Beaton was enormously relieved to find his adored Elizabeth 'in her most jovial mood, enjoying every nuance of the play's humour with a hearty relish, and alert to all the twists of the mechanical plot. She was having a "night out" and in such good spirits that she chuckled at many things that the audience would take for granted, and roared at the things that amused her most.' The Queen sat 'relaxed and hunched, with head cocked backwards to listen concentratedly to the play', or to think about opening Parliament or having the Archbishop to lunch or whether the design for her Coronation gown was quite right. Margaret, with 'straight neck and back' was miles away.

In the interval Beaton asked the Queen Mother whether she had enjoyed her holiday.

'Oh, I've bought a villa in the most remote part of the world!'

'How brave of you to have nothing between you and the Atlantic!'

'I've taken this villa to get away from everything, but I don't expect I shall ever be able to get there!'[4]

Everyone roared with laughter. It was that kind of evening.

Peter Townsend divorced his wife in December on the grounds of adultery with John de Laszlo, son of the man responsible for the most idealised and popular portrait of Elizabeth ever painted. The royal family was discreetly sympathetic. At Christmas they stayed at Sandringham as usual, but eighty-five-year-old Queen Mary felt unequal to the jollifications and remained in her room. She had recently made a new Will, leaving everything previously bequeathed to Bertie to her eldest granddaughter. Now she thought how tiresome it would be to spoil Lilibet's Coronation by dying in the middle of it: ('How careless of him to die in the middle of the season,' she had once remarked on hearing of the death of some public figure). She would make a memo: Coronation not to be postponed or upset in any way because of mourning.[5]

Queen Mary in her later years became the most regal of matriarchs. Elizabeth would soon be faced with taking over that rôle but would have to play it quite differently. She had no supporting sons; brother-in-law Harry, though immensely conscientious in his duties, was hardly a shoulder to lean on; her son-in-law was a Mountbatten, not at all what she needed. There were friends, of course, but they were all outsiders. She must have a completely trustworthy man in her inner circle, a man in the know who would complement her femininity in public. Not a lover – that went without saying – but a confidante, a protector, someone who would look after her while she worked out the best way of tackling the future. She had made Peter Townsend Comptroller of her Household in order that he might fulfil this position. Peter's affection for Bertie and stabilising influence on Margaret, his rather melancholy good looks, his efficiency in dealing with all the boring trivia and the good fortune that he was no longer married were perfect qualifications for a lifetime as *chevalier servant* to a Queen Mother.

The more worldly Queen Mary (who had danced the Hokey Cokey with Peter at Balmoral and thought him a nice young man) would have seen the dangers in a trice and something would have been done to stop, or at least deflect, the course of human nature. Elizabeth, having a more optimistic and complacent personality, never thought about such things. She must have known how painfully Margaret missed her father, that she was jealous of her sister and piqued by her boyfriends' precipitate dashes to the altar with other people. She must have sensed, at least, that Peter was deeply unhappy about his divorce. Perhaps her inability to see the outcome was due to simple ignorance. While her own sexual approach worked wonders, her actual experience was extremely limited for a woman of fifty-two. Whatever the explanation, she was not aware that Townsend and her daughter were in that vulnerable state in which falling in love or off a high building seem the only solutions. Left alone at Sandringham or Windsor, they found it easier to fall in love.[6]

It is impossible for a normal mother to sit smiling placidly while sexual fireworks explode over the Canasta and zip across the dinner table. If Elizabeth noticed a change in the atmosphere it sounds as though she must have put it down to the weather. Margaret confided in her eventually, but even then Townsend could only 'imagine' the Queen Mother's reaction.[7] She made no sign that she felt angered or outraged or, on the other hand, that she acquiesced. She didn't say 'I thought so' and she certainly didn't send for Mr Churchill and greet him with, 'Well, Prime Minister. *This* is a pretty kettle of fish!' The subject gnawing at their souls was not one she would discuss with the Comptroller of her Household and as a mother she appeared to opt out completely. Lilibet, head of the family and realm, must deal with it.

Although Townsend was the perfect Comptroller of a royal household, his divorce made him ineligible as a member of the Royal

Family and it did not make a jot of difference that he had been 'the innocent party'. In any case Margaret was bound by the Royal Marriages Act of 1772 which stipulated (and still does, as far as I know) that until the age of twenty-five all potential successors to the throne must have the Sovereign's permission to marry; for the subsequent two years they have to ask the approval of Parliament and cannot do what they like until they are twenty-seven. Margaret was twenty-two, Townsend forty. Five years of enforced celibacy did not appeal to either of them.

The Princess asked the Queen and the Queen asked the Prime Minister. Churchill had burned his fingers over the Abdication and maintained that it was quite impossible for Margaret to marry a divorced member of the Household. She must wait until she was twenty-five and apply again. He advised Townsend to depart meanwhile for the equivalent of Oklahoma. The Queen took the first part of his advice but not the second. She insisted that Townsend should keep his position in her mother's ménage – a well-meant but naïve gesture from an elder sister who seems to have felt that if she herself had a husband and children and the Crown, Margaret could at least have Townsend. The couple were even invited to dinner in the Belgian Suite as a further sign of goodwill. Philip, to whom the consequence must have seemed obvious, amused himself with witticisms about the affair, but otherwise it was a pleasant enough evening.

Queen Mary was unaware of these deplorable events. She did not venture out in the bitter weather of early 1953 and by March it was clear to those around her that she was dying. On the night of 24 March the crowd waiting in fog and darkness outside Marlborough House watched in awestruck silence as the Queen's personal standard was lowered from the masthead. 'The glorious old girl' was dead. She was buried in St George's Chapel and that night there was a dinner party for twenty-eight members of the family at Windsor Castle. Prince Paul of Yugoslavia, his wartime treachery forgiven and forgotten, sat between the Queen and the Queen Mother. The Duke of Windsor, who had followed his mother's coffin and watched it lowered into the familiar vault, was not invited.

The Queen and her family remained at Windsor while a large army of workmen moved into Buckingham Palace to refurbish it for the Coronation. During this time Cecil Beaton went to take more pictures of Elizabeth and found that in her daughter's absence the Queen Mother was being given 'quite casual treatment' by the remaining staff. If Margaret and Townsend were there, they were not in evidence. Elizabeth's old rooms were bare, the furniture taken away; the whole place smelled of paint, electricians whistled in the Picture Gallery, it was bitterly cold. Some of the staff complained to Beaton's assistants that they 'couldn't think why the Queen Mother stayed on here so long – not that she will relish the move to Clarence House for there won't be the number of servants there that she's accustomed to.'[8] When Beaton asked for a vase of flowers he was told there wasn't a flower in the place.

Beaton was concerned for himself, as well as the Queen Mother. The photographer Baron was a friend of Prince Philip's and had been taking recent pictures of the family; he might get the job of doing the Coronation, which Beaton badly wanted. When the session was over he stopped at his favourite florist and ordered a huge bouquet of spring flowers to be sent to 'that adorable human being living in that cold, bleak Palace.' Beaton got the job, and meeting Elizabeth at the American Embassy ball a few days later thanked her for helping to bring this 'coup' about. 'She laughed knowingly with one finger high in the air.'[9]

On 18 May 1953 the Queen Mother, together with her House-hold and Margaret, finally moved into Clarence House. Townsend's account of this period is mainly concerned with the hostility of the Queen's Private Secretary, Tommy Lascelles, and the negligence of her press secretary, Richard Colville. He says nothing about his curious status, but presumably divided his time between mother and daughter, hoping for the best.

This would be the first televised Coronation and it must not only be right but seen by millions of viewers to be right. Rehearsals were top of the agenda. The Duke of Norfolk, Earl Marshal of England – whose job it is to reproduce history on these occasions – was a Roman Catholic. He got on with co-ordinating, planning, choreographing and rehearsing the operation while Geoffrey Fisher, Archbishop of Canterbury, thought up ideas such as reintroducing Armills (or bracelets) used in the Coronation of Elizabeth I. Fisher took great delight in instructing the Press about mysteries such as the Recognition, the Oath, the Anointing, the Investiture, the Crowning and the Enthronement, not forgetting the Ampulla, the Spoon and, of course, the Armills. He also released confidences such as that Elizabeth I's Armills were much too cumbersome for Elizabeth II, so it had been suggested to the Commonwealth that it might give her enough gold to make daintier ones.[10] He also confided that George VI had used up all the anointing oil, so a Bond Street chemist was busy concocting some more from King Charles I's recipe; in order that his sense of smell should not be impaired the good man had given up smoking for a month. The Press transferred the information, suitably adapted, to the pagan hordes who for the first time would participate in these ancient ceremonies.

Buckingham Palace Ballroom was marked out with posts and tapes in order that the Queen, a large sheet pinned to her shoulders, might rehearse her moves to the accompaniment of gramophone records of her father's Coronation. Presumably she had read his account and was on the look-out for accidents. On 28 May the Queen Mother and Princess Margaret rehearsed the procession to their seats in the Abbey and there was a final dress rehearsal the following day with stand-ins for the principal performers. The Queen's understudy was the Duchess of Norfolk, the first time since the Reformation that a Roman Catholic had taken the rôle. According to her husband she gave 'a superb performance'.[11]

> In she came, glittering from top to toe, diamonds everywhere, a two-foot hem of solid gold on her open dress – the Queen Mother playing second-lead as beautifully as she had played the first. On she came up the aisle with a bow here to Prince Bernhard, a bow there to a row of ambassadors, and up those tricky steps with no looking down like the Duke of Gloucester, no half turn to check on her train like the Duchess of Kent, no hesitation at the top like Princess Margaret, no nervous nod of the head like Princess Mary . . .[12]

Channon, not for the first time but extraordinary in the context, was cruel: 'Queen Mum was OK, but compared badly with Queen Mary's entry last time.'[13] Cecil Beaton saw 'The Mistress of the Robes to the Queen Mother, of towering height . . . minimised by the enormous presence and radiance of the petite Queen Mother. Yet in the Queen Widow's expression we read sadness combined with pride.'[14] Harold Nicolson watched it on television in the comfort of the Travellers' Club, but went outside to see the procession. It was pouring with rain and he expressed no particular sympathy for the Queen Mother and Margaret, drenched in their open carriage, but commented that 'the procession characteristically . . . ended by an ambulance for any horses that might get hurt.'[15] Brigadier Clark, in the Abbey, saw a grandmother managing her four-and-a-half-year-old grandson. Charles, in an oyster-coloured satin suit with a Coronation medal pinned to his shirt and his hair slicked down with brilliantine, hung perilously over the Royal Gallery until Elizabeth hauled him back; then he disappeared altogether. His grandmother, searching for him with one foot and muttering entreaties, kept devotedly looking at the crowning of her daughter. At last the child emerged, triumphantly holding her handbag,[16] and from then on pestered his grandmother and aunt with questions. Someday in the next century, a different world, he would be in his mother's place. In the meanwhile, Charles must be kept quiet.

News arrived that day that Hillary and Tenzing had reached the summit of Everest, but by early evening the international Press were on to a story of far greater significance: Princess Margaret had picked a piece of fluff off Peter Townsend's uniform in full view of the Royal Family and Coronation guests. This astounding gesture was headlined in the New York papers the following morning. The British Press, as in 1936, kept quiet for ten days. On Sunday, 14 June *The People* opened fire:

> It is high time for the British public to be made aware of the fact that newspapers in Europe and America are openly asserting that the Princess is in love with a divorced man and that she wishes to marry him. The story is of course utterly untrue. It is quite unthinkable that a royal princess, third in line of succession to the throne, should ever contemplate a marriage with a man who has been through the divorce courts.

Even forty years ago the power of the Press over our inviolable Royal Family and their Establishment was remarkable: a paragraph such as this could change their lives and cause their policies to be reversed overnight. The next day Townsend, who had been due to leave for Rhodesia with the Queen Mother and Margaret on 30 June, found himself posted as air attaché to Brussels. Patrick Plunket, the Queen's equerry, replaced him in the Clarence House entourage.

# Chapter Thirty-Three

A promise had been given that Townsend need not leave for Brussels until Margaret returned from Rhodesia on 17 July so in fact it was to be only just over two weeks' parting. The Queen Mother and the Princess, accompanied by Lady Hambleden, Lord Plunket, Private Secretary Captain Oliver Dawnay and Margaret's lady-in-waiting flew to Salisbury on 30 June as planned. After a State drive down Third Street – known as Royal Mile since Bertie and Elizabeth drove down it in 1947 – they relaxed, or discussed their problems, and on the following morning visited the farm of a Mr Miller, one of the leading cattle breeders in the country, and took morning tea with Mr Miller and his friends.

That night they boarded their train – its name changed from 'White' to 'Ivory' in the past six years – and arrived at Bulawayo at half past ten the next morning. The Queen Mother opened the Rhodes Centenary Exhibition before a crowd of 25,000 people. The impulse which drove Rhodes on to the north, she said, was no mere desire for territorial expansion; it was something more than political; in its essence it was a *spiritual* motive. The Exhibition showed the 'wonderful progress' that had taken place in Central Africa; 'the whole development has been that of a tiny white community, surrounded by primitive Africans, growing into a young and flourishing nation.' The *Times* leader was considerably more ironic:

> Starting from the current Victorian agnosticism, [Rhodes] chose to believe in God upon a balance of probabilities, and found it 'obvious' that God was trying to produce a type of humanity most fitted to bring peace, liberty and justice to the world. He did not doubt that the race into which he had been born was alone on the earth in fulfilling the qualifications. This was his justification of Empire.

The next day, to prove her whole-hearted support for Rhodes' opinions, the Queen Mother made a last-minute decision to join the procession to his grave in Matapos. Wreaths were procured to lay on the hallowed spot. Photographs show the Queen Mother with the inevitable fur stole and peep-toes, looking merry, Margaret glum. To cheer her up Elizabeth decided to give a party at Government House for pressmen, broadcasters and local journalists. The only creature in which Margaret appeared to take the slightest interest was a leopard cub.

From Bulawayo they travelled by train to Gwelo, where there was a triumphal arch proclaiming GREETING GREAT WHITE QUEEN AND GREAT WHITE PRINCESS and a choir from Johannesburg singing an anthem in praise of 'all descendants of Queen Victoria'. Then a night run through Salisbury, Marandellas and Rusapi to Umtali in Southern Rhodesia, a town comprising 7,000 whites and 18,000 Africans. Here the Queen Mother unveiled a memorial to Kingsley Fairbridge, originator of the Fairbridge farm schools, reputedly 'one of the most successful child migration schemes in Africa.' Then a day's break to the Leopard Rock Hotel in the Vumba Mountains, where they received the news that Townsend had been told to report for duty in Brussels on 15 July, two days before they were due to go home.

Anyone who has been a spoiled girl in love – or the mother of one, come to that – can imagine the scene. Margaret raged, wept and took to her bed. Her mother explained that she had a bad cold. Two days later Margaret was flown back to Salisbury in the Prime Minister's Dakota, where she was attended by a Dr Michael Gelfand, 'a specialist in the Government medical service'.

By the time her mother joined her on 12 July Margaret had recovered sufficiently to attend a display by the British South African Police, enlivened with Highland dancing performed by the local Caledonian Society; but although Elizabeth was enthusiastic about the Harare African Township her daughter couldn't face it. Meanwhile in Kenya, a thousand or so miles to the north, Mau Mau had stolen binoculars, blankets and tins of food from TreeTops Hotel and attacked Royal Lodge at Sagana, where only last year the prospective Queen had watched floodlit elephants.

It couldn't have been a very enjoyable trip, for all the benevolent smiles and bland speeches. A ball at Government House in Margaret's honour was attended by 850 'young guests' from all over the colony, some chosen by ballot. The Princess was as sophisticated as her social drawbacks would allow and by no means stupid. If she put a brave face on that evening she too was a chip off the old block. The next day they drove to the village of Mrewa 'in the heart of the native area', where they were much diverted by Chief Mangwande's welcoming address: 'Welcome, mother of our gracious Queen and British Empire, in which space and distance have become of small account when words and works may encircle the globe as does the sun, so that no part of the Empire may brood in darkness . . . Welcome also to the daughter of our honoured Empire!' An eighty-year-old chief with a long white beard did an impromptu caper for their benefit but unfortunately collapsed with the strain.

On 15 July, while they were attending a tobacco auction in Salisbury, Peter Townsend arrived in Brussels. Three days later mother and daughter were at Ascot with the Queen and Prince Philip. The Queen Mother looked flourishing, but the stress of the last few months required her suddenly to take to her bed and Margaret toured the gardens of Stoke Newington, Holloway and Finsbury in her place.

This was Elizabeth's fourth Coronation Year. Apart from the Atom Bomb and television and the fact that machines went faster and higher, there was little change in the basic pattern. God was still active, drowning 307 people in British floods in January and 1,794 in the Netherlands. There were earthquakes in Persia and the Greek Islands, tornadoes in Texas, Michigan and Ohio, tremors in Ethiopia. The Russians exploded an H-Bomb in Siberia, the United States dropped the biggest ever Atom Bomb over Nevada and the British dropped a couple more on Woomera, Australia. A more ancient method of warfare was revived by the United Nations Command in Korea with the offer of $50,000 reward for every Communist 'plane delivered intact to non-Communist territory and a further bonus of $50,000 to the first Communist pilot to arrive. The jackpot was won by a North Korean pilot, who flew his MiG-15 to an air base near Seoul and retired a rich man. The Korean war ended on 27 July after three years and twenty-five days.

Accidents were unspectacular: eleven people killed in a collision on the Central Line, forty-three in a BOAC Comet crash near Calcutta, twenty-seven in a BEA Viscount crash in Belfast, 133 drowned when the mail ferry *Princess Victoria* foundered off the coast of County Down. Julius and Ethel Rosenberg were executed as spies on 19 June, John Halliday Christie sentenced to death on 25 June for the murder of six women. More happily, Dilys Cadwaladr won the Bardic Crown at the

Rhyl Eisteddfod and the International Court of Justice unanimously decided that sovereignty over the islets and rocks of the Ecrehous and Minquiers in the Channel Islands belonged to the United Kingdom.

Practically nobody was assassinated except the heir to the Bey of Tunis and the vice-chairman of the Tunis municipal council. Even the revolutions didn't come off, though they were attempted in Bolivia, Bulgaria and Cuba. There were the usual riots, skirmishes and emergencies – the situation in Kenya was known as the latter. On 8 April Jomo Kenyatta was sentenced to seven years' hard labour. Stalin died from cerebral haemorrhage and was briefly succeeded by Malenkov. Eisenhower took over from Harry Truman. Marshal Tito was voted President of Yugoslavia by 568 votes to one. British royalty came into the limelight with the Coronation, Queen Mary's death, the Townsend affair and the Queen's trip to Australia and New Zealand at the end of the year, during which time the Queen Mother was one of the five Counsellors of State and deputised for her daughter. Carol of Rumania died in Portugal, King Ibn Saud died in Riyadh, King Faysal II took the oath in Baghdad, King Husain took it in Jordan, King Norodom Sihanouk of Cambodia fled to Siam on 13 June and returned on 21 June; the Shah of Persia fled to Baghdad on 16 August and returned on 22 August; King Sisavang Vong of Laos fled from his capital of Luang Prabang on 10 May and never returned. The Egyptian monarchy was abolished. Prince Jean of Luxembourg married Princess Josephine Charlotte of Belgium and Princess Ragnhild of Norway married Erling Lorentzen, a commoner. Apart from the Coronation it was all relatively poor stuff.

Our great-grandchildren will know more what the royal family thought of it than we do, and I doubt whether our great-grandchildren will care much. One of the last entries in Channon's published journal was, for him at least, a happy valediction: 'Goodbye, wonderful Coronation Summer. I have revelled in you and drunk your pleasure to the dregs.'[1]*

*Chips was knighted in 1957. He died two years later at the age of sixty-one.

# Chapter Thirty-Four

By 1954 Margaret had taken up again with friends she had abandoned for Townsend – Billy Wallace, Peter Ward, Henry Porchester, Colin Tennant, Judy Montagu, the Fifties equivalent of the Bright Young Things. She was smoking her cigarettes through an exaggeratedly long tortoiseshell holder (Queen Mary's idea, she said), staying out late at insalubrious nightspots, behaving with a flamboyance unsuited to a twentieth-century British princess however unremarkable in anyone else. The Press never tired of her; a lot of other people did.

In June that year Judy Montagu put on Edgar Wallace's *The Frog* 'in aid of charity' at the Scala Theatre. The leads were played by Lords Porchester and Norwich, Billy Wallace and Mrs Gerald Legge, the step-mother of Elizabeth's future granddaughter-in-law, with *vignettes* by Elsa Maxwell and Douglas Fairbanks. Margaret, ironically not allowed to perform in public, was Associate Director. 'The whole evening was one of the most fascinating exhibitions of incompetence, conceit and bloody impertinence that I have ever seen in my life,' wrote Noël Coward, a close friend of the Kents and Mountbattens as well as the Queen Mother and seldom disposed to criticise the *haute monde*. '. . . In the dressing-room afterwards, where we went civilly to congratulate Porchy, we found Princess Margaret eating *foie gras* sandwiches, sipping champagne and complaining that the audience laughed in the wrong places. We commiserated politely and left.'[1]

Margaret would soon be twenty-four – one more year to go and she would be free of her sister's veto. It would be nice to think that at this juncture she had a moment of active rebellion and sent Townsend an SOS; more likely that he, rebelling against being parted from his young sons, decided that exiled or not he was going to visit England. He arrived under the name of 'Carter' and after an elaborate cloak-and-dagger scheme involving Harrods bookshop where Brigadier Norman Gwatkin waited to take him to a waiting car, he was reunited with Margaret at Clarence House. A month or so later Margaret spent the night at Balmoral, unchaperoned, in the proximity, if not the company, of Colin Tennant. This, and the newspaper headlines, frightened Tennant so much that he fled to Venice. 'Dominic Elliot took over with Princess Margaret,'[2] he said laconically.

The crucial birthday was on 21 August. Crowds converged expectantly on Balmoral, perhaps hoping to see Townsend descend by parachute. All they saw was a Sale of Work at Abergeldy in aid of Craithie Church, with the Queen Mother, the Queen, her children and her sister selling the work. On 1 October Anthony Eden, himself divorced and remarried, arrived at Balmoral with the news that certain members of the Cabinet, headed by the Marquess of Salisbury – that same 'Bobbety' who had provided the Comet for Elizabeth's amusement – threatened to resign if the Princess married the divorced Group Captain; also, if she persisted, it must be made clear that she would forfeit her right to succession, her Civil List allowance and her domicile in the United Kingdom.

Margaret had already arranged to meet Townsend in London on 13 October. On 9 October the Queen Mother flew to the Castle of Mey. On the 13th, as arranged, Townsend turned up at Clarence House.[3] Elizabeth was back before the weekend and on Sunday Margaret and her mother walked round the garden at the Royal Lodge for forty minutes. That may not sound long, but anyone who has spent forty minutes walking round the garden with their daughter or mother knows that something more than the floribundas is being discussed. Apart from the ravening packs of reporters, Townsend and Margaret spent a normal evening with the Mark Bonham Carters on Monday. On Wednesday they didn't meet; Margaret had dinner at Lambeth Palace with Archbishop Fisher, her mother, the Queen and the Duke of Edinburgh. On Thursday the Cabinet assembled to discuss a Bill of Renunciation to free the Princess of her responsibilities under the Royal Marriages Act and enable her to marry Townsend in a civil ceremony. The consequences were unaltered. Apart from Lord Salisbury's resignation, which might considerably weaken Eden's government, she would have to live abroad, possibly for five years, on an air attaché's pay. Uncle David's example was not encouraging.

On Friday, in driving rain and bitter wind, the family gloomily gathered together for the unveiling of King George VI's statue in

Carlton Gardens. On Monday the *Times*, more hurt than angry, pointed out that the Royal Family 'is a reflection of our better selves' – if the Queen's sister entered into a union which our better selves could not 'in conscience regard as a marriage', that reflection would become distorted. As for the young woman's happiness, we must not forget 'that happiness in the full sense is a spiritual state and that its most precious element may be the sense of duty done.' Meanwhile the Church was bellowing for its strayed lamb with phrases like 'an affront to religion' and 'contrary to the law of Christ'.

Given the particular personalities and circumstances, the result was inevitable. Margaret, or Townsend, or both, decided the game wasn't worth the candle. On the evening of the *Times* leader they gave up. For some obscure reason 'the royal advisers' were against making the decision public. On Thursday Margaret went to see Archbishop Fisher and officially returned to the fold, but it was not until the following Monday evening that the BBC broke into its programmes to broadcast her renunciation statement:

> I would like it to be known that I have decided not to marry Group-Captain Peter Townsend. I have been aware that, subject to my renouncing my rights to succession, it might have been possible for me to contract a civil marriage. But, mindful of the Church's teaching, that Christian marriage is indissoluble, and conscious of my duty to the Commonwealth, I have resolved to put these considerations before any others. I have reached this decision entirely alone, and in doing so have been strengthened by the unfailing support and devotion of Group-Captain Townsend. I am deeply grateful for the concern of all those who have constantly prayed for my happiness.

Even, she might have added, if those prayers have been unavailing.

No doubt the Queen Mother had interceded on her daughter's behalf, if not necessarily on behalf of her happiness, and was heartily grateful for the result. She had always been a pious Christian, and since entering the Royal Family had made many friends in the upper echelons of the Church of England. The support of Archbishop Fisher in this sad business must have seemed a direct sign of God's co-operation and concern.

The Archbishop, however, was unable to leave well alone. He may have been haunted by the spectre of his predecessor, Cosmo Lang, but it clearly didn't warn him. On a television programme purporting to be about Lambeth Palace, he prattled to Richard Dimbleby about 'the Townsend affair'. Feeling that he might have been indiscreet, he followed this up with a letter to the *Times* the following day:

Of course she took advice. She got plenty of advice, asked for, and a good deal more unasked for . . . She was seeking all the time what God's will was, and when it became clear what God's will was, she did it, and that is not a bad thing for people in general to take note of . . . she especially thanked those who had prayed for her. Only people who have been praying for her can really understand the decisions demanded of her, the problems she had to face, and the tearing of the heart one way or another. Those who prayed for her know what she has been through, and those who have not do not.[4]

This arrogant gobbledegook got the Press on the raw. On 4 November the *Daily Sketch* accused the Archbishop of throwing words 'like a bundle of incendiaries on a dying fire' and suggested that the disestablishment of the Church would be no bad thing. The *Daily Mirror* positively demanded it: 'CRISIS HAS COME TO THE SERENE CLOISTERS OF THE CHURCH OF ENGLAND – Slowly a wave of anger mounts against the Primate, bringing with it a tide of doubt about the teachings of the Church on divorce . . .' The *Daily Express* said that the Princess's romance and heart had been 'broken by ecclesiastical influence'.[5] The ebullient Archbishop survived. Like many survivors, he was expert at juggling with the truth. When asked in Cape Town whether all the fuss had been justified, he replied cheerily, 'The whole thing – and you can quote me – was purely a stunt.'[6]

Five years later Margaret married Antony Armstrong-Jones (later first Earl of Snowdon) in Westminster Abbey. Apart from the Princess's status and its attendant publicity the marriage followed much the same course as innumerable other marriages: two children, eighteen years of increasing rancour, collapse. The Queen Mother, as fond of her son-in-law as she had been of Peter Townsend, watched in dismay. But there was no Mabell Airlie to bring Margaret to her senses and in May 1978 she was granted a decree nisi. Just over six months later Lord Snowdon married Lucy Lindsay-Hogg. The 'pretty and dashing' Margaret Rose has remained single for the rest of her life.

As far as the country was concerned the only constructive result of all this was that the official attitude to divorce became more tolerant, the Church lost much of its authority and the divorce laws themselves were eventually made more humane. The image of a King who sacrificed the throne for the woman he loved had been replaced in the mythology of the New Elizabethans by the Princess who sacrificed the man she loved for the sake of duty, a title, and £15,000 a year. This was exactly what Elizabeth had prayed for. How perplexing, then, to see David Windsor devotedly faithful to Wallis until his death; Peter Townsend married to a beautiful young Belgian, living happily ever after; her divorced son-in-law content with his family and his work; and her dutiful daughter, brought up on the highest moral principles, with her mother's shining example always before her, growing older alone, unappreciated and unloved. Most of us would ask ourselves where we went wrong. To Elizabeth, unaware of far worse disasters to come, it must have seemed that God Himself had blundered.

# Chapter Thirty-Five

It is one thing to drift, smiling radiantly, in the wake of a King; quite another to take the responsibility alone. In October 1954 the Queen Mother flew to the United States to receive a fund collected in commemoration of King George VI. During that week she accepted a cheque at the Waldorf-Astoria banquet wearing one of Hartnell's crinolined creations and smothered in priceless jewellery, unveiled a couple of portraits, met Senator McCarthy and Richard Nixon at the British Embassy, stayed with the Eisenhowers in Washington, received an honorary Doctor of Laws degree at Columbia, trudged through forty-four galleries of the Metropolitan Museum of Art, expressed much admiration for the Guggenheim and was received by Congress.

But it was her lack of 'side' that endeared her to the American people. At the Commonwealth Ball she requested the band to play 'Hey there (you with the stars in your eyes)' and 'Hernando's Hideaway'. She 'adored' the Empire State Building, bought a steam shovel and dolls' plastic tea-set at FAO Schwarz, jewelled cashmere sweaters for Margaret and Lilibet at Hammacher Schlemmer, a magnetic bottle-opener, a Scrabble set on a turntable, a decanter equipped with an automatic measure – gifts for the Castle that had everything. A New York taxi driver, stuck in a traffic jam on Broadway, watched her arrival to see *The Pajama Game*, all sparkles and graciousness and royal fun. 'If she wasn't a Queen there's many a man who'd like to marry her,' he said. 'She'd be a pleasing handful at playtime.'[1]

Fired by the success of her first solo performance, the Queen Mother decided to go on tour. She appeared nine times in Canada, twice in Honolulu and Fiji, Australia, New Zealand, Tunisia and the Caribbean. In February 1965 she went to Jamaica to receive an honorary Doctorate of Letters bestowed on her by the eighty-two-year-old Princess Alice Countess of Athlone – the Alice who had marched her up a Scottish mountain so long ago – who sailed to Jamaica on a banana boat every January to fulfil her duties as Chancellor of the University College of the West Indies. The ceremony was hilarious. Princess Alice had a fit of giggles and nice Mr Adlai Stevenson, their distinguished speaker, was most droll. 'Well, Mr Stevenson,' the Queen Mother said, cocking her head and twinkling up at him, 'we were together at Oxford six weeks ago, and now we meet here. Where shall it be next?' 'You name the place, Ma'am,' he replied gallantly, 'and I'll be there.'[2]

A few days later the Queen Mother and her entourage drove to lunch with her dear friend Noël Coward. They had bullshots on the verandah and delicious curry served in steaming coconuts, followed by strawberries and rum cream pie. 'I am at her feet,' Coward wrote in ecstasy. 'She has infinite grace of mind, charm, humour and deep-down kindness, in addition to which she looks enchanting . . . The houseboy – by his special request – wore white gloves and a white coat. It was all tremendous fun . . . and she left behind her five gibbering worshippers.'[3]

Britain's African protectorates were the Queen Mother's favourite charity, run by old friends. To those of her own class, creed and colour in Rhodesia, Kenya, Uganda and Nyasaland, she brought reassurance that they were not forgotten and everything was still as it should be. 'Loving them as a Queen Mother should',[4] she presented herself to black Africans as *Mambo Kazi*, instructing them with suitably simple, if incomprehensible, parables such as 'When one ox pulls this way and the other that, nothing is achieved. It may even be that the yoke is broken. But when all bow their yokes the plough moves and the work for the harvest has begun.'

Sadly, Africa had to be removed from the Queen Mother's itinerary. Uganda declared its independence in 1962, Kenya the following year. Nyasaland became Malawi and Rhodesia, after endless troubles, emerged as Zambia and Zimbabwe. It was abundantly clear that even those independent republics which had once benefited from British rule, and were now members of the Commonwealth, no longer appreciated her loving care.

Deprived of Africa, between 1956 and 1985 the Queen Mother played Germany, Rome, Paris, Cyprus, and Iran as well as frequent guest appearances in the French provinces, the Channel Islands, the Isle of Man and Northern Ireland. A month before her eighty-fifth birthday she flew to Canada on an eight-day official visit and made larger headlines than usual by dropping her glove and picking it up. She then toured Ontario, Saskatchewan and Alberta, opened the fifth World Angus Forum, watched the 126th running of the Queen's Plate and insisted on being taken up the 850 foot CN Tower in Toronto in spite of the fact that he view was almost totally obscured by smog. The following month she visited Venice looking very overweight, as though her stiff little legs, absurdly shod in high-heeled peep-toes, could hardly support the trussed, baby-blue bolster of her body. Except for the automatic smile her expression was curiously stunned, her head nodding by clockwork as she listened to a long and voluble description of the great west window in the Basilica of San Marco. Climbing in and out of gondolas was precarious and although, after a moment's bewilderment, she cautiously accepted an ice-cream cornet from a gondolier she didn't seem to find it amusing. Viscount Norwich of Aldwick, bent from the hips, sidled along beside her except on the occasion when the royal launch got stuck in a canal and he was forced to leave her sitting in it by herself for a few minutes. She looked decidedly testy, as though she longed to be in Caithness playing charades or walking briskly with her dogs over the heather. From then on, as she gradually began to withdraw from a world she no longer understood, her engagements became less arduous. Apart from sailing to the Isles of Scilly she filled in the rest of that year by visiting supermarkets, stirring a celebratory cake for the Royal Navy, christening a new railway train and scattering a trowelful of token gravel on the roof of King's College Hospital.

Two of the Queen Mother's favourite rôles at home have been as Chancellor of London University and Lord Warden and Admiral of the Cinque Ports, neither of which parts had previously been played by a woman. The first, which she took over in 1955, lasted thirty-five years and was a resounding success. The second, which she still holds, entitles her to any flotsam and jetsam washed up between Shore Beacon, Essex, and Redcliffe in Sussex. It had been performed at various times in the past by Sir Robert Menzies, Sir Winston Churchill (he wore his costume to the Coronation of Elizabeth II) and the one-time Liberal Leader, Earl Beauchamp KG, though it is unlikely that this particular Warden was mentioned since in June 1931 he absented himself in a great hurry after being accused of homosexual practices by his brother-in-law, the Duke of Westminster – 'I thought fellows like that shot themselves,' King George V exclaimed in astonishment. The Earl was certainly not in the Queen Mother's thoughts when she declared, 'I feel both proud and humble to follow these great men,' while a nineteen-gun salute boomed through the sea mist and the new flag was broken above Dover Castle.

In the past forty years she has been associated, either as President or Patron, with 312 organisations, ranging from the Royal Agricultural Society to the Dachsund Club. She is Lady of the Order of the Garter, Lady of the Thistle, Dame Grand Cross of the Order of St John, Colonel-in-Chief of more than a dozen regiments, Commander-in-Chief of the Women's Army, Navy and Air Force and Royal Air Force Central Flying School, Honorary Colonel of the Inns of Court and City Yeomanry and Constable of Dover Castle. Well-known as a patron of the Arts, eleven years after his death she unveiled a memorial stone to 'Noël Coward, Playwright, Actor and Composer' in Westminster Abbey. The Address was given by Sir Richard Attenborough CBE, flowers laid at the foot of the stone by Lord Olivier OM and at its four corners by Miss Joyce Carey OBE, Sir John Mills CBE, Miss Evelyn Laye CBE and Dame Anna Neagle DBE. Penelope Keith gave The Toast from *Cavalcade* and the ancient Abbey, home of the Lords Spiritual, coronation place of monarchs, shrine of Shakespeare and Milton, filled with the nostalgic melodies of 'Someday I'll Find You' and 'I'll See You Again'. By the time the Ambrosian Singers had finished 'London Pride', there wasn't a dry eye in the house.

Until the 1990s her itinerary gave the impression of a hectic succession of commitments not possible to fulfil by any other woman of her age. How, people asked, did she do it? Mainly by helicopter. Sometimes in the Royal Yacht. Wherever she went a lady-in-waiting went with her, and she was nearly always accompanied by her faithful Private Secretary and friend, Sir Martin Gilliat. Their responsibility was to dispose of all the minute difficulties that might impede the royal progress, to keep their eyes peeled, ears to the ground, noses to windward. The organisation was impeccable, though sometimes upset by the lady's vagueness about time. The Queen Mother image was dressed, coiffured, made up, transported, deposited. When the performance was over it was fetched, transported, deposited, fed, cleaned and carefully put away for the night. If the Queen Mother beckoned, someone noticed; if she called, someone came. All she had to do when she dropped fresh as a daisy from the sky was to generate love, delight and enthusiasm. As this is her nature anyway and she thoroughly enjoyed it, it was not most people's idea of work, which is usually associated with effort and often with a dragging reluctance. Ceremonies conducted by the Queen, when she was one of the royal crowd, came low on the Queen Mother's list of priorities.

If one asked people what they thought lay behind this appearance of ceaseless activity, many would hazard a guess at suffering: 'She's been through it,' they would say knowingly. The Queen Mother has an instinctive distaste for disease, maiming, malformation of any kind,[5] which must have made her patronage of the British Home and Hospital for Incurables one of her more trying duties. Fortunately she has encountered less physical unpleasantness than many women of her age. Her appendix was removed in 1964 and in 1982 she choked on a fishbone during a dinner party at the Royal Lodge and had to be whisked to hospital to have it removed under a general anaesthetic. In 1966 she had a colostomy, a painful operation in which part of the colon is brought through an incision in the abdominal wall to form an artificial opening so that faeces can be discharged into a bag attached to the skin. For the next thirteen years this was euphemistically referred to as the Queen Mother's 'major abdominal surgery'. When Helen Cathcart, one of her numerous biographers, eventually revealed the facts the Colostomy Welfare Group was delighted: 'We always knew about the Queen Mother. That it has now become public knowledge will encourage the 20,000 or so people who have this operation every year . . . what a pity they don't talk about it.'

In the first decade of her widowhood, when she needed a little more comfort than usual, she was prone to stumbling or walking into unexpected furniture; in 1956 she fell down at Clarence House and twisted her ankle, in 1960 she knocked her leg at the Royal Lodge, in 1961 she fell during an Ascot houseparty at Windsor and broke a bone in her foot, in 1962 she 'stumbled' at Birkhall and broke it again. She then seems to have kept her balance until just before her grandson's wedding in 1981, when she tripped over at Ascot and wounded herself so severely that she ran a high temperature. After similar mishaps in her nineties she walks with a stick and her right leg is permanently bandaged.

One of the penalties of Elizabeth Bowes-Lyon's chosen profession has been to suffer her misfortunes in the public eye. Unpleasant though that may be, it is unlikely that she would have preferred the public ward. At the age of ninety-five sensible court shoes have replaced the peep-toes but she still dresses in the customary pastels, hat and jewellery. The Queen Mother, old and frail as she is, remains resolutely feminine.

The House of Windsor would not starve or go homeless without the £8,722,000 net they receive from the Civil List. A wealthy woman in her own right, the Queen Mother's portion of this sum is £643,000 a year tax-free – the largest allotted to any member of the family bar the Queen. Both the Queen and Prince Charles, at last forced to acknowledge a discrepancy between the royal lifestyle and the resources that support it, now pay tax 'on a voluntary basis'; the State rooms of Buckingham Palace have been opened to the (paying) public and the Royal Yacht will shortly be decommissioned instead of having its regular £17 million refit. The Queen Mother is not required to make such stringent economies. Her household, the family's second largest, consists of a Lord Chamberlain, a Private Secretary Comptroller and Equerry, an Assistant Private Secretary Comptroller and Equerry, a Treasurer and equerry, an equerry and extra equerries, an Apothecary, a Mistress of the Robes, ladies of the bedchamber, women of the bedchamber, extra women of the bedchamber, a Clerk Comptroller, a Clerk Accountant, an Information Officer and a number of minor clerks. A selection of these retainers accompanies her on visits to her country properties, the Royal Lodge in Windsor Great Park and the Castle of Mey in Caithness.

One does not have to be Goneril or Regan to question why all this should be necessary to an old lady who might, if it weren't for a whim of fate, be struggling to make ends meet on £1,720 a year Bereavement benefit. Comparison may be the best way of recognising differing standards, but is nevertheless odious. It is almost universally believed that the Queen Mother is invaluable as the last symbol of a secure monarchy and should therefore enjoy its privileges.

# Chapter Thirty-Six

Lady Airlie's advice had been right. Though Bertie may not have satisfied Elizabeth's longing for romance their marriage became an affectionate partnership, glowing ever brighter in hindsight. Those who failed to achieve this sensible compromise were moral failures and deserved little sympathy. Unfortunately, even in the days when the majority of people felt the same, many couples persisted in thinking themselves incompatible. Long before her own daughter's divorce Elizabeth was faced with a number of such cases in the family: in 1948 her niece Anne Anson, Jock's eldest girl and Patrick Lichfield's mother, divorced her husband to marry Prince George of Denmark; another niece, Nancy Moira, divorced in 1950 and remarried four years later, while Margaret and Townsend were enduring their enforced separation; in 1967 Lord Harewood, the Queen's cousin, was divorced by his wife and married Patricia Tuckwell, mother of his two-year-old son. In 1978 another royal nephew, Prince Michael of Kent, married the divorced Roman Catholic Baroness Marie-Christine von Reibnitz who was immediately accorded the title of Her Royal Highness, thereby invalidating Elizabeth's ostensible reason for the embargo on Wallis Windsor.

Gently but firmly, the Queen Mother dissociated herself from all these problems. 'When her niece married a Danish Prince,' Archbishop Fisher confided, 'she didn't disapprove; but she wouldn't go. Didn't want to get muddled up in it, if you see what I mean.'[1] Neither did she want to get muddled up in irregular marriages or any sort of unsuitable behaviour, such as the sad history of her nephew Timothy 16th Earl of Strathmore. Timothy Bowes-Lyon's mother died while preparing to move to Glamis after her husband's succession. His sister, Lady Harrington, who was to take her place as first lady of Glamis, died in Switzerland shortly afterwards; his elder brother, John Patrick, was killed in action in 1941. Crushed by these disasters added to his inherited melancholy, the elder Lord Strathmore became a recluse. He died in 1949 and Elizabeth, then Queen, went to his funeral. Nine years later Timothy married a nurse at the Home where he was being treated for alcoholism. Mary Bridget Brennan was a Roman Catholic, but at least she had not been divorced; there was no just cause or impediment why she should not be the Countess of Strathmore. Elizabeth ignored the wedding; so, therefore, did everyone else. When she was three weeks old the Countess' baby daughter died of bronchial pneumonia at Glamis. The Countess committed suicide shortly afterwards.[2] The Queen Mother sent a wreath, her sole acknowledgement of Timothy's existence from the day of his marriage until she attended his funeral five years later.

*

> The Duchess of York
> Said bother the stork!
> But the Kents cried with joy
>   It's a boy, it's a boy!

Whether I have quoted this doggerel correctly, or where it comes from, I have no idea; but it must mean that in the distant past somebody, somewhere, was concerned about the Yorks not having a son. If Elizabeth felt the same, her grandson the Prince of Wales reaped the benefit. It was said he reminded her of Bertie – as a young man Charles certainly displayed the same diffidence and apparent reluctance to be royal – but he was much more promising material. Jonathan Dimbleby, his authorised biographer, records the unusual fact that as a toddler the Prince would climb on to his grandmother's lap to listen with rapt attention to her stories.[3] Charles himself wrote 'Ever since I remember my grandmother has been the most wonderful example of fun, laughter, warmth, infinite security and, above all else, exquisite taste in so many things' – qualities which were perhaps not conspicuous in his immediate family.

The Queen Mother made no secret of her disapproval of the choice of Gordonstoun, with its emphasis on surviving physical hardship, as a school for the sensitive lad. (It was a typical Mountbatten idea. What was wrong with Eton?[4] Too near Windsor and Fleet Street said his father.[5]) No one could have been more appalled by his ordeal of being ducked, fully clothed, in a cold bath or sympathised more with his loneliness and fears.[6] On his frequent visits to Birkhall from Gordonstoun Charles implored her to persuade his parents to take him away, but the Queen Mother wouldn't do that. She would, she said, help him face it.[7] This was how she had made one King; now, happily, she was making another.

Charles was thirty-two when he married Diana Spencer, granddaughter of Ruth, Lady Fermoy, one of the Queen Mother's few close women friends and, since 1960, her Woman of the Bedchamber. Although shortly before her death Lady Fermoy disclosed that she had been against the marriage,[8] she and the Queen Mother were much in favour of it at the time. The birth of two great-grandsons over the next three years seemed to prove that her hopes had been well founded. If she sensed a deepening melancholy in the Prince of Wales it was probably only the Coburg in him coming out.

Charles had followed his grandfather's example and married a commoner. The Queen Mother's two younger grandchildren, Anne and Andrew, did the same. Unlike Elizabeth Bowes-Lyon, however, Diana Spencer, Mark Phillips and Sarah Ferguson could not adapt themselves, or be adapted to, the royal way of life. In June 1987 millions of incredulous television viewers of *It's A Royal Knockout* watched as the Duke and Duchess of York, the Princess Royal and her youngest brother Prince Edward jumped about in sacks and hit each other on the head with sausage balloons.[9] The Prince of Wales's marriage was on the rocks and the Princess Royal divorced by the time the Duchess of York beat a hasty retreat from Balmoral after the *Daily Mirror* ran a picture showing a wealthy admirer sucking her toes. In March 1992 the Yorks announced their separation. In June 1992 Andrew Morton published *Diana: Her True Story*, a book which threw the first shadow of the guillotine over the House of Windsor. The media pounced on the slightest rumour to feed an avid public and the Prince and Princess of Wales, icons guaranteeing the monarchy's survival, were seen for the first time as fallible people behaving in a way infallible commoners could condemn.

In December that year Buckingham Palace announced with regret that the Prince and Princess of Wales had decided to separate. Three days later the Princess Royal married Commander Timothy Laurence. The Queen lost her voice, but managed to croak that 1992 had been an *annus horribilis*. Two of the three great crises in the Queen Mother's life had been over marriage and divorce; the third not only involved her favourite grandson but threatened her whole way of life. The Queen Mother made no comment.

At the age of thirteen Princess Anne 'volunteered'[10] to go to Benenden, where she got very respectable A'level results and made up her mind to become the best eventing rider in the world, which she did. Perhaps it is not so necessary to be an example of 'infinite security' to girls. Anne's reaction to her grandmother is similar to her great-aunt Marina's: 'Sometimes when I think of her I find it depressing because I can't see any way that I could do what she's done,' she told Kenneth Harris in 1980. 'I'm not the best person to talk about her; it wouldn't be the same as the Prince of Wales talking. There is a rather special relationship between the eldest grandson and a grandmother, I think, which is not true of granddaughters.'[11]

The Princess Royal is definitely not *espiègle*, nor is she happy to be a royal figurehead. Never wasting time on her image, sensibly dressed, scowling if she feels like it, business-like and brusque, she attracts attention to her cause rather than her performance. While Charles is frequently photographed holding his grandmother's arm to help her along, protective and adoring, Anne is very seldom seen with the rest of the family.

The Prince of Wales occasionally takes his sons to Scotland but otherwise, as far as we know, the Queen Mother has little contact with her great-grandchildren as does their grandmother, the Queen. Peter and Zara Phillips seem to lead a reasonably normal life, apart from the fact that their mother is usually off saving other people's children, but the other four appear to spend their school holidays being whisked from place to place, one parent or the other competing as to which can give them the better time. This is so usual that it would not be worth remarking on if it weren't for the contrast with royalty's traditional upbringing. Perhaps it is an improvement. Perhaps in the future some distant Mountbatten-Windsor will become a teacher, statesman or astronaut, but that thought can give little comfort to a woman whose belief in the uniqueness of royalty was inspired by her family relationship with George V and Queen Mary.

The Windsors remained chronic discomforts until their deaths. In June 1967 the Queen invited Wallis to accompany the Duke to the unveiling of a Memorial plaque to Queen Mary – the first official recognition the Duchess had ever received from the royal family and the first time she and the Queen Mother had come face to face for over thirty years. The three elderly stars of 1936 – Elizabeth nearly sixty-seven, Wallis almost seventy and David seventy-three – greeted each other in public with undimmed antipathy and fierce smiles. The Queen Mother and her brother-in-law brushed cheeks for an instant. Wallis refused to curtsey to her, but accepted and dropped a proffered hand. She did curtsey to the Queen who, doubtless for good reason, looked furious throughout the ceremony. It was left to Marina, Dowager Duchess of Kent to give the Windsors lunch before they returned to Paris. The Queen Mother, the Queen and the Duke of Edinburgh went to the Derby.

Archbishop Fisher claimed that 'the Queen Mother's attitude to life is to make everything as easy as possible,'[12] but harboured resentment can never be made easy. The Queen's official acceptance of the Duchess of Windsor, the fact that her grandson Charles had actually visited Wallis and that Wallis was said to be fond of him, the threat of a reconciliation after all these years, was hard to take.

In November 1971 the Duke of Windsor was found to have inoperable cancer of the throat. Six months later the Queen, Prince Philip and the Prince of Wales went to see the old man in Paris. The Duke was dying, happy that his request for Wallis to be buried next to him at Frogmore had been granted. At the end of May his coffin was flown home in a VC10 jet, met by a Royal Guard of Honour, the Duke and Duchess of Kent and members of the government. He lay in state for two days, while 57,000 people filed past the catafalque. On 2 June Wallis, to whom the Duchess of York had refused so much as a cup of tea or a *petit-four*, was flown from Paris in an aeroplane of the Queen's Flight, met at Heathrow by Lord Mountbatten and driven to Buckingham Palace, where she was given the State Suite. Wallis was heavily sedated for this first visit to her husband's family. After the burial at Frogmore she wandered among the guests asking 'Where's the Duke? Why isn't the Duke here?' The Queen Mother is said to have taken her arm, murmuring, 'I know how you feel. I've been through it myself.'[13] This could have been construed as a pointed reminder, but certainly was not meant as such. Wallis flew back to Paris that afternoon and struggled on, becoming sicker in body and mind, for fourteen more years before being flown over to be ceremonially buried with her husband in Frogmore. Elizabeth never saw her again.

Whether the Queen Mother has 'forgiven' the Windsors or not is a sentimental speculation. They never harmed her; there is nothing to forgive. It would be more appropriate to wonder whether she has ever felt any remorse; any indication, if only between herself and the Almighty, of sackcloth and ashes. Humility is not listed among her many virtues, even by her most fervent admirers. The Windsors are among the subjects that are never, even obliquely, mentioned in her presence. They may be corpses in her wake or unfortunate spectres for whom she is not responsible; in either case the impression is that she says 'Poor souls', and walks buoyantly on.

# Chapter Thirty-Seven
# HER OWN VICTORY

> Yesterday, on the anniversary of VE-Day, it was for the Queen Mother that the vast crowds gathered outside Buckingham Palace. With the passing of a generation of wartime leaders, she remains a living link to those terrible times. Her courage and serenity then inspired the nation; her steadfast endurance now commands the love and respect of a generation not yet born when she came out on the balcony of Buckingham Palace in 1945. Churchill told the crowds then: 'This is your victory.' Yesterday it was hers.[1]

Vietnam, Korea, Cambodia, the Gulf War, the endless fratricide in Lebanon and Yugoslavia, even our wonderful defence of the Falklands, have not moved the Queen Mother anything like as much as 'her' war. As a nonagenarian she has specialised in commemorating it, regularly touring old bomb-sites in the East End, reminiscing with survivors, admiring their great-grandchildren. On the fiftieth anniversary of VE-Day, shortly before her ninety-fifth birthday, she hobbled out onto the balcony of Buckingham Palace. Standing between her two daughters in the place of honour she looked down on the vast crowd packing The Mall, her expression slightly bewildered, almost apprehensive, the smile tentative, as though she was trying to remember how to wear it. When Vera Lynn, the other heroine of that age, launched into 'White Cliffs of Dover' the Queen Mother began shyly mouthing the words. Her daughters, clasping their handbags, stared fixedly ahead.

'Reconciliation' was the theme of this three-day celebration. The President of Croatia sat next to the President of Bosnia in the VIP stand in Hyde Park, the Prince of Wales kissed his estranged wife for the cameras, leaders of fifty world states solemnly signed olive branches while pigeons of peace, more reliable than doves, flew overhead. Leaders of Christianity's various factions participated in a brilliantly staged Service of Reconciliation in Westminster Abbey, the Prime Minister, on his way to Berlin, was apparently untroubled by his reputed refusal to attend the celebratory Victory Parade in Moscow. While wartime aircraft laboured across the sky, fireworks, invisible in bright sunlight, exploded on the Palace roof in a fair imitation of anti-aircraft fire. At night beacons provided a nostalgic reminder of the Blitz and only corpses and burning buildings were missing from street-parties otherwise complete with sandbags, search lights, sirens and ration books. An advertisement for the *Sunday Times* ran the caption 'On VE night my mother was brought home from the pub in a wheelbarrow' under a picture of a winsome child with a daisy-chain in her hair. Presumably the woman was drunk, not dead; either way it was unclear why this should have been one of the paper's 'Intimate memories of Britain's finest hour'. No one was in the mood to notice such things. Spitfires over the white cliffs of Dover had turned into bluebirds at last.

It was an orgy of nostalgia to those with partial recall and very entertaining to those with no memory of the reality. The Queen Mother broke a long silence: 'This day will bring back many memories to many people. I do hope that all those who go to the many ceremonies will remember with pride and gratitude the men and women, armed and unarmed, whose courage really helped to bring us to victory. God bless them all.' Thunderous cheers echoed across the decades: cheers for her father-in-law, who reigned for a quarter of a century before realising that he was loved; cheers for her brother-in-law, the uncrowned King; cheers for Bertie as he sailed into Valetta harbour and stood beside her on the balcony that first VE-Day; cheers for her daughter and grandson, petering out as the wind changed but back in full strength now people could again see an image to adore. 'Queen Of All Our Hearts', the little old lady modestly waved her acknowledgment. Elizabeth appeared to have saved the monarchy for the second time.

But who is the adulation actually for? The shrewd, fairly intelligent upper-class girl who happened to marry a King, or an image created by people's longing for an inaccessible but sympathetic sweetheart, a Queen Mother of their own? Since the vast majority of admirers know very little about her beyond hagiography from the media and sycophantic biographies it is not unreasonable to suppose the latter, which proves nothing about the woman herself: she remains a smile, a coquettish wave, an endearing decoration on her time. No individual can merely be that. The Queen Mother has

participated in some of the major events of the century but the
memories that drift round in that old head may be even more
significant: the long-gone idyll of Edwardian summers, the ghosts
of Glamis; foxtrot melodies of the Twenties, the feel of silk stockings, the singed smell of a Eugene wave fighting with the scent of
a gardenia corsage, tennis parties and shooting parties, the guilty
excitement of being in love; walking down the aisle on Bertie's
arm as Duchess of York, the cool, papery texture of Queen Mary's
cheek, the crowds, Mr Szlumper and Mr Bushrod; arriving in Belgrade for Peter's christening, dimpling at Archdukes, gossiping with
forgotten Queens, keeping Bertie's spirits up; opening the ball with
David, Wallis Simpson's hideous gown, Wallis Simpson suggesting
changes to the garden, Wallis Simpson playing hostess at Balmoral,
Wallis Simpson; Bertie, diffident, pessimistic, irascible and always
adoring; the war they won together, the Roosevelts and Churchills,
dead friends who ruled the world. These fragments of the Queen
Mother's treasure would repay all the devotion that has been lavished
on her over a lifetime, but she will undoubtedly take the key to her
grave.

The Queen Mother's choice for her eight-fifth birthday radio programme reveals at least one side of the personality that has enchanted
the British public for almost a century. It is a scene from Noël Coward's *Private Lives*:

| | |
|---|---|
| *Elyot:* | You mustn't be serious, my dear one. It's just what they want. |
| *Amanda:* | Who's 'they'? |
| *Elyot:* | All the futile moralists who try to make life unbearable. Laugh at them. Be flippant. Laugh at everything – all their sacred shibboleths. Flippancy brings out the acid in their damned sweetness and light. |
| *Amanda:* | If I laugh at everything, I must laugh at us too. |
| *Elyot:* | Certainly you must. We're figures of fun all right . . . |
| *Amanda:* | And what happens if one of us dies? Does the one that's left still laugh? |
| *Elyot:* | Yes – yes, with all his might. |
| *Amanda:* | That's serious enough, isn't it? |
| *Elyot:* | No. No, it isn't. Death's very laughable – such a cunning little mystery. All done with mirrors. |
| *Amanda:* | Darling. I believe you're talking nonsense. |
| *Elyot:* | So is everyone else, in the long run. Let's be superficial and pity the poor Philosophers. Let's blow trumpets and squeakers, and enjoy the party as much as we can, like |

very small, quite idiotic schoolchildren. Let's savour the delights of the moment. Come and kiss me, darling, before your body rots and worms pop in and out of your eye-sockets . . .

'I suppose,' Queen Mary asked Lady Shaftesbury one day, 'one must force oneself to go on to the end?' Sooner or later the image of Queen Elizabeth the Queen Mother will be lowered with pomp and ceremony and lamentation into the Royal Vault, before it lies beside Bertie in his own Memorial Chapel forever. But the implacable end anticipated by Queen Mary is not part of Elizabeth's itinerary. It may be increasingly difficult to climb into a helicopter, but once air-borne the flight is effortless, skimming over the dull pedestrian world, skimming empty spaces and uneasy silences, neglect and indifference, landing only where the lights shine and the climate is entirely dependable. One day she will simply spin out of sight, emerging God knows where to carry on with the angels.

# Notes

*Chapter One*

1. Interview with Sir Martin Gilliat, the Queen Mother's Private Secretary, Clarence House, 1983.
2. *Forfar Herald*, 24 August 1900.
3. Philippe Julian, *Edward and the Edwardians*, (London 1967).
4. Leonard Woolf, *Sowing*, (London 1970).
5. Princess Alice, Duchess of Gloucester, *Memoirs*, (London 1983).
6. Lady Cynthia Asquith, *Queen Elizabeth*, (London 1937).
7. Ibid.
8. *The Diaries of Sir Henry Channon*, (London 1967).
9. James Wentworth Day, *The Queen Mother's Family Story*, (London 1967).
10. Interview with the Rt. Hon. Harold Macmillan PM, 1983.
11. Lady Cynthia Asquith, op. cit.
12. Ibid.
13. Ibid.
14. *Daily Express*, 1 July 1909.
15. Lady Cynthia Asquith, op. cit.

*Chapter Two*

1. Christopher Hibbert, *Edward VII: A Portrait*, (London 1982).
2. Kenneth Rose, *King George V*, (London 1983).
3. HRH the Duke of Windsor, *A King's Story*, (London 1951).
4. *Ottoline, the Early Memoirs of Ottoline Morrell*, (London 1974).
5. Lady Cynthia Asquith, *Queen Elizabeth*, (London 1937).
6. Princess Alice, Duchess of Gloucester, *Memoirs*, (London 1983).
7. Frances Donaldson, *King George VI and Queen Elizabeth*, (London 1977).
8. Helen Cathcart, *The Queen Mother Herself*, (London 1979).

*Chapter Three*

1. Kenneth Rose, *King George V*, (London 1983).
2. Ibid.
3. Ibid.
4. Lady Cynthia Asquith, *Queen Elizabeth*, (London 1937).
5. James, Viscount Stuart of Findhorn, *Within the Fringe*, (London 1967).
6. Princess Alice, Duchess of Gloucester, *Memoirs*, (London 1983).
7. Lady Cynthia Asquith, op. cit.
8. Lady Cynthia Asquith, *Diaries 1915–1918*, (London 1968).
9. James, Viscount Stuart of Findhorn, op. cit.
10. A J P Taylor, *English History 1914–1945*, (London 1970).
11. Elizabeth Longford, *The Queen Mother*, (London 1981).

*Chapter Four*

1. John Wheeler-Bennett, *King George VI*, (London 1958).
2. J G Lockhart, *Cosmo Gordon Lang*, (London 1949).
3. Sir John Wheeler-Bennett, op. cit.
4. Ibid.
5. HRH the Duke of Windsor, *A King's Story*, (London 1951).
6. Sir John Wheeler-Bennett, op. cit.
7. Mabell, Countess of Airlie, *Thatched with Gold*, (London 1962).
8. Sir John Wheeler-Bennett, op. cit.
9. Ibid.
10. Ibid.
11. Frances Donaldson, *Edward VIII*, (London 1974).
12. Sir John Wheeler-Bennett, op. cit.
13. Ibid.
14. Ibid.
15. Ibid.
16. Ibid.
17. Ibid.
18. Ibid.
19. Frances Donaldson, op. cit.
20. Sir John Wheeler-Bennett, op. cit.
21. Ibid.
22. Ibid.
23. Ibid.
24. Ibid.

25. Ibid.
26. Ibid.
27. Ibid.

*Chapter Five*

1. James, Viscount Stuart of Findhorn, *Within the Fringe*, (London 1967).
2. Sir John Wheeler-Bennett, *King George VI*, (London 1958).
3. Ibid.
4. Elizabeth Longford, *The Queen Mother*, (London 1981).
5. *The Lady*, June 1920.
6. Elizabeth Longford, op. cit.
7. Robert Graves & Alan Hodge, *The Long Weekend: A Social History of Great Britain 1918–1939*, (London).
8. Mabell, Countess of Airlie, *Thatched With Gold*, (London 1962).
9. *The Diaries of Sir Henry Channon*, (London 1967).
10. Elizabeth Longford, op. cit.
11. *The Diaries of Sir Henry Channon*, op. cit.
12. James, Viscount Stuart of Findhorn, op. cit.
13. Sir John Wheeler-Bennett, op. cit.
14. Elizabeth Longford, op. cit.
15. Ibid.
16. Letter from Queen Victoria to her seventeen-year-old grand-daughter, Princess Victoria, 8 December 1880.
17. Robert Sencourt, *The Reign of Edward VIII*, (London 1962).
18. Barbara Cartland, *We Danced All Night*, (London 1970).
19. James, Viscount Stuart of Findhorn, op. cit.
20. Helen Cathcart, *The Queen Mother Herself*, (London 1979).
21. *Tatler*, 13 October 1920.
22. Mabell, Countess of Airlie, op. cit.

*Chapter Six*

1. David Sinclair, *Queen and Country*, (London 1979).
2. James, Viscount Stuart of Findhorn, *Within the Fringe*, (London 1967).
3. Mabell, Countess of Airlie, *Thatched With Gold*, (London 1962).
4. Sir John Wheeler-Bennett, *King George VI*, (London 1958).
5. Ibid.
6. Ibid.
7. Ibid.

8. James Pope-Hennessy, *Queen Mary*, (London, 1959).
9. Ann Edwards, *Matriarch*, (London 1984).
10. Mabell, Countess of Airlie, op. cit.
11. *Tatler*, 16 March 1921.
12. Richard Hough, *Edwina*, (London 1983).
13. *Tatler*, 10 August 1921.
14. Mabell, Countess of Airlie, op. cit.
15. Ibid.
16. Robert Sencourt, *The Reign of Edward VIII*, (London 1962).
17. Martin Gilliatt.
18. Rachel Bowes-Lyon.
19. Harold Macmillan.

*Chapter Seven*

1. Robert Lacey, *Majesty*, (London 1977).
2. David Sinclair, *Queen and Country*, (London 1979).
3. Helen Hardinge, *Loyal to Three Kings*, (London 1967).
4. *Tatler*, 21 September 1921.
5. Helen Cathcart, *The Queen Mother Herself*, (London 1979).
6. James Pope-Hennessey, *Queen Mary*, (London 1959).
7. Ibid.
8. Brian Masters, *Great Hostesses*, (London 1982).
9. Ann Edwards, *Matriarch*, (London 1984).
10. Sir John Wheeler-Bennett, *King George VI*, (London 1958).
11. J C C Davidson, *Memoirs of a Conservative 1910–1937*, (London 1969).
12. Ibid.
13. Ibid.
14. Ibid.
15. Ibid.
16. Robert Sencourt, *The Reign of Edward VIII*, (London 1962).
17. HRH the Duke of Windsor, *A King's Story*, (London 1951).
18. Frances Donaldson, *King George VI and Queen Elizabeth*, (London 1977).
19. Kenneth Rose, *King George V*, (London 1983).
20. Mabell, Countess of Airlie, *Thatched With Gold*, (London 1962).
21. Ibid.
22. Ibid.

*Chapter Eight*

1. HRH Princess Alice Countess of Athlone, *For My Grandchildren*, (London 1980).
2. James, Viscount Stuart of Findhorn, *Within the Fringe*, (London 1967).
3. James Pope-Hennessey, *Queen Mary*, (London 1959).
4. Theo Aronson, *Royal Family: Years of Transition*, (London 1983).
5. Kenneth Rose, *King George V*, (London 1983).
6. Ibid.
7. Ibid.
8. Ibid.
9. *The Diaries of Sir Henry Channon*, (London 1967).
10. James Pope-Hennessey, op. cit.
11. Ibid.
12. Mabell, Countess of Airlie, *Thatched With Gold*, (London 1962).
13. James Pope-Hennessey, op. cit.
14. James Bryan & Charles J V Murphy, *The Windsor Story*, (London 1979).
15. James Pope-Hennessey, op. cit.
16. Ibid.
17. Kenneth Rose, op. cit.
18. Sir John Wheeler-Bennett, *King George VI*, (London 1958).
19. Mabell, Countess of Airlie, op. cit.
20. Ibid.
21. M C Carey, *Princess Mary*, (London 1922).
22. Frances Donaldson, *Edward VIII*, (London 1974).
23. James Pope-Hennessey, op. cit.
24. Truman Capote interviewed by *Esquire* magazine, March 1983.
25. HRH the Duke of Windsor, *A King's Story*, (London 1951).
26. Ibid.
27. Frances Donaldson, op. cit.
28. HRH the Duke of Windsor, op. cit.
29. Frances Donaldson, op. cit.
30. Noble Frankland, *Prince Henry Duke of Gloucester*, (London 1980).
31. Ibid.
32. *Durable Fire: The Letters of Duff and Diana Cooper 1913–1950*, (London 1983).
33. Noble Frankland, op. cit.
34. Ibid.

*Chapter Nine*

1. *The Diaries of Sir Henry Channon*, (London 1967).
2. *The Star*, 17 January 1923.
3. *Daily Sketch*, 18 January 1923.
4. Ibid.
5. Ibid.
6. Ibid.
7. J A Frere, *The British Monarchy at Home*, (London 1963).
8. HRH the Duke of Windsor, *A King's Story*, (London 1951).
9. Helen Cathcart, *The Queen Mother Herself*, (London 1979).
10. Ibid.
11. Ibid.
12. Helen Hardinge, *Loyal to Three Kings*, (London 1967).
13. Ibid.
14. Kenneth Rose, *King George V*, (London 1983).
15. HRH the Duke of Windsor, op. cit.
16. Ibid.
17. Lady Cynthia Asquith, *Queen Elizabeth*, (London 1937).
18. Dorothy Laird, *Queen Elizabeth The Queen Mother*, (London 1966).
19. Kenneth Rose, op. cit.
20. *The Lady*, 26 April 1923.

*Chapter Eleven*

1. Brian Masters, *Great Hostesses*, (London 1982).
2. Ibid.
3. Ibid.
4. Sir John Wheeler-Bennett, *King George VI*, (London 1958).
5. HRH Duke of Windsor, *A King's Story*, (London 1951).
6. James Pope-Hennessey, *Queen Mary*, (London 1959).
7. HRH Duke of Windsor, op. cit.
8. James Pope-Hennessey, op. cit.
9. Lady Cynthia Asquith, *Queen Elizabeth*, (London 1937).
10. Helen Hardinge, *Loyal to Three Kings*, (London 1967).
11. Sir John Wheeler-Bennett, op. cit.
12. Aubrey Buxton, *The King in his Country*, (London 1955).
13. Robert Sencourt, *The Reign of Edward VIII*, (London 1962).
14. Sir John Wheeler-Bennett, op. cit.
15. Ibid.

*Chapter Twelve*

1. Sir John Wheeler-Bennett, *King George VI*, (London 1958).
2. J R Clynes, *Memoirs*, Vol. 2, (London 1937).
3. Kenneth Rose, *King George V*, (London 1983).
4. Harold Nicolson, *King George V*, (London 1952).
5. Harold Nicolson, *Diaries and Letters 1930–1939*, (London 1952).
6. A J P Taylor, *English History 1914–1945*, (Oxford, 1965).
7. Sir John Wheeler-Bennett, op. cit.
8. Ibid.
9. Ibid.
10. Ibid.
11. Ibid.
12. Ibid.
13. HRH Princess Alice Countess of Athlone, *For My Grandchildren*, (London 1980).

*Chapter Thirteen*

1. Harold Nicolson, *King George V*, (London 1952).
2. Ibid.
3. Elizabeth Longford, *Elizabeth R*, (London 1983).
4. Kenneth Rose, *King George V*, (London 1983).
5. Sir John Wheeler-Bennett, *King George VI*, (London 1958).
6. PD, Vol. 202 1231.
7. Sir John Wheeler-Bennett, op. cit.
8. Ibid.
9. Ibid.
10. Dermot Morrah, *The Work of the Queen*, (London 1958).
11. Sir John Wheeler-Bennett, op. cit.
12. Dorothy Laird, *Queen Elizabeth The Queen Mother*, (London 1966).
13. *Durable Fires: The Letters of Duff and Diana Cooper 1913–1950*, (London 1983).
14. Dorothy Laird, op. cit.
15. James Pope-Hennessey, *Queen Mary*, (London 1959).
16. Sir John Wheeler-Bennett, op. cit.
17. James Lees-Milne, *Harold Nicolson: A Biography 1886–1929*, (London 1980).
18. Mabell, Countess of Airlie, *Thatched With Gold*, (London 1962).
19. Sir John Wheeler-Bennett, op. cit.

*Chapter Fourteen*

1. David Duff, *George and Elizabeth*, (London 1983).
2. *Time* magazine, 11 June 1923.
3. Aldo Castellani, *Microbes, Men and Monarchs*, (London 1963).
4. Lord Harewood, *The Tongs and the Bones*, (London 1981).
5. Aldo Castellani, op. cit.
6. HRH Duke of Windsor, *A King's Story*, (London 1951).

*Chapter Fifteen*

1. Rebecca West, *1900*, (London 1982).
2. André Maurois, *Memoirs*, (London 1970).
3. Stella King, *Princess Marina: Her Life and Times*, (London 1969).
4. *The Diaries of Sir Henry Channon*, (London 1967).
5. Kenneth Rose, *King George V*, (London 1983).
6. Princess Alice Duchess of Gloucester, *Memoirs*, (London 1983).
7. Dermot Morrah, *The Work of the Queen*, (London 1958).
8. Sir Robert Bruce Lockhart, *Diaries*, (London 1973).
9. Gloria Vanderbilt & Thelma Furness, *Double Exposure, (London 1959)*.
10. Ibid.
11. Elizabeth Longford, *Elizabeth R*, (London 1983).
12. Sir Robert Bruce Lockhart, op. cit.
13. Stella King, op. cit.
14. *The Diaries of Sir Henry Channon*, op. cit.
15. Kenneth Rose, op. cit.
16. Princess Alice Duchess of Gloucester, op. cit.
17. Kenneth Rose, op. cit.
18. The Duchess of Windsor, *The Heart Has Its Reasons*, (London 1956).

*Chapter Sixteen*

1. HRH Duke of Windsor, *A King's Story*, (London 1951).
2. Harold Nicolson, *King George V*, (London 1952).
3. J G Lockhart, *Cosmo Gordon Lang*, (London 1949).
4. Ibid.
5. Ibid.
6. Kenneth Rose, *King George V*, (London 1983).
7. Helen Hardinge, *Loyal to Three Kings*, (London 1967).
8. The Duchess of Windsor, *The Heart Has Its Reasons*, (London 1956).
9. *The Diaries of Sir Henry Channon*, (London 1967).

10. The *Times*, 21 January 1936.
11. HRH Duke of Windsor, op. cit.
12. The Duchess of Windsor, op. cit.
13. Marion Crawford, *The Little Princesses*, (London 1950).
14. HRH Duke of Windsor, op. cit.

*Chapter Seventeen*

1. Harold Nicolson, *King George V*, (London 1952).
2. Francis Watson, *Dawson of Penn*, (London 1950).
3. *The Diaries of Sir Henry Channon*, (London 1967).
4. Harold Nicolson, *Diaries and Letters 1930–1939*, (London 1952).
5. Sir John Wheeler-Bennett, *King George VI*, (London 1958).
6. The Duchess of Windsor, *The Heart Has Its Reasons*, (London 1956).
7. Helen Hardinge, *Loyal to Three Kings*, (London 1967).
8. The Duchess of Windsor, op. cit.
9. Ibid.
10. Marion Crawford, *The Little Princesses*, (American edition 1950).
11. Ibid (British edition 1950).
12. *The Diaries of Sir Henry Channon*, (London 1967).
13. Princess Alice, Duchess of Gloucester, *Memoirs*, (London 1983).
14. Helen Hardinge, op. cit.
15. Ibid.
16. Harold Nicolson, *King George V*, (London 1952).
17. HRH Duke of Windsor, *A King's Story*, (London 1951).
18. James Pope-Hennessey, *Queen Mary*, (London 1959).
19. Helen Hardinge, op. cit.
20. Ibid.
21. Marie Belloc Lowndes, *Diaries*, (London 1971).
22. Helen Hardinge, op. cit.
23. J A Frere, *British Monarchy at Home*, (London 1963).
24. Keith Middlemas & John Barnes, *Baldwin: A Biography*, (London 1969).
25. Helen Hardinge, op. cit.
26. Ibid.
27. HRH Duke of Windsor, op. cit.
28. Ibid.
29. Ibid.

*Chapter Eighteen*

1. Helen Hardinge, *Loyal to Three Kings*, (London 1967).

2. *Time* magazine, 9 November 1936.
3. HRH Duke of Windsor, *A King's Story*, (London 1951).
4. Helen Hardinge, op. cit.
5. The Duchess of Windsor, *The Heart Has Its Reasons*, (London 1956).
6. Frances Donaldson, *Edward VIII*, (London 1974).
7. The Duchess of Windsor, op. cit.
8. Frances Donaldson, op. cit.
9. Harold Nicolson, *Diaries and Letters 1930–1939*, (London 1952).
10. HRH Duke of Windsor, op. cit.
11. Ibid.
12. Ibid.
13. Diana Moseley, quoted by Alastair Forbes, *The Spectator*, 4 January 1980.
14. Dorothy Laird, *Queen Elizabeth The Queen Mother*, (London 1966).
15. Sir John Wheeler-Bennett, *King George VI*, (London 1958).
16. *The Diaries of Sir Henry Channon*, (London 1967).
17. Ibid.
18. Ibid.
19. Sir John Wheeler-Bennett, op. cit.
20. Ibid.
21. Ibid.
22. Ibid.
23. Ibid.

*Chapter Nineteen*

1. Sir John Wheeler-Bennett, *King George VI*, (London 1958).
2. Dorothy Laird, *Queen Elizabeth The Queen Mother*, (London 1966).
3. Philip Ziegler, *Crown and People*, (London 1978).
4. Sir John Wheeler-Bennett, op. cit.
5. Denis Judd, *King George VI*, (London 1982).
6. *The Diaries of Sir Henry Channon*, (London 1967).
7. Alastair Forbes, *The Spectator*, 4 January 1980.
8. Cecil Beaton quoted in Brian Masters' *Great Hostesses*, (London 1982).
9. Harold Nicolson, *Diaries and Letters 1930–1939*, (London 1952).
10. Keith Middlemas & John Barnes, *Baldwin: A Biography*, (London 1969).
11. *The Diaries of Sir Henry Channon*, op cit.
12. Philip Ziegler, *Diana Cooper*, (London 1981).
13. Winston Churchill, *The Gathering Storm*, (London 1948).

14. Frances Donaldson, *King George VI and Queen Elizabeth*, (London 1977).

*Chapter Twenty*
1. Lord Gorrell, *One Man Many Parts*, (London 1956).
2. Marion Crawford, *The Little Princesses*, (London 1950).
3. James Pope-Hennessey, *Queen Mary*, (London 1959).
4. Sir John Wheeler-Bennett, *King George VI*, (London 1958).
5. Ann Morrow, *The Queen Mother*, (London 1984).
6. Ibid.
7. J G Lockhart, *Cosmo Gordon Lang*, (London 1949).
8. Robert Lacey, *Majesty*, (London 1977).
9. David Duff, *Elizabeth of Glamis*, (London 1973).
10. Brian Masters, *Great Hostesses*, (London 1982).
11. The *Sunday Times*, 25 May 1980.
12. Janet Flanner, *London Was Yesterday*, (London 1975).
13. William L Shirer, *Berlin Diary*, (New York 1941).
14. James Pope-Hennessey, op. cit.

*Chapter Twenty-One*
1. Lord Harewood, *The Tongs and the Bones*, (London 1981).
2. Alastair Forbes, *Times Literary Supplement*, 4 January 1980.
3. Ibid.
4. Frances Donaldson, *Edward VIII*, (London 1974).
5. Cecil Beaton, *Self Portrait with Friends*, (London 1979).
6. Frances Donaldson, *King George VI and Queen Elizabeth*, (London 1977).
7. Ibid.
8. *Cavalcade*, 5 June 1937.

*Chapter Twenty-Two*
1. Frances Stevenson, *Lloyd George*, (London 1971).
2. Meryle Secrest, *Kenneth Clark*, (London 1984).
3. Ibid.
4. Ibid.
5. Ibid.
6. Michael Holroyd, *Augustus John*, (London 1974).
7. Ibid.
8. Diana Cooper, *The Light of Common Day*, (London 1959).
9. Ibid.
10. Ibid.

11. Sir John Wheeler-Bennett, *King George VI*, (London 1958).
12. William L Shirer, *Berlin Diary*, (London 1941).
13. Sir John Wheeler-Bennett, op. cit.
14. Ibid.
15. Lady Cynthia Asquith, *Diaries 1915–1918*, (London 1968).
16. James Pope-Hennessey, *Queen Mary*, (London 1959).
17. Harold Nicolson, *Diaries 1930–1939*, (London 1966).
18. James Pope-Hennessey, op. cit.
19. Sir John Wheeler-Bennett, op. cit.

*Chapter Twenty-Three*

1. Helen Cathcart, *The Queen Mother Herself*, (London 1979).
2. James Pope-Hennessey, *Queen Mary*, (London 1959).
3. Andrew Barrow, *Gossip 1920–1970*, (London 1978).
4. Robert Lacey, *Majesty*, (London 1977).
5. James Pope-Hennessey, op. cit.
6. Marion Crawford, *The Little Princesses*, (London 1950).
7. Sir John Wheeler-Bennett, *King George VI*, (London 1958).
8. Ibid.
9. Eleanor Roosevelt, *Autobiography*, (London 1962).
10. Ibid.
11. Marion Crawford, op. cit.
12. Harold Nicolson, *Diaries and Letters 1930–1939*, (London 1952).
13. Cecil Beaton, *Self Portrait with Friends*, (London 1979).
14. Sir John Wheeler-Bennett, op. cit.
15. Ibid.
16. Ibid.
17. Aubrey Buxton, *The King in his Country*, (London 1955).
18. Ibid.
19. Sir John Wheeler-Bennett, op. cit.
20. Winston Churchill, *The Gathering Storm*, (London 1948).

*Chapter Twenty-Four*

1. Robert Lacey, *Majesty*, (London 1977).
2. Sir John Wheeler-Bennett, *King George VI*, (London 1958).
3. Ann Morrow, *The Queen Mother*, (London 1984).
4. Sir John Wheeler-Bennett, op. cit.
5. Ibid.
6. Winston Churchill, *The Gathering Storm*, (London 1948).
7. Sir John Wheeler-Bennett, op. cit.

8. Ann Morrow, op. cit.
9. Andrew Duncan, *The Reality of Monarchy*, (London 1970).
10. Sir Eric St Johnston, *One Policeman's Story*, (London 1978).
11. Philip Ziegler, *Crown and People*, (London 1978).
12. Sir John Wheeler-Bennett, op. cit.
13. *By Safe Hand: Letters of Sybil and David Eccles 1939–1942*, (London 1983).
14. Princess Alice the Countess of Athlone, *For My Grandchildren*, (London 1980).
15. Marion Crawford, *The Little Princesses*, (London 1950).
16. *The Diaries of Sir Henry Channon*, (London 1967).
17. Sir John Wheeler-Bennett, op. cit.
18. Helen Cathcart, *The Queen Mother Herself*, (London 1979).
19. Sir John Wheeler-Bennett, op. cit.
20. Chester Wilmot, *The Struggle for Europe*, (London 1952).
21. Sir John Wheeler-Bennett, op. cit.
22. Chester Wilmot, op. cit.
23. Dorothy Laird, *Queen Elizabeth The Queen Mother*, (London 1966).
24. Sir John Wheeler-Bennett, op. cit.
25. Andrew Duncan, op. cit.
26. Chester Wilmot, op. cit.
27. Sir John Wheeler-Bennett, op. cit.
28. Ibid.
29. Ibid.
30. Ibid.
31. Alan Jenkins, *The Forties*, (London 1977).
32. Sir John Wheeler-Bennett, op. cit.
33. Ibid.
34. Ibid.
35. Ibid.
36. Ibid.
37. Ibid.
38. Ibid.
39. Ibid.
40. Ibid.
41. Ibid.

*Chapter Twenty-Five*

1. Princess Alexandra of Yugoslavia, *Prince Philip*,
2. Elizabeth Longford, *Elizabeth R*, (London 1983).

3. J G Lockhart, *Cosmo Gordon Lang*, (London 1949).
4. Sir John Wheeler-Bennett, *King George VI*, (London 1958).
5. Noble Frankland, *Prince Henry Duke of Gloucester*, (London 1980).
6. Ibid.
7. Ibid.
8. *The Diaries of Sir Henry Channon*, (London 1967).
9. Sir John Wheeler-Bennett, op. cit.
10. Stella King, *Princess Marina: Her Life and Times*, (London 1969).
11. PD Vo. 385 1894.
12. Sir Robert Bruce Lockhart, *Diaries*, (London 1973).
13. Osbert Sitwell, *Queen Mary and Others*, (London 1974).
14. James Pope-Hennessey, *Queen Mary*, (London 1959).
15. Osbert Sitwell, op. cit.
16. James Pope-Hennessey, op. cit.
17. Ibid.
18. Ibid.
19. Ibid.

## Chapter Twenty-Six

1. Michael Bloch, *The Duke of Windsor's War*, (London 1982).
2. Stephen Birmingham, *Duchess*, (London 1981).
3. Ibid.
4. Sir John Wheeler-Bennett, *King George VI*, (London 1958).
5. Leslie Hore-Belisha, *Private Papers*, (London 1960).
6. Michael Bloch, op. cit.
7. Ibid.
8. Frances Donaldson, *Edward VIII*, (London 1974).
9. The Duchess of Windsor, *The Heart Has Its Reasons*, (London 1956).
10. Michael Bloch, op. cit.
11. The Duchess of Windsor, op. cit.
12. Martin Gilbert, *Finest Hour: Winston Churchill 1939–41*, (London 1983).
13. Ibid.
14. Michael Bloch, op. cit.
15. Ibid.
16. James Pope-Hennessey, *Queen Mary*, (London 1959).
17. Michael Bloch, op. cit.

## Chapter Twenty-Seven

1. Sir John Wheeler-Bennett, *King George VI*, (London 1958).

2. David Duff, *Elizabeth of Glamis*, (London 1973).
3. Mabell, Countess of Airlie, *Thatched With Gold*, (London 1962).
4. Ibid.
5. Sir John Wheeler-Bennett, op. cit.
6. James Cameron, *The Best of Cameron*, (London 1981).
7. Ibid.
8. Peter Townsend, *Time and Chance*, (London 1978).
9. Ibid.
10. Ibid.
11. Basil Boothroyd, *Philip*, (London 1971).
12. William Purcell, *Fisher of Lambeth*, (London 1969).
13. Ibid.
14. James Lees-Milne, *Caves of Ice*, (London 1983).
15. Christopher Hibbert, *Edward VIII: A Portrait*, (London 1976).
16. Sir John Wheeler-Bennett, op. cit.
17. Richard Hough, *Mountbatten, Hero of our Time*, (London 1980).

## Chapter Twenty-Eight

1. HM Queen Alexandra of Yugoslavia, *Prince Philip: A Family Portrait*, (London 1949).
2. Marion Crawford, *The Little Princesses*, (London 1950).
3. Geoffrey Wakeford, *Thirty Years a Queen*, (London 1968).
4. Peter Townsend, *The Last Emperor*, (London 1975).
5. Sir John Wheeler-Bennett, *King George VI*, (London 1958).
6. Eleanor Roosevelt, *Autobiography*, (London 1962).
7. Ibid.
8. *The Diaries of Sir Henry Channon*, (London 1967).
9. Peter Townsend, op. cit.
10. Robert Lacey, *Majesty*, (London 1977).
11. Sir John Wheeler-Bennett, op. cit.
12. Anthony Holden, *Charles, Prince of Wales*, (London 1979).

## Chapter Twenty-Nine

1. Sir John Wheeler-Bennett, *King George VI*, (London 1958).
2. Ibid.
3. HM Queen Alexandra of Yugoslavia, *Prince Philip: A Family Portrait*, (London 1949).
4. *The Diaries of Sir Henry Channon*, (London 1967).
5. Basil Boothroyd, *Philip*, (London 1971).
6. Brigadier Stanley Clark, *Palace Diary*, (London 1958).

7. Harold Nicolson, *Diaries 1930–1964*, (London 1980).

*Chapter Thirty*

1. James Pope-Hennessey, *Queen Mary*, (London 1959).
2. Peter Townsend, *Time and Chance*, (London 1978).
3. Ibid.
4. James, Viscount Stuart of Findhorn, *Within the Fringe*, (London 1967).
5. The *Times*, 12 February 1952.
6. *The Diaries of Sir Henry Channon*, (London 1967).
7. Rebecca West, *1900*, (London 1982).
8. Dermot Morrah, *The Royal Family in Africa*, (London 1947).
9. Sir Henry Channon, op. cit.
10. From a letter from Queen Elizabeth to Edward Seago, quoted by Elizabeth Longford in *The Queen Mother*.
11. Robert Lacey, *Majesty*, (London 1977).

*Preface to Part Four*

1. James Lees-Milne, *Caves of Ice*, (London 1983).

*Chapter Thirty-One*

1. *The Diaries of Sir Henry Channon*, (London 1967).
2. James Pope-Hennessey, *Queen Mary*, (London 1959).
3. James Cameron, *The Best of Cameron*, (London 1981).
4. Ibid.
5. Robert Lacey, *Majesty*, (London 1977).
6. Brigadier Stanley Clark, *Palace Diary*, (London 1958).
7. Mabell, Countess of Airlie, *Thatched With Gold*, (London 1962).
8. James Pope-Hennessey, op. cit.

*Chapter Thirty-Two*

1. Victoria Glendinning, *Edith Sitwell: A Unicorn Among Lions* (Oxford 1983).
2. Peter Lane, *The Queen Mother*, 1979).
3. Ibid.
4. Cecil Beaton, *Self Portrait with Friends*, (London 1979).
5. James Pope-Hennessey, *Queen Mary*, (London 1959).
6. Peter Townsend, *Time and Chance*, (London 1978).
7. Ibid.

8. Cecil Beaton, op. cit.
9. Ibid.
10. William Purcell, *Fisher of Lambeth*, (London 1969).
11. Brigadier Stanley Clark, op. cit.
12. *Daily Express*, 2 June 1953.
13. *The Diaries of Sir Henry Channon*, (London 1967).
14. Cecil Beaton, op. cit.
15. Harold Nicolson, *Diaries 1930–1964*, (London 1980).
16. Brigadier Stanley Clark, op. cit.

*Chapter Thirty-Three*

1. *The Diaries of Sir Henry Channon*, (London 1967).

*Chapter Thirty-Four*

1. Noël Coward, *Diaries*, (London 1982).
2. Nigel Dempster, *Princess Margaret*, (London 1981).
3. Peter Townsend, *Time and Chance*, (London 1978).
4. William Purcell, *Fisher of Lambeth*, (London 1969).
5. Ibid.
6. Peter Townsend, op. cit.

*Chapter Thirty-Five*

1. Cecil Beaton, unpublished diary, October 1954.
2. Theo Aronson, *Princess Alice, Countess of Athlone*, (London 1981).
3. Noël Coward, *Diaries*, (London 1982).
4. Elizabeth Longford, *The Queen Mother*, (London 1981).
5. Dorothy Laird, *Queen Elizabeth The Queen Mother*, (London 1966).

*Chapter Thirty-Six*

1. James Pope-Hennessey, *A Lonely Business*, (London 1981).
2. *Forfar Dispatch*, 21 October 1972; *Daily Express*, 30 August 1977.
3. Jonathan Dimbleby, *Prince Charles*, (London 1994).
4. Dorothy Laird, *Queen Elizabeth The Queen Mother*, (London 1966).
5. Anthony Holden, *Charles, Prince of Wales*, (London 1979).
6. Ibid.
7. Ibid.
8. Jonathan Dimbleby, op. cit.
9. *It's a Royal Knockout*, BBC TV.

10. HRH Princess Anne interviewed by Terry Wogan, BBC TV, 22 March 1985.
11. James Pope-Hennessey, op. cit.
12. Ibid.
13. James Bryan & Charles J V Murphy, *The Windsor Story*, (London 1979).

*Chapter Thirty-Seven*

1. The *Times*, 9 May 1995.

# Bibliography

Alexandra of Yugoslavia, HM Queen, *Prince Philip: A Family Portrait*, (London 1949).

Alice, HRH Countess of Athlone, *For My Grandchildren*, (London 1980).

Alice, HRH the Duchess of Gloucester, *Memoirs*, (London 1983).

Aronson, Theo, *Princess Alice, Countess of Athlone*, (London 1981). *Royal Family: Years of Transition*, (London 1983).

Asquith, Lady Cynthia, *Queen Elizabeth*, (London 1937).

Barrow, Andrew, *Gossip 1920–1970*, (London 1978).

Beaton, Cecil, *Self Portrait with Friends*, (London 1979).

Belloc Lowndes, Marie, *Diaries*, (London 1971).

Birmingham, Stephen, *Duchess*, (London 1981).

Bloch, Michael, *The Duke of Windsor's War*, (London 1982).

Boothroyd, Basil, *Philip*, (London 1971).

Bryan, James & Murphy, Charles J V, *The Windsor Story*, (London 1979).

Buxton, Aubrey, *The King in his Country*, (London 1955).

*By Safe Hand: Letters of Sybil and David Eccles 1939–42*, (London 1983).

Cameron, James, *The Best of Cameron*, (London 1981).

Carey, M C, *Princess Mary*, (London 1922).

Cartland, Barbara, *We Danced All Night*, (London 1970).

Castellani, Aldo, *Microbes, Men and Monarchs*, (London 1963).

Cathcart, Helen, *The Queen Mother Herself*, (London 1979).

Churchill, Winston, *The Gathering Storm*, (London 1948).

Clark, Brigadier Stanley, *Palace Diary*, (London 1958).

Clynes, J R, *Memoirs*, Vol. 2, (London 1937).

Cooper, Diana, *The Light of Common Day*, (London 1959).

Coward, Noël, *Diaries*, (London 1982).

Crawford, Marion, *The Little Princesses*, (London 1950).

Davidson, J C C, *Memoirs of a Conservative 1910–1937*, (London 1969).

Dempster, Nigel, *Princess Margaret*, (London 1981).

*Diaries of Sir Henry Channon*, (London 1967).

Dimbleby, Jonathan, *Prince Charles*, (London 1994).

Donaldson, Frances, *King Edward VIII*, (London 1974).
  *King George VI and Queen Elizabeth*, (London 1977).

Duchess of Windsor, The, *The Heart Has Its Reasons*, (London 1956).

Duff, David, *Elizabeth of Glamis*, (London 1973).

HRH the Duke of Windsor, *A King's Story*, (London 1951).

Duncan, Andrew, *The Reality of Monarchy*, (London 1970).

*Durable Fire: The Letters of Duff and Diana Cooper 1913–1950*, (London 1983).

Edwards, Ann, *Matriarch*, (London 1984).

Flanner, Janet, *London Was Yesterday*, (London 1975).

Frankland, Noble, *Prince Henry Duke of Gloucester*, (London 1980).

Frere, J A, *The British Monarchy at Home*, (London 1963).

Gilbert, Martin, *Finest Hour: Winston Churchill 1939–41*, (London 1983).

Glendinning, Victoria, *Edith Sitwell: A Unicorn Among Lions*, (Oxford 1983).

Gorrell, Lord, *One Man Many Parts*, (London 1956).

Graves, Robert & Hodge, Alan, *The Long Weekend: A Social History of Great Britain 1918–1939*, (London).

Hardinge, Helen, *Loyal to Three Kings*, (London 1967).

Harewood, Lord, *The Tongs and the Bones*, (London 1981).

Hibbert, Christopher, *Edward VIII: A Portrait*, (London 1982).

Holden, Anthony, *Charles, Prince of Wales*, (London 1979).

Hore-Belisha, Leslie, *Private Papers*, (London 1960).

Hough, Richard, *Mountbatten, Hero of our Time*, (London 1980).
  *Edwina*, (London 1983).

Jenkins, Alan, *The Forties*, (London 1977).

Judd, Denis, *King George VI*, (London 1982).

Julian, Philippe, *Edward and the Edwardians*, (London 1967).

King, Stella, *Princess Marina: Her Life and Times*, (London 1969).

Lacey, Robert, *Majesty*, (London 1977).

Laird, Dorothy, *Queen Elizabeth the Queen Mother*, (London 1966).

Lane, Peter, *The Queen Mother*, (London 1979).

Lees-Milne, James, *Harold Nicolson: A Biography 1886–1929*, (London 1980).
  *Caves of Ice*, (London 1983).

Lockhart, J G, *Cosmo Gordon Lang*, (London 1949).

Lockhart, Sir Robert Bruce, *Diaries*, (London 1973).

Longford, Elizabeth, *Queen Elizabeth The Queen Mother*, (London 1981).

Mabell, Countess of Airlie, *Thatched With Gold*, (London 1962).

Masters, Brian, *Great Hostesses*, (London 1982).

Maurois, André, *Memoirs*, (London 1970).

Middlemas, Keith & Barnes, John, *Baldwin: A Biography*, (London 1969).

Morrah, Dermot, *The Royal Family in Africa*, (London 1947).
   *The Work of the Queen*, (London 1958).

Morrow, Ann, *The Queen Mother*, (London 1984).

Nicolson, Harold, *King George V*, (London 1952).
   *Diaries and Letters 1930–1939*, (London 1952).

*Ottoline: The Early Memories of Ottoline Morrell*, (London 1974).

Pope-Hennessey, James, *Queen Mary*, (London 1959).

Purcell, William, *Fisher of Lambeth*, (London 1969).

Roosevelt, Eleanor, *Autobiography*, (London 1962).

Rose, Kenneth, *King George V*, (London 1983).

Secrest, Meryle, *Kenneth Clark*, (London 1984).

Sencourt, Robert, *The Reign of Edward VIII*, (London 1962).

Shirer, William L, *Berlin Diary*, (New York 1941).

Sinclair, David, *Queen and Country*, (London 1979).

Sitwell, Osbert, *Queen Mary and Others*, (London 1974).

St Johnston, Sir Eric, *One Policeman's Story*, (London 1978).

Stevenson, Frances, *Lloyd George*, (London 1971).

Stuart, James, *Within the Fringe*, (London 1967).

Taylor, A J P, *English History 1914–1945*, (London 1970).

Townsend, Peter, *Time and Chance*, (London 1978).
   *The Last Emperor*, (London 1975).

Vanderbilt, Gloria & Furness, Thelma, *Double Exposure*, (London 1959).

Wakeford, Geoffrey, *Thirty Years A Queen*, (London 1968).

Watson, Francis, *Dawson of Penn*, (London 1950).

Wentworth Day, James, *The Queen Mother's Family Story*, (London 1967).

West, Rebecca, *1900*, (London 1982).

Wheeler-Bennett, Sir John, *King George VI*, (London 1958).

Wilmot, Chester, *The Struggle of Europe*, (London 1952).

Woolf, Leonard, *Sowing*, (London 1970).

Ziegler, Philip, *Crown and People*, (London 1978).
   *Diana Cooper*, (London 1981).

# Index